'This research-based book fills a gap by exploring the ambiguous space between coaching and therapy in a thoughtful but well applied way. It is critical but accessible and is a must read for those interested in examining the boundaries and overlaps between the two professions.'

Paul Stokes, *PhD, Associate Professor of Coaching and Mentoring, Sheffield Hallam University, UK*

'*Coaching in the Grey Space* aims to enhance the work of helping professionals across different settings, from the beginner to the experienced practitioner. This book offers a timely contribution for those encountering and navigating the Grey Space in their coaching practice, to explore their ways of working and the boundaries of where coaching and therapy intersect. This evidence-based perspective highlights the preparatory and preventative aspects of the Grey Space. A key resource for anyone interested in enhancing their understanding of this complex landscape.'

Siobhain O'Riordan, *PhD, Chartered Coaching Psychologist*

'As we learn more about the nature of "everyday trauma" we can see how it contributes to stress overload, dysfunctional behaviours, anxiety and depression – all widespread today. To make a clear separation between therapy and coaching is no longer feasible, so coaches need to be well supported to work in this "grey area". This important book will do just that – it is a welcome contribution to the coaching profession.'

Hetty Einzig, *Founder-Director, Transpersonal Leadership Coaching, AC Publications Strategy Director, and author of* The Future of Coaching: Vision, Leadership and Responsibility in a Transforming World

Coaching in the Grey Space

Coaching in the Grey Space is set to enhance the practice of coaching psychology, by defining the previously unidentified grey space – where boundaries between the coaching and therapeutic terrain intersect.

This book navigates how we as coaches can negotiate this complex terrain, to improve the management of boundaries and ethics for coaches within the practice and safeguard clients. It also describes how coaching within the grey space can have both preparatory and preventative effects with the potential for far-reaching positive outcomes. With extensive research, enquiries and experiments and wide-reaching case studies, the book will equip a reader with a thorough understanding of an often complex and fast-moving industry.

Promoting a much-needed evidence-based debate on the ethical boundaries of coaching and therapy, this book will be an original and practical resource of interest for coaching practitioners, both established and those undergoing training in the field.

Dr Lauretta Greer is a trauma-informed Coaching Psychologist specialising in personal development, transitions and stress management, with a particular interest in stress management and prevention. She holds a BSc in Counselling and Psychology, an MSc in Occupational Psychology and a DProf in Coaching and is a qualified bereavement counsellor and an accredited psychometric and personality practitioner. Her mission is to support people through enhancing and developing their skills, so that they can improve their mental and physical health and take charge of their lives for the better.

Coaching Psychology
Series Editor: Stephen Palmer

Coaching psychology is a distinct branch of academic and applied psychology that focuses on enhancement of performance, development and wellbeing in the broader population. Written by leading experts, the **Coaching Psychology** series will highlight innovations in the field, linking theory, research and practice. These books will interest professionals from psychology, coaching, mentoring, business, health, human resources and management as well as those interested in the psychology underpinning their coaching and mentoring practice.

https://www.routledge.com/Coaching-Psychology/book-series/COACHPSYCH

Titles in the series:

Neurodiversity Coaching
A Psychological Approach to Supporting Neurodivergent Talent and Career Potential
Nancy Doyle and Almuth Mcdowall

Schema Coaching
Overcoming Deep-seated Challenges
Iain McCormick

Arts-based Coaching
Using Creative Tools to Promote Better Self-expression
Andrea Giraldez-Hayes and Max Eames

The Wise Team Coach
Crafting a Personal Approach to Team Coaching
Paul Lawrence

Coaching in the Grey Space
Exploring Boundaries, Ethics and Complexity when Coaching and Therapy Intersect
Lauretta Greer

Coaching in the Grey Space

Exploring Boundaries, Ethics and
Complexity when Coaching and
Therapy Intersect

Lauretta Greer

Routledge
Taylor & Francis Group

LONDON AND NEW YORK

Designed cover image: Commissioned thesis artwork for
Dr. Lauretta Greer by TM The Studio.

First published 2026
by Routledge
4 Park Square, Milton Park, Abingdon, Oxon OX14 4RN

and by Routledge
605 Third Avenue, New York, NY 10158

Routledge is an imprint of the Taylor & Francis Group, an informa business

© 2026 Lauretta Greer

The right of Lauretta Greer to be identified as author of this work has been
asserted in accordance with sections 77 and 78 of the Copyright, Designs and
Patents Act 1988.

British Library Cataloguing-in-Publication Data
A catalogue record for this book is available from the British Library

Library of Congress Cataloging-in-Publication Data
Names: Greer, Lauretta, author.
Title: Coaching in the grey space : exploring boundaries, ethics and complexity
when coaching and therapy intersect / Lauretta Greer.
Description: Abingdon, Oxon ; New York, NY : Routledge, 2026. |
Series: Coaching psychology | Includes bibliographical references and index.
Identifiers: LCCN 2025012123 (print) | LCCN 2025012124 (ebook) |
ISBN 9781032835334 (hardback) | ISBN 9781032835341 (paperback) |
ISBN 9781003509776 (ebook)
Subjects: LCSH: Personal coaching. | Psychology, Applied.
Classification: LCC BF637.P36 G74 2026 (print) | LCC BF637.P36 (ebook)
LC record available at https://lccn.loc.gov/2025012123
LC ebook record available at https://lccn.loc.gov/2025012124

ISBN: 978-1-032-83533-4 (hbk)
ISBN: 978-1-032-83534-1 (pbk)
ISBN: 978-1-003-50977-6 (ebk)

DOI: 10.4324/9781003509776

Typeset in Times New Roman
by Newgen Publishing UK

Dedicated to Max Gunn
Space, time and distance is insignificant, I love you
always and forever!

Contents

Acknowledgements

I would like to thank Mary Hartog, my supervisor, for her belief and steadfast guidance throughout this research process.

To my family the GioCundy's, the Audouin-Leightons and friends for their unwavering support and love. To all my co-enquirers and critical friends, without whom this would not be possible.

With special thanks to Andrew Meeker, Dr Siobhain O'Riordan and Professor Sarah Corrie, for their generous counsel in the development of this work.

I would like to extend my heartfelt thanks to Tina-Lee McDougall, Director of TM The Studio (tmthestudio.com), for her incredible vision and unwavering support throughout this journey. From designing the book cover to shaping my brand and marketing, her expertise has been invaluable in bringing this work to life and ensuring this book reached publication on time.

Finally, I would like to thank my editor, Louis Molloy, for bringing my PhD to life in this book, and his continued hard work to make this piece of work what it is today.

Preface

For years, there has been controversy surrounding the role of coaching: the role it plays, the territory it occupies and the ethics and safety regarding its practice. With a rapidly growing and developing coaching industry, research in understanding the navigation of the boundaries where coaching and therapy intersect has struggled to keep up. This book brings together years of thought-provoking research and examples of practice for those professionals who want to deepen and develop their practice and keeping up -to-date through real-world practitioner examples and applied research. This will equip practitioners to navigate the space where coaching and therapy intersect, with confidence.

Coaching in the Grey Space offers a clear definition to a previously undefined area of coaching/coaching psychology: the grey space, where the boundaries between coaching and therapeutic terrain intersect. This book offers direction as to how we, as coaches, can negotiate this complex terrain, to improve the management of boundaries and ethics for coaches within the practice and safeguard clients, drawing on research findings which explore these moments of intersection. Furthermore, it outlines that the client brings the whole of themselves into the coaching room and, therefore, it is not always possible to know if a client is "coachable" right away and offers insight into how to manage these complexities sensitively and collaboratively with our clients. In addition, it brings to light how coaching within the grey space can have both preparatory and preventative effects with the potential for far-reaching positive outcomes. With extensive research, enquiries and case studies, the book will give a reader a thorough understanding of an often confusing and fast- moving industry.

Introduction

I am a coaching psychologist offering personal consulting focused on health, well-being, transformation, resilience, stress management and prevention. My mission is to support people through enhancing and developing their skills, so that they can improve their mental and physical health and take charge of their lives for the better – to thrive.

My motivation and rationale for conducting this research was because of questions and experiences I was having within my own practice. I was working with several clients, who I would have been advised to 'refer' to therapy by coaching training, coaching bodies/boards or textbooks. However, in my experience, to do so was not necessarily the best thing for the client.

The research outlined in this book gave me the opportunity to explore and understand how others experienced and worked in the space where therapy and coaching intersect: the grey space. What emerged from my initial motivations and curiosity began to shape a study based on an action research enquiry with others and also a first-person enquiry/autoethnographic enquiry around my own practice.

Through this research, many themes were presented. They highlight the complexities of the terrain of the grey space, the concerns coaches bring and the need to ensure that their clients are not left without support. In doing so, the coaches act as a bridge – stepping into the role of 'helper' to facilitate finding support, through to their disillusion with systemic issues and inherited terms such as 'referral'. I go on to suggest that the term 'referral' is outdated within the future profession of coaching. As we 'grow up' as a profession, we have the opportunity to choose which narratives, discourses and rhetoric we keep – and those which no longer serve – and, finally, to call for training such as foundational mental health, basic psychology and trauma-informed training. Additionally, this book aims to emphasise the need for robust supervision, such as dual-trained supervisors who can illuminate the path that coaches traverse.

Coaches of all kinds working in the grey space should be actively engaging in reflective and reflexive practice, bringing to light "everyday taken-for granted" (Schön, 1983), as will be demonstrated through this research. In addition, in Chapters 4 and 5 a map is offered through the lived experience of all the co-enquirers to assist coaches in navigating this space. Lessons can be taken, utilising

DOI: 10.4324/9781003509776-1

ways in which co-enquirers navigated this terrain and sought to improve their own practices.

What this research aims to highlight is that we as coaches can and do work in productive ways with our clients within this complex intersection where the boundaries between therapy and coaching intersect: the grey space.

Navigation of chapters

Chapter 1, 'Am I the pioneering grey space client?' undertakes a narrative enquiry informed by autoethnography to place myself and my own story within the context of my research. The personal nature of the enquiry as you will see from the autoethnography is informed by my lived experience and, as such, it took time to find the words, the narrative and to make the decision about how I would tell and craft this piece and what I would wish to share in the public domain.

Chapter 2, 'Mapping the terrain of the grey space', considers the terrain of the grey space, the tensions and concerns within the psychological/therapeutic and wider community with the emergence of coaching, with many of these concerns questioning good practice. It argues that creating a distinguishing line between the therapeutic and coaching terrain is not possible, and not necessarily in the client's best interest.

Chapter 3, 'How and when we may encounter the grey space', provides a brief overview of the literature currently surrounding the grey space, giving important context to my research. This review of current guidance highlights the importance of my work. A case is presented for stress being a 'wicked problem', viewing coaching psychology and coaching as being well positioned as practice. It is here that the need to consider how and when we may encounter and then navigate this 'grey space' terrain is discussed.

In Chapter 4, 'Navigating the grey space: Part I The grey space compass: the process of how coaches explore and plot this territory', I plot the terrain, offering a recalibration of our compass as coaches, charting and mapping how coaches explore and navigate this grey space, including exploring when and how coaching continues, or when to signpost to other professional interventions, such as therapy. It can be surmised that this is not a one-size-fits-all approach. Questions are contemplated such as: What are the similarities and differences between various coaches when managing and approaching the grey space with their clients? How and when do coaches signpost? Extracts presented are representative of the collaborative enquiry of group workshops and cross-boundary experts' one-to-one conversations, exploring the lived experiences of coaches navigating this terrain.

Chapter 5, 'Navigating the grey space: Part II Surveying the grey space', and Chapter 6, 'Navigating the grey space: Part III Further surveying, and charting what emerges', charts the grey space, explores the findings and what emerged within it, facilitating the voices of various coaches from a range of positions. I bring to the fore and illuminate hidden experiences and an understanding of their practice, and how these coaches work in the grey space. The conversations are wide-ranging, with a variety of views given across different areas of coaching and therapy. Coaches felt strongly about normalising mental ill health and the need for more mental health education; 'giving voice' to normalising mental health within the ethical considerations, limits and boundaries as a coach. Coaches indicated that the grey space is a dynamic and complex space, with questions arising regarding 'signposting' and holding juxtapositions regarding therapy, traditional psychology and systemic issues, coaches' stance of facilitating, 'giving voice on behalf of their client' and what is required to traverse the complexities of the grey space.

Chapter 7, 'Viewing beyond trauma', seeks to describe real-world examples of trauma and how we may encounter this within our practices, through an illustrative case study. This is vital when considering the presence of trauma and the management of boundaries between the coach and coachee. Once again, the navigation of the grey space and the role of the coach comes into play. Through this illustrative example a case is presented of how coaching can be 'preparatory'. Furthermore, I suugest due to the acquisition of tools learnt within this coaching space the client may be better positioned and resourced, creating greater 'willingness' (Hayes, et al., 2004) to engage in further therapeutic work surrounding their trauma, even if this is at a later date. I also suggest that trauma is inherent to the grey space, with a greater likelihood of trauma being present, therefore it is vital that coaches be trauma informed. This is recommended in order to practice safely and ethically.

Chapter 8, 'Regular navigational updates and conclusion' accepts that navigation outdates very quickly, so any map is only a guide. I argue that it is essential across the helping professions that our skills navigating the grey space complexities are developed. The idea that mental health *should* not show up in the coaching space and that coaches *should* only be working with clients who have no mental health problems is redundant and unrealistic. The map of the terrain that coaches are presented with due to the contextual issues is outdated. We need to remember that "the map is not the territory" (Bateson, 1972). Bateson and Bateson further suggest that there is a tendency to mistake the map for the territory: "The name is not the thing named" (Bateson & Bateson, 1987, p.21), and that we must at times confront the map-like boundaries, as the landscapes and terrain shift, so our maps need to be updated. Lastly, I provide suggestion as to how we as coaches and the profession may need to revise our maps. As the world we live in becomes more complex, we too as coaches need to ensure that we have the relevant tools necessary to map our terrain so that we can navigate this ethically.

In Chapter 8, I conclude that the grey space can be both preparatory and preventative when journeyed in an ethical way. Preparatory in terms of instances where clients whose coaching journey touches on trauma – 'coaching the client towards' therapy – also in terms of the ameliorative/preventative aspects presented, such as the mental health issues linked to long-term stress. I demonstrate that there are treasures to be found for clients in being able to plot, map and navigate this space with clients. Finally acknowledging the ever-changing nature of the world around us, and the impact this has on coaching psychology as a whole, creates a greater sense of importance surrounding the theory of the grey space in coaching psychology.

References

Bateson, G. (1972). *Steps to an ecology of mind.* London: The University of Chicago Press.
Bateson, G. & Bateson, M. (1988). *Angles fear: Towards an epistemology of the scared.* New York, NY: Bantam Dell Pub Group.
Hayes, C. & Fulton, J.A. (2015). 'Autoethnography as a method of facilitating critical reflectivity for professional doctorate students'. *Journal of Learning Development in Higher Education, 8.*
Schön, D.A. (1983). *The reflective practitioner: How professionals think in action.* New York, NY: Basic Books.

Chapter 1

Am I the pioneering grey space client?

Overview

The following narrative offers a glimpse into my lived experience on multiple layers as a person, as a coach and as a researcher; exploring how my personal stories, and those of my clients, are intrinsically linked to my research of the grey space and my own development. This self-study enquiry is informed by using an autoethnographic approach. "Autoethnographic approaches are flexible, reflexive and reflective of life as lived; they do not follow a rigid list of rule-based procedures; frequently they are multivocal" (Ellis & Bochner, 2020, p.6).

When conducting a self-study, drawing on a first-person action enquiry, it is particularly important as a researcher to step back and consider what our motivations are for conducting any piece of research. Why this topic? Why this enquiry? Reason and Marshall (1987) suggest that, as researchers, we select topics consciously or unconsciously resulting from the 'baggage' we carry around, with an underlying drive: "a bid for personal development" (p.115). Through this autoethnography, my wish is to offer the wider coaching community a view into how and why I navigate this terrain as I do, so that they too may take something from this lived experience and add value to their coaching practices and clients. Through this approach, I, as a researcher, can consider my experience as a practitioner within the grey space, with the view that the reader can construct lessons within their own sphere of practice (McIlveen, 2008). Ellis and Bochner (2000) propose that we can learn about our own lives through reading about the lives of others: "autoethnography offers the potential to expand scholarship about human experience" (p.7). This further suggests that through tales of how individuals manoeuvre and navigate losses, disappointments and traumas, we are assisted in living fuller lives. With narratives offering companionship and ways of coping, we gain understanding, insight and the opportunity to reframe and live more fully through the challenges of life.

Chapters 1 and 7 explore elements of my story and how they sit within my research. I will also be giving accounts from my first-person perspective on interaction with co-enquirers from this research and from clients. The elements of my story include the following: exploring when trauma shows up in the coaching room and how this impacts and relates to my experience; the stance I adopt, and why; the

DOI: 10.4324/9781003509776-2

importance of awareness of self as a coach, and the moments when I am still grappling with it in terms of my own story; the significance of preparing for disclosure; the responses these disclosures may bring; and the parallel reaction I faced through my lived experience.

Bochner and Ellis (2016) speak of the connection to others that an author can create using vulnerability in autoethnography. Through writing in the first person rather than the third person, which one traditionally sees in academic writing, the reader is offered the opportunity to "enter into dialogue with the writer's existence, as well as their own" (p.82). Furthermore, by claiming that this third-person prose strives for objectivity, thereby creating a distance and an asymmetrical position, a gap is created between self and other. Rather, "autoethnographic writing resists this kind of emotional distancing" (Bochner & Ellis, 2016, p.82). Through this process, the writer requests that the reader joins them for a journey that includes the twists, turns, emotional highs and lows of life; evoking feelings and engendering the reader to make a personal connection to the stories told. "Our writing is not simply academic; it's personal and artistic too" (Bochner & Ellis, 2016, p.80). From this viewpoint, the "authors use their own experience in the culture of reflexivity to bend back on self and look more deeply at self-other interactions" (Ellis & Bochner, 2000, p.740). Through this narrative, both wide-angle (cultural context) and intimate (self) positions will be considered (Winkler, 2018).

Ethical considerations regarding others and self within this narrative have been deliberated on. As a result, I have taken great care in how I represent those people who form part of my story, and who are not able to offer their perspective. Therefore, the source of this narrative and how it is constructed is exclusively from my first-person account, narrated through my voice and experience. Furthermore, when selecting which aspects to share and how best to convey them, a level of challenge and emotional discomfort was experienced, which is not uncommon (Dashper, 2015); resulting in reflecting on how best to take care of myself and others represented in this narrative (Chatham-Carpenter, 2010). Therefore, to protect myself and others, censoring aspects of the story became essential. I have drawn inspiration from the stylistic approach in Ellis' (2020) piece " 'I hate my voice': coming to terms with minor bodily stigmas" when writing elements of this chapter.

As Bochner (2012) proposes,

> autoethnographies are not intended to be received but, rather, to be encountered, conversed with and appreciated. My concern is not with better science but with better living and therefore I am not so much aiming for some goal called 'truth' as for an enlarged capacity to deal with life's challenges and contingencies.
>
> (p.161)

And so, I invite you to receive the following chapters in the spirit in which they are intended.

I am the pioneering grey space client

My path to healing and integration has been a long and winding one. Not only am I a researcher, but I am also a seeker. A seeker for well-being and a thriving life. There is a belief and a drive that motivates and propels me forward, that my circumstances and my experience will not define me. I have pushed against what others have suggested my life would be or how I would 'turn out'; be that family members or clinicians. And I believe that this drive for my personal wellness is the force that has led me down this path of coach and researcher. What started off as a journey just for me at the age 24 has now ended up as a journey for others too.

Let me explain. I have learned, and am still learning, to heal and overcome severe neglect and years of sexual abuse I experienced as a child. I have been in some form of therapy, counselling and 'self-work' since the age of 11. Some of these approaches were not my choice but, as the years have gone by, others have been. I have been on an active, conscious quest since I was 24 years old to understand the impacts my experiences have had and how I could reverse or overcome them. At times, I see the 'mad scientist' in me willing to try anything to see if it creates any change and progress. I have tried/been through and seen numerous varieties of therapies, including clinical psychology, integrative, psychodynamic, person-centred and transactional analysis, as well as other practices that may be seen as fringe or alternatives, such as mindfulness (18 years ago, when it was seen as a weird, 'hippy' thing), functional medicine, shamanic clearings and rituals, family constellations, breathwork, sound healing, reiki, tapping and acupuncture. Most recently, I attended legal psilocybin-based therapy retreats in the Netherlands, with integration therapy and biodynamic psychotherapy, with my constant companion being coaching. All in an attempt to seek relief, insight and tools to overcome and move to a life of regulation and then towards thriving.

I believe that each of these experiences gave me 'something' – some more than others. At times, all that I might have received was kindness and compassion from another, and that was invaluable, for example, when experiencing reiki. I have had negative experiences too; ones that could have ultimately derailed my journey to thriving. Two such incidents come to mind; the first, regarding a clinical psychologist 'closing the book on me', which was my first experience of someone in a helping role. Now I understand that, in those days, research into and understanding of the abuse I had experienced was limited. However, this did negatively affect me, until the day I took charge. As I repeatedly entered abusive intimate relationships, hitting a low point, I knew that something had to change. This led me to coaching.

> One way counsellors can induce shame in their clients is through pathologizing or labelling them. This has the effect of dehumanising or objectifying the client and rendering them invisible. This will re-trigger early shame experiences or humiliation. This can be reinforced by the therapist interpretations, especially if they are primarily theory driven.
>
> (Sanderson, 2015, p.219)

Additionally, Sanderson (2015) highlights that "shame is ubiquitous in therapy due to the inherent unequal power dynamic in the therapeutic relationship" (p.169), with clients seeking help and, through the therapeutic process, being asked to reveal themselves fully, while the therapist's narrative remains hidden. Furthermore, clients who have been traumatised are more prone to shame than those who are non-traumatised. In addition, there may be

> clusters around vulnerabilities such as feelings of helplessness, powerlessness, dependency needs and disclosure of intimate thoughts, feelings and past behaviours which may be a source of shame and humiliation. This is especially the case in clients who have experienced physical or sexual abuse or domestic violence or who have a history of self-destructive behaviours … These become a source of shame, adding layer upon layer.
>
> (Sanderson, 2015, p.175)

The second incident that stands out in my mind is that of having an initial session with a therapist, disclosing my story and having to console the therapist, who was sobbing because of my disclosure, leaving me feeling that I was too much or that I needed to take care of the therapist. (Side note: I have experienced a therapist shed a tear with me in mutual sadness. This was not that.) And so, I personally do not initially judge more highly the person who is a therapist than those who do alternative healing in meeting me as a human being with compassion and professionalism. Yes, there may be more evidence for those tried and tested methods, yet this does not dismiss the value received from the others, even though that value may not be quantifiable.

Furthermore, had these other individuals (non-therapists) adopted a stance of not being able to work with me as a result of the disclosure of my trauma and suggested that I seek therapy, this would have unintentionally reinforced the shame-inducing belief I held for many years of 'being broken'. Instead, they all worked within the remit of their craft and met me as a human being with compassion and care, which, as previously mentioned, in and of itself was incredibly healing. And so, I come to understand why I am doing this research in this space – the grey space – and why I feel so strongly about how we signpost and the positions we adopt with our clients as coaches, so that we do not unintentionally reinforce a client's shame or unhelpful belief system. Rather, we become and offer that restorative experience of meeting our clients with compassion, love and kindness, which is intrinsically a therapeutic experience, even if what we are doing is working on their coaching goals.

Many times, my reasons for disclosure were so that the practitioner was informed, should this be relevant for the treatment they offered. For example, in functional medicine this is vital information because health is looked at systemically, seeing every aspect of one's experience as part of one's health picture. In my case, this made a huge difference in dealing with my gut issues, which stemmed from a dysregulated nervous system due to living in a state of hypervigilance.

I would highlight that my goal here is not to dismiss therapy and the value it holds. I am currently in therapy and find it hugely beneficial. What I am highlighting is the value coaches and non-therapeutic practitioners offer, as well as highlighting that, in my experience, just because an individual holds a counselling, therapy or psychology title does not automatically qualify them as being good, healing or therapeutic.

Coaching was my companion and stabiliser: a preparatory root to dealing with my trauma

As mentioned above, there came a point in my journey when I began to take matters into my own hands. I had no means for private therapy, and access to therapy was difficult, to say the least. I remember going to the GP and discussing that I felt that I needed support due to my earlier experiences. At the time I was put on an eight-week waiting list and received six sessions. My therapist was lovely, but we could not even scratch the surface in six sessions. I came away feeling that I had had good conversations with someone willing to listen, yet nothing much had changed in me. It was at this point that I became an 'active seeker'. Bailey and Taylor (2022) report: "exploring the experiences of women who sought support for their mental health after rape or abuse" presents two themes – "a long waiting list and support not available" and "sought own support for mental health after sexual violence" (pp.1&41). I relate to both themes.

As a good companion does, coaching acted as a stabiliser, through empowerment, which enabled me to develop resource and resilience. For the first time, I could imagine what I might like my life to look like, in addition to being able to put actionable stretching goals towards making change. Even if at the time it felt like I was dreaming about a better future, it offered me hope. Hopefulness is a life-sustaining human strength, consisting of goal striving and pathway thinking, which when combined ignite agency; the motivation for change (Snyder et al., 1991).

Only in the last seven years have I been able to dive deep into my trauma with the appropriate support. This is due to my life feeling more stable, having the support I need and finding the right (for me) therapeutic support. My experience resonates with the theme 'Coaching towards therapy' from the collaborative enquiry groups, Cycle 5 (see page 60).

I believe that coaching can facilitate self-directed learning, skills and tools development (Grant, 2008), so one becomes one's "own self-coach" (Palmer & Neenan, 2005). This happened to me.

Divorced with two children under the age of 6, no formal education, no family support, a lack of therapeutic support, having recently immigrated from South Africa and life not working, I took matters into my own hands. Unable to afford books, when I could, I would go to Waterstones (which had a Costa Coffee), and, while the children were in school, would order a coffee and spend all the time

I could devouring self-help and personal development books, and whatever else they had in the psychology section, creating an "upward spiral" of positivity (Fredrickson & Joiner, 2002).

Sitting in Waterstones reading the self-help books written by authors such as Tony Robbins gave me the courage to study for a life coaching diploma. From this, I gained coping skills, including thinking and behavioural skills, that were under-developed or lacking due to my early environment. Therefore, I gained companionship through coaching, as these writers and this knowledge became the needed role models I so sorely lacked. Concepts such as raising standards, changing limiting beliefs, emotional, physical, relationship, financial and time mastery issues (Robbins, 2001) were being revealed to me, with questions posed such as "What will this cost me if I *don't* change?", "Ultimately what will I miss out in my life if I don't make the shift? and "What is it already costing me mentally, emotionally, physically, financially, spiritually?" (Robbins, 2001, p.128). I cannot overstate the positive impact this experience has had on me. I truly feel that I would not have had the courage or conviction to take chances or find opportunities, such as physically knocking on the university door to figure out how to become a mature student, had it not been for this. I view coaching as not only resourcing me to develop the life skills I require to make change but also providing me with resilience so that I have the capacity to work through my trauma at a later point. To this day, coaching is my constant companion, supporting and showing me the way. Enabling me to increase my "willpower", determination and "waypower", devising pathways to achieve a goal (Snyder, 2002).

Disclosure: the misplaced responsibility

The knot in my stomach, the deep breath I take, steading myself … which response will I receive this time? How will this person view me now that they have this information? This experience has lessened over time; I am far more equipped nowadays to manage it, having learned that the shame I once felt is not mine to own. That this experience – my experience – is not my responsibility, and that I should not be the one who carries it. Yet, sadly in the world in which we live, there are times when I still do. "Women and girls who are subjected to sexual violence or abuse are likely to have heard many different forms of victim blaming, either directed at them or women and girls in general" (Taylor, 2022, p.39). During those moments when I have disclosed my experience to others, there has been a range of responses: from disgust, pity, shock, horror, rejection and being viewed as damaged goods, all the way through to overprotection and awe. In the extreme, it has been seen that, through my presence, I highlight the darker side of what humans are capable of; bursting the idyllic bubble they have worked so hard to create. Now I know that the response I receive is more a reflection of the other than of me and those who receive this information with love, awe or neutrality have greater self-awareness and emotional capacity.

Why is this relevant, you may ask? Vaughan-Smith (2019) suggests that there are moments when one may "feel unprepared to deal with the issues" clients bring. "For some coaches, their anxiety and trauma survival defences get in the way, and they stop coaching ... becoming inactive, overactive, or avoidant or directive" (p.17) due to the disclosure the client has made. Furthermore, our greatest tool in the coaching dynamic is "using self as coach", as a navigational tool for how to adapt and adjust to the coachee's needs (O'Broin & Palmer, 2006). Therefore, it is vital that we do our personal work, to build our awareness, gain insights into our biases, preconceptions and presumptions and sharpen our tools, so that our wounds are not triggered or activated by our clients and what they may disclose to us; so that we can meet them, with compassion and empathy, whatever they bring or disclose. This does not mean working beyond our capability; rather, meeting human being to human being.

My lived experience informs how I approach my clients, and the position that I take. The stance I adopt with my clients continues to evolve and this research process has influenced that stance further; particularly in becoming more trauma-informed/sensitive. By incorporating my lived experience and this newly acquired knowledge, I hope that I have learned what not to do from the negative experiences I have been on the receiving end of, as mentioned above. Likewise, what to do, in offering compassion, and that restorative relational experience.

And so, with this narrative I encourage coaches to consider how we hold space for what our clients share. Also, that we can see beyond the trauma, that our 'eyes' do not get clouded by the lens of trauma they may have experienced, enabling us to be free to reflect to our clients their strengths and capabilities.

Summary

In this chapter, I have sought to recount my own personal experiences, observations and thoughts in order to establish the path my research has travelled down. My own challenges through life have not only helped me gain a better understanding of myself, but also enabled further investigation of how I – and my peers – can support our clients through our coaching. Understanding my personal experience is important for a reader to reflect on my research, which will be contained in later chapters.

Discussion points

1. How does your 'life story' influence your choices regarding areas of practice?
2. How do you currently manage disclosure? Is there room for improvement?

Recommended reading

O'Broin, A.O. & Palmer, S. (2006). The coach-client relationship and contributions made by the coach in improving coaching outcomes. *The Coaching Psychologist*, 2(2), 16–20.
Taylor, J. (2022). 'Views and perspectives. On being trauma informed'. Dr Jessica Taylor | About (Accessed: January 2022).
Vaughan-Smith, J. (2019). *Coaching and trauma. From surviving to thriving*. London: Open University Press.

References

Bailey, C.A. & Taylor, J. (2022). 'I needed to know I wasn't crazy': Exploring the experiences of women who sought support for their mental health after rape or abuse, VictimFocus, UK. Available at: VictimFocus Report 2022 I needed to know that I wasnt crazy MH SV Bailey Taylor FINAL.pdf (cdn-website.com) (Accessed: November 2022).
Bochner, A.P. (2012). On first-person narrative scholarship: Autoethnography as acts of meaning. *Narrative Inquiry*, 22(1), 155–164.
Bochner, A.P., & Ellis, C. (2016). *Evocative autoethnography: Writing lives and telling stories*. New York, NY: Routledge.
Chatham-Carpenter, A. (2010). "Do thyself no harm": Protecting ourselves as autoethnographers. *Journal of Research Practice*, 6(1), 1–13.
Dashper, K. (2015). 'Revise, resubmit and reveal? An autoethnographer's story of facing the challenges of revealing the self through publication'. *Current Sociology*, 63(4), 511–527. https://doi.org/10.1177/0011392115583879
Ellis, C.S. & Bochner, A.P. (2000). 'Autoethnography, personal narrative, and personal reflexivity'. In N.K. Denzin & Y.S. Lincoln (eds.), *Handbook of Qualitative Research*, 2nd edn. Thousand Oaks, CA: Sage.
Fredrickson B. L. & Joiner T. (2002). 'Positive emotions trigger upward spirals toward emotional well-being'. *Psychological Science*, 13(2), 172–175.
Grant, A.M. (2008). 'Past, present and future: The evolution of professional coaching and coaching psychology'. In S. Palmer & A. Whybrow (eds.), *Handbook of coaching psychology: A guide for practitioners*. Hove: Routledge.
McIlveen, P. (2008). 'Autoethnography as a method for reflexive research and practice in vocational psychology'. *Australian Journal of Career Development*, 17(2), 13–20.
O'Broin, A.O. & Palmer, S. (2006). The coach-client relationship and contributions made by the coach in improving coaching outcomes. *The Coaching Psychologist*, 2(2), 16–20.
Palmer, S. & Neenan, M. (2005). 'Cognitive-behavioural coaching'. Paper presented at Cognitive Therapy Conference, Gothenburg, Sweden.
Reason, P. & Marshall, J. (1987). 'Research as personal process'. In D. Boud & V. Griffin (eds.), *Appreciating adult learning: From the learner's perspective*. London: Kogan Page.
Robbins, T. (1992). *Awaken the giant within: How to take immediate control of your mental, emotional, physical and financial destiny*. New York, NY. Simon & Schuster.
Sanderson, C., (2015). *Counselling skills for working with shame*. London: Jessica Kingsley Publishers.
Snyder, C.R. (2002). Hope theory: Rainbows in the mind. *Psychological Inquiry*, 13(4), 249–275.
Snyder, C.R., Cheavens, J. & Michael, S.T. (1999). 'Hoping'. In C.R. Snyder (ed.), *Coping: The psychology of what works*. New York: Oxford University Press.

Taylor, J. (2022). 'Views and perspectives. On being trauma informed'. Available at: Dr Jessica Taylor | About (Accessed: January 2022).

Vaughan-Smith, J. (2019). *Coaching and trauma. From surviving to thriving*. London: Open University Press.

Winkler, I. (2018). 'Doing autoethnography: Facing challenges, taking choices, accepting responsibilities'. *Qualitative Inquiry*. https://doi.org/10.1177/1077800417728956

Chapter 2

Mapping the terrain of the grey space

This chapter considers the terrain of the grey space, describing the tensions and concerns that arise within the psychological/therapeutic and wider community with the emergence of coaching. Many of these concerns question what makes good practice. It lays out that creating a distinguishing line between the therapeutic and coaching terrain is not possible, and not necessarily in the client's best interest. Here, a consideration of the knowledge landscape and relevant literature is explored. It advises that coaches are not seen to be colluding with the "tyranny of the positive" (Einzig, 2011), rather they should be aware and competent in navigating the complexities of the grey space.

Learning through education

When I embarked on a full-time Master's degree in Occupational Psychology at Birkbeck University (2012), this provided: insight into organisational dynamics; a deeper understanding for my current clients and what they may bring to the process; an understanding of how stress affects this sphere; and knowledge of the tools to draw on to cultivate awareness. At the end of my degree, I trained as a psychometric test user.

The notion of 'embodied understanding of, and in practice', and unfolding circularity, was fundamental to my approach. Dall'Alba and Sandberg (2006)) argue that understanding from this perspective is not "limited to cognitive content or actives; rather, it instead involves intuitive assessment of each situation against the background of previous experience" (pp.389–390). Whilst training, I could follow this method as I was still working at an organisational psychology company; administering psychometric tests, shadowing wash-ups and panel interviews and observing theory in practice.

As a practitioner, critical reflection is of great importance because it creates a process for gaining awareness through exploration of 'everyday taken-for granted'. By obtaining new awareness, we may confirm or reconstruct our identities. I do this through a critical narrative approach, including drawing on metaphors. Lakoff (1992) states that metaphors help to conceptualise the world. I use a nautical/sailing metaphor to conceptualise my experience as a practitioner, and I have incorporated

DOI: 10.4324/9781003509776-3

visual 'tricks' to assist understanding, particularly when it comes to articulating the intangible.

Having completed my Master's degree, I looked through my metaphorical telescope for the next direction to navigate towards, and an internal 'mutiny' occurred. The earlier influence of the critical psychology module, which brought to light the interplay of power and the position of 'expert' (Foucault, 1982), meant that the current routes I could follow on the map were undesirable. And so, a decision to chart new territory happened, and my voyage to become a coaching psychologist began.

Minnows and whales – coaching versus therapy, counselling psychology and clinical psychology: my position

There are tensions within the psychological community regarding the emergence of coaching. Arguments include: a lack of clarity regarding what professional coaching is, and what constitutes effective and reputable coaching (Sherman & Freas, 2004); coaches that may cause harm to those with unrecognised mental health issues (Bergals, 2002; Cavanagh, 2005); and non-regulated 'certification' programmes (Walker, 2004). This raises concerns regarding credibility and professionalism, particularly regarding life coaches because they appear to hold the least level of credibility (Salerno, 2005, cited in Palmer & Whybrow, 2008, p.27). Many of these concerns centre around good practice and are therefore valid. However, as a sub-discipline of psychology, coaching psychology offers professionalism, established qualifications and training. I wish to map out an ontological position highlighting my view on why coaching psychology is distinctly different from other applied psychologies.

During my undergraduate degree, I undertook a critical psychology module which had a considerable influence on me. As a result, when I coach, I am always mindful and question what sort of reality I am co-authoring with my client. Burr (2003) suggested that our identities are a construction from culturally available discourses, which are obtained through our communication with others. One cannot move away from the culturally available discourse, or social structures, but one can learn to claim or resist various identities on offer within the prevailing discourses.

As a result of coaching psychology developing interventions for the non-clinical population by drawing on existing psychological theories and techniques (Grant, 2008), I view my work as offering up discourses that may not have been available previously. Willig (1999) proposes: "Individuals are constrained by available discourses because discursive positions pre-exist the individual whose sense of 'self' (subjectivity) and range of experiences are circumscribed by available discourses" (p.00). Therefore, by drawing on newly available discourse, the client can 're-author' the 'self', through 'crafting' and reconstructing how they produce their story, and ultimately their identity (Burr, 2003; Foucault, 1972; Parker, 1992; Willig, 1999). I will demonstrate this through a case study.

Case study 1

Client B1 undertook coaching for stress management after experiencing anxiety when the relationship with his fiancée of seven years broke down, months before their wedding. He had no prior mental health issues and reported having always managed challenges well. Our coaching took place in weekly 60-minute sessions over five months. A narrative theme emerged: one of referring to himself as a 'delicate flower'. This was the result of experiencing strong emotions and becoming anxious for having these emotions. It became apparent that his narrative was causing him more distress because he felt that something fundamental in him had been broken.

I drew on a range of coaching techniques: mindfulness breathing to manage his anxiety; using a psycho-educational approach (Neenan & Dryden, 2002) to educate and normalise the emotions he was experiencing; Socratic questioning (Neenan & Dryden, 2002) for him to reflect on his reasons for ending the relationship; and exploring what he valued within a relationship. What became apparent was that he held guilt for having been the one that made the final decision to end the relationship. Using cognitive behavioural coaching (CBC) (Palmer, Cooper & Thomas, 2003; Palmer & Cooper, 2010), he began to challenge the narrative he was forming about himself. At the end of our sessions, he reconstructed his identity as being 'an emotionally mature and capable man' with a strong sense of what he valued for himself and therefore what he valued in relationships.

It is important for me to critically reflect on the influence and impact that coaching psychology has from a broader viewpoint. Brookfield (1995) suggested that socially based disciplines come from the point of view that "we teach to change the world" (p.1). However, one is unable to be sure, even with the best of intentions, that this guarantees effective and suitable practice. Therefore, I am constantly aware – holding the question in mind throughout my coaching work – of what "objects of knowledge" (Foucault, 1972) are being offered up and drawn on during our work together. Not only is it vital for me to be critically reflective as to what objects of knowledge are being made available through my coaching, but it is also imperative to hold an awareness of the position of privilege and power granted to me as a coaching psychologist. Foucault (1982) proposes that "names", particularly those accepted as legitimate disciplines of knowledge, such as "psychologist", hold a position of privilege. This is because coaching as a sub-discipline draws its "expert knowledge" (Foucault, 1982) from a range of psychological disciplines (Grant, 2008).

Therapy, particularly the field of psychology, still holds negative connotations for many people. As Foucault (1982) suggests, madness is viewed in our culture as belonging to, or 'owned' by, the disciplines of psychology/psychoanalysis and psychiatry. Moreover, resulting from the expert position adopted by these disciplines, a hierarchical relationship is formed; one that has the power to determine and judge another's behaviour, with lasting consequences. It is here that the power dynamic between patient and therapist/psychologist can be argued to be distributed towards the expert; resulting in wariness when it comes to the willingness of individuals to seek help and support.

As a coaching psychologist, my position of expert is not seen to be of the same standing as that of a clinical/counselling psychologist. Coaching psychology offers a different power dynamic: one of shared power. The coach-client relationship developed during the coaching process is one of full transparency and equality (Kearns, Gardiner & Marshall, 2008). "Coaching requires a sophisticated set of skills and the ability to draw on expert knowledge, while at the same time facilitating the self-directed learning which lies at the core of the coaching enterprise …" (Grant, 2008, p.34) and ultimately empowering the client to become their own self-coach (Palmer & Neenan, 2005); resulting in coaching having a more positive image with less perceived corrective power. Consequently, individuals may be more open to addressing the improvement of issues earlier – for example, stress – before the problem becomes clinical (Palmer & Cooper, 2013).

Another question I hold is, does coaching help maintain a societal status quo by placing the onus on the individual to take responsibility for what is in fact a societal issue? (Foucault, 1982; Rose, 1999). For example, an individual learning to manage stress at work, when it is the organisational structure which is fundamentally flawed. That is why I view my role as facilitating self-directed learning (Grant, 2008) through drawing on a range of theories and tools; enabling the client to obtain additionally available discourse (Burr, 2003; Foucault, 1972; Parker, 1992; Willig, 1999), gaining 'self-reflexivity', and enabling the client to determine 'self' to 'author' (Foucault, 1997). It could be claimed that, through the coaching process, I facilitate a disruption of the status quo, resulting from offering up objects of knowledge that were once only available to the expert; thereby providing a basis for my clients themselves to challenge and resist power structures (Foucault, 1997).

Navigating through the fog: the uncharted territory of the grey space

As any skipper knows, certain processes and procedures need to be followed when sailing in uncharted territory. Currently, navigating my practice within an emerging sub-discipline makes plotting my trajectory challenging at times! One such area is the boundary between personal development coaching and therapy, the 'grey space'. Distinguishing similarities and differences in these fields when working with individuals who are navigating change, whether in personal or transformational coaching, is highly pertinent.

Figure 2.1 represents the 'blur' I experience when undertaking personal/ transformational coaching work. It highlights my difficulty in defining where the clear line of demarcating territory is when stepping into 'life coaching' because my clients may bring many issues that sit very close to therapeutic territory; the figure represents how the practice of distinguishing boundaries between therapy and life

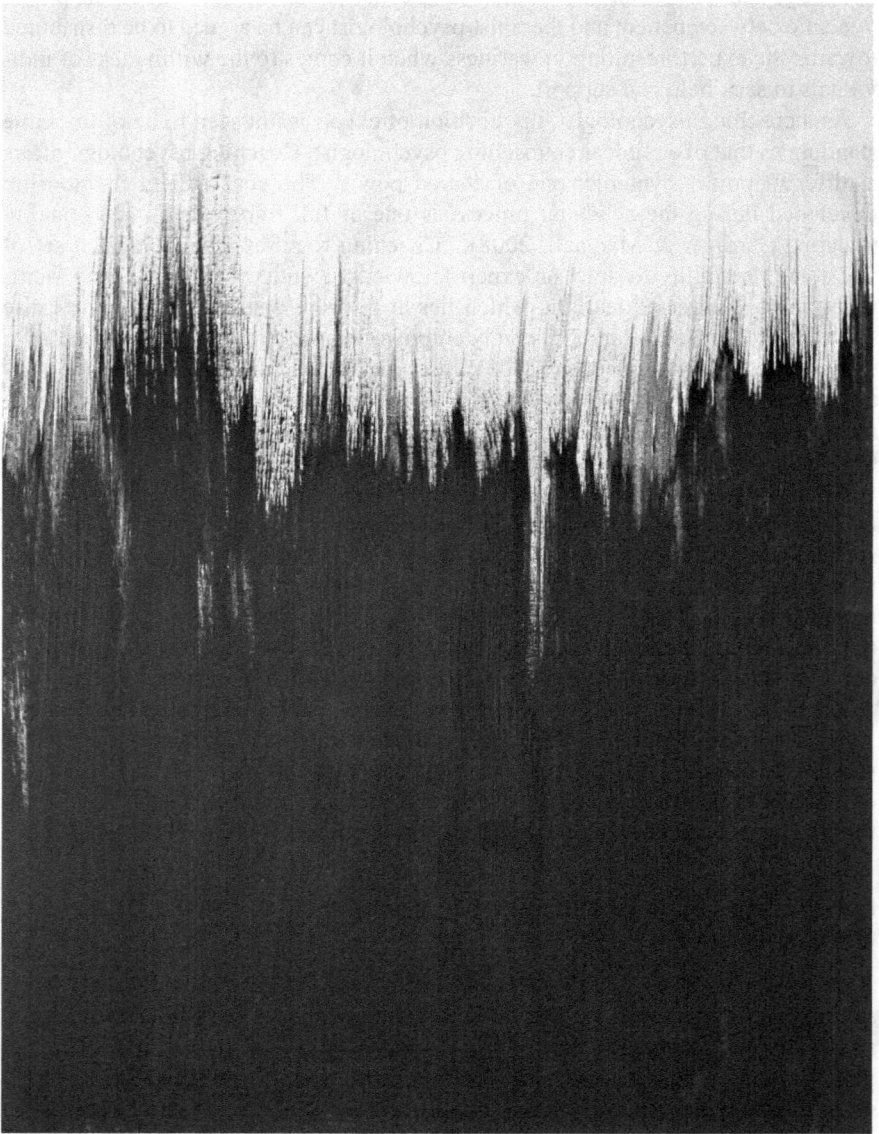

Figure 2.1 Conceptual overlap of therapeutic and coaching practices
Source: https://danslelakehouse.com/2012/02/simple-but-striking-diy-painting.html

coaching is not as simple as it might appear to be in theory. Research suggests that the boundaries between clinical and non-clinical clients may not be clear-cut. Grant (2007) suggests there is "discrepancy between the espoused ideas of what coaching 'should' be and the reality of what happens in real-life coaching practice" (p.177); suggesting that there is a blur in the boundary between the practices of coaching and therapy. Moreover, studies suggest that clients who voluntarily seek life coaching have higher levels of psychopathology than those who enter coaching through workplace coaching programmes (Grant, 2007).

I believe that I am in a strong position to navigate this issue because I have a grounding in counselling and therapy, having been a bereavement counsellor and having also learned the theoretical and practical elements of counselling. I can distinguish between a client who may be dealing with clinical issues, and one who has non-clinical issues. Therefore, I feel able to identify those individuals who, after further exploration, will be coachable because they have internal resources to engage in the coaching process. Coaching is proactive, with clearly defined 'action steps' (Palmer & Whybrow, 2008). Action steps entail the client's ability to: implement learning, tools or strategies gained through coaching; be agentic; and take practical steps towards change, which are in alignment with their coaching goals. The ability to implement action steps is one of the determining factors as to whether or not a client is coachable, or needs to be referred for therapy.

Client-first coaching

Sometimes, there is a fine line between what constitutes coaching and what starts to become therapeutic territory. A major distinction in the coaching process is the declared intention of working towards my clients' goals. Grant (2007) proposes that previous approaches to distinguish between coaching and therapy did not consider recent developments in modalities in which coaching goal-striving and mental health/mental illness sit side by side (Keyes, 2003). Furthermore, Grant (2007) proposes keeping within the boundaries of coaching: "coaching psychologists' primary focus is not on alleviating psychopathology or concentrating on distress; instead, [it is] in the assistance of helping clients articulate goals and supporting them to systematically strive for goal attainment" (p.178).

For me to navigate such murky waters, my own supervision process and continual practice development (CPD) play a vital role, in addition to contracting with my clients. My memberships of the British Psychological Society (BPS), the Division of Coaching Psychology, the International Society for Coaching Psychology and the Association for Coaching are key factors in my professional life, especially the guidance of the BPS's Code of Ethics and Conduct and their Practice Guidelines. Additionally, when working in this grey space, my 'North Star' has been whether the client is able to implement action steps, as previously mentioned. The example below considers ethical issues and the importance of contracting and supervision.

Case study 2

Client A2 undertook coaching with personal development and stress management goals, due to work-related stress, which was affecting his personal life. He also had goals regarding his intimate relationships, such as boundary setting and developing self-care skills. He disclosed that he had previously suffered mental health issues, which resulted in a failed suicide attempt, adding that he had already seen a therapist. He now felt he could cope with the situation. Our coaching took place in weekly 60-minute sessions over six months. The early sessions focused on his relationship goals; working with cognitive behavioural coaching (CBC), self-care practices, assertive communication, and personal self-awareness drawing on mindfulness. Later sessions concentrated more on stress management, using the multimodal-transactional model of stress (adapted from Palmer & Dryden, 1995).

I received a message from A2 after our sixth session, stating that he had again experienced suicidal thoughts due to work pressure. I responded with a coaching call. In the course of the conversation, it became apparent that there had been no attempt on his part to implement any action, but rather he was 'hitting a low' and the thoughts did not remain. From an ethical position, I explained that A2 may need to seek additional support should this continue, and made an agreement that he would contact A&E and speak to his family should he experience these thoughts again. He felt that the support he was receiving from me was sufficient for the time being and agreed to several action steps relating to self-care.

Once the conversation was over, I immediately contacted my supervisor, who affirmed what I had said to my client and confirmed that I was behaving ethically.

A2 and I spoke candidly regarding this incident during the following months, and he has not since experienced suicidal thinking again. I was transparent regarding my role and the support on offer, to maintain the boundaries of coaching.

At the end of our coaching work together, A2 successfully achieved his coaching goals and is still maintaining them.

I believe that the work within this grey space has a preventative essence. The coaching process is empowering the client to take up a new 'subject position', and craft an alternative identity; one that is more congruent with the goals they set out for themself (see pp. 15).

Knowledge landscape/relevant literature

So far, I have described the formative process of my own research, as well as a couple of real-life situations I encountered. We will now look at previous studies in the area of coaching, exploring the knowledge landscape which informed this research.

Coaching psychology is a young discipline in relative terms, with many tensions surrounding it as laid out above, and with debates questioning the need for such a sub-discipline; in particular, concerns have been raised as to whether there may be an overlap with other more established sub-disciplines of psychology. However, when treated as a sub-discipline of psychology, coaching psychology offers competence, reputable qualifications and training (Palmer & Whybrow, 2008). Coaching has been recognised within the BPS through the creation of a dedicated Division for Coaching Psychology (established in 2021), which is a great milestone for the profession. Other similar organisations have also recognised coaching, for example the British Association for Counselling and Psychotherapy (BACP), which has a dedicated coaching division.

Much of the research surrounding coaching psychology has investigated the effectiveness of the facilitation of goal striving, performance improvement and life-experience enhancement in the non-clinical population – where the aims of the therapy are to treat psychological issues or other matters relating to psychopathology (Bachkirova & Cox, 2004; Grant, 2007). Consideration has also been given to the differences between coaching and therapy. Grant (2007) suggests that the primary concern of coaching is to enrich goal striving and well-being, rather than remedial treatment of mental illness and distress. This is an important and central philosophical assumption about coaching and coaching psychology, and reflects the espoused viewpoint of a large number of organisations, including the Association of Coaching (AC), the European Mentoring and Coaching Council (EMCC), the International Coach Federation (ICF) and the Worldwide Association of Business Coaches (WABC). In addition, considerable endeavour has been – and continues to be – made to ensure that coaching as a practice is responsible and ethical. Continual development and research into coaching as a practice is carried out within many establishments that are not necessarily linked to the psychological community (such as those mentioned above, to name but a few). They look to address some of the apprehensions mentioned here regarding the overall field of coaching. There is, however, much more to do in this discipline as this arena grows – such as the development of practice – and to improve the further understanding and managing of ethics and boundaries.

Coaching emotions: entering the grey space

Due to this continual pursuit for ethical practice, concerns have been highlighted by Einzig (2011), a transpersonal executive coach, suggesting that coaches may be unintentionally facilitating the repression or punishment of anything deemed to be negative. This situation may lead to examples of unconscious mass denial and corporate excess if coaches position themselves as exclusively contributing to high performance.

Einzig (2011) further suggests that we live in a "cut-it-out or fix-it society", which emphasises the current societal expectation of conformity, where "talking openly and authentically about feeling depressed or anxious, of losing interest and pleasure in life, of our despair at the state of the world, is not generally welcome". One is expected to give the response "Fine" when asked "How are you?" (p.41).

Therefore, there is a call for coaches to be 'brave' and to step into the space of emotions, particularly those that are challenging, so as not to collude with the "tyranny of the positive" (Einzig (2011, p.41). The challenge is to do this within the ethical considerations of what it is to be a coach, recognising one's own limits and boundaries, while ensuring a basic awareness of psychological and personality disorder, with the ability to recognise the potential presence of such disorders. Einzig (2011, p.41) goes on to suggest that we can take on board a lesson from indigenous cultures who "have a different view of illness or emotional distress, seeking to learn and integrate them" rather than avoid such factors. Posing the question "What if the answers we seek lay in the darkness?" supports the client to overcome their fear of this space and instead entertain a different perspective; one that assists in finding meaning.

In transpersonal coaching – which sits closely with my own work as a coaching psychologist – the coach can use this space to help the client reframe pain, failure and crises, viewing them as essential elements for growth and meaning-making, which can offer valuable opportunities for learning. The coach is therefore shifting the paradigm by bearing in mind such questions as: What is its purpose (pain, failure, crises)?, What potential is trying to emerge?, What creative possibility is hidden within?, thereby supporting the client in developing resilience in moments of stress. However, it is here that as coaches we enter into what I call the 'grey space', where defining the boundaries between coaching and therapy becomes extremely important. The ability to know and navigate this space is essential. However, as Grant (2007) suggests, the boundaries between clinical and non-clinical clients may not be so clear-cut.

Another approach to distinguishing coaching from therapy considers the distribution of psychopathology within the general population (Krabbendam et al., 2004). From these authors' stance, the population is divided into four sections, with the extreme end of the distribution viewed as the psychiatric population, with progressively less affected populations being deemed clinical, moving into counselling, and finally through to coaching populations. It is the section of the coaching population located just before one reaches the counselling population that is of great interest to me (see Figure 2.2). Here, one could consider the boundary of the population as being a blurred line, between what constitutes the ending of the counselling population and the beginning of the coaching population; thereby working within a grey space.

As discussed, coaching holds less stigma than counselling. I am interested in investigating the grey space because it is one that I often find myself wrestling with in my work, and I believe that there is a need for more understanding and best practice to be developed.

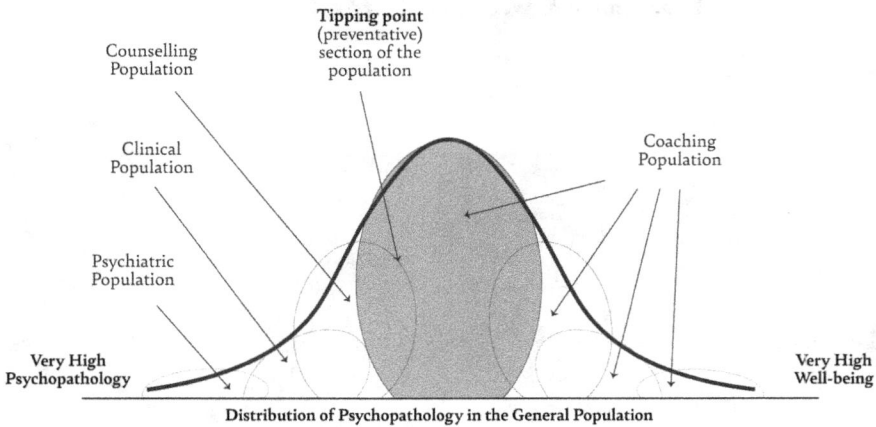

Figure 2.2 Distribution of psychopathology in the general population

Framework analysis

Grant (2007) provides a framework that can be used as a guide to navigate the terrain of the grey space. He puts forward an Engagement/Well-being Matrix (see Figure 2.3), which presents a four-dimensional framework where individuals can move between the different dimensions (dependent on context in life and various moments in time), rather than being 'in' or 'out' of each quadrant. It further highlights that coaching may help reduce distress and improve levels of well-being, while preserving performance outputs. This suggests that coaching lends itself well to those individuals who sit in the 'Distressed but Functional' quadrant (Grant, 2017). Individuals who are allowed to operate in this quadrant for too long may subsequently move into the 'Distressed and Dysfunctional' quadrant (Grant, 2007). Here, the task of the coach is to have the ability to differentiate between issues that might be amenable to coaching techniques, and to refer on those who require other expert interventions.

Theeboom et al. (2013) put forward evidence for solution-focused cognitive-behavioural coaching as having tangible ameliorative effects on stress and anxiety, and developing resilience as well as a range of correlated cognitive processes.

Additionally, a form of this matrix can be applied when coaching individuals who are seeking personal developmental coaching or life coaching; the Proposed Model of Goal Striving and Mental Health (see Figure 2.4). For the purpose of this proposal, the quadrant of 'Distressed but Functional' is of considerable interest. Here, individuals entering coaching have high levels of intentional goal striving; they may be highly functioning yet still be experiencing distress, such as anxiety or depression. This scenario seems to be congruent with what I deem to be the grey space. Compare that with the quadrant on the lower left, 'Major Psychopathology',

Engagement & Well-being Matrix, (adapted) Grant (2007)

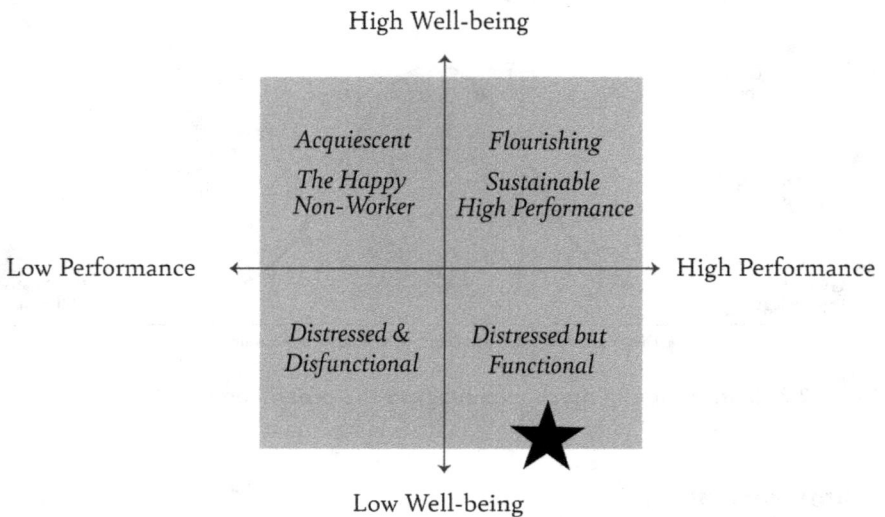

High Well-being

Acquiescent *The Happy* *Non-Worker*	*Flourishing* *Sustainable* *High Performance*
Distressed & *Disfunctional*	*Distressed but* *Functional*

Low Performance ←——————————————→ High Performance

Low Well-being

Figure 2.3 Engagement /Well-being Matrix
Source: Grant, 2007, p.255.

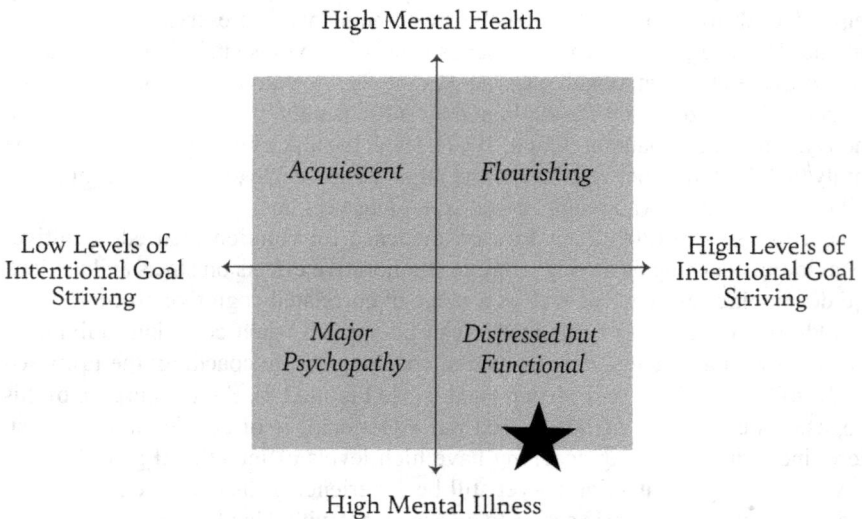

High Mental Health

Acquiescent	*Flourishing*
Major *Psychopathy*	*Distressed but* *Functional*

Low Levels of
Intentional Goal ←——————————————→ High Levels of
Striff   Intentional Goal
                                    Striving

Low Levels of
Intentional Goal
Striving

High Levels of
Intentional Goal
Striving

High Mental Illness

Figure 2.4 Proposed Model of Goal Striving and Mental Health
Source: Grant, 2007, p.257.

where there are high levels of mental illness and low levels of intentional goal striving: this is clearly therapeutic territory, in which case clients entering coaching may need to be referred on.

Grant (2003) conducted a study into the impact of life coaching on goals attainment, metacognition and mental health. Results showed that participants in the programme reported associated increased levels of insight, enhanced mental health, quality of life and goal attainment. There have also been questions posed as to whether life coaching can add to the recovery process and become a valued part of mental health services. Essentially, it can support individuals who have experienced long-standing mental illness, with coaching adding to the support system of recovery: it provides a foundation of self-management, self-care (Bora et al., 2010) and discovering personal resourcefulness (Higgins & McBennett, 2007). The study concluded that life coaching principles lend themselves well to the core recovery principles. In this context, coaching "puts equal or more weight on that a person is recovering 'towards' and on the need and value of building a meaningful life and pattern of living apart from the illness" (Grant 2003 (pp.460–461).

In a case study conducted by Campone (2014), a client suffering from dissociative identity disorder benefited greatly from attending both psychotherapy and life coaching. The psychotherapy centred on managing past trauma, while the life coaching focused on progressing and implementing life goals.

Some people who work within the context of mental health or emotion along with other health care providers criticise coaching due to a perceived lack of clinical training (Jenner, 2014). However, a positive benefit could be argued: the coach focuses on the person, rather than the 'illness' (Bishop, 2018). This is a result of self-directed learning and the equality in the coach-client relationship, factors which are paramount to the development of empowerment (Campone, 2014); once again suggesting that coaching offers up discourses that may not have been otherwise accessible, thereby instituting an ability to re-author the self (discussed later) through crafting and reconstructing how the person produces their story and, ultimately, their identity (Burr, 2003; Foucault, 1972; Parker, 1992; Willig, 1999).

However, for coaches to be effective in this space, it is advised that they have the appropriate training and skills to a satisfactory level (Bora et al., 2010), while maintaining strong ethical and boundary considerations (Dryden, 2011).

Discussion points

1. How familiar are you with the current literature surrounding the idea of 'the grey space?
2. How has the grey space presented itself in the context of your own practice?
3. What ways do you navigate this space, if/when you encounter it?

Suggested reading

Campone, F. (2014). 'At the border: Coaching a client with dissociative identity disorder'. *International Journal of Evidence Based Coaching and Mentoring,* 12(1), 72–81.

Einzig, H. (2011). 'The beast within'. *Coaching at Work,* 6(3), 40–43.

Foucault, M. (1972). *The archaeology of knowledge.* London: Tavistock.

Foucault, M. (1982). *Madness and civilization: A history of insanity in the age of reason.* London: Tavistock.

Foucault, M. (1997). *Ethics: Essential works of Foucault 1954–1984, Volume 1* (ed. P. Rabinow). London: Penguin.

Grant, A.M. (2007). 'A languishing-flourishing model of goal striving and mental health for coaching populations'. *International Coaching Psychology Review* 2(3), 250–264.

Grant, A.M. (2017). 'Solution-focused cognitive-behavioural coaching for sustainable high performance and circumventing stress, fatigue and burnout'. *Consulting Psychology Journal: Practice and Research,* 69(2), 98–112.

References

Bachkirova, T. & Cox, E. (2004). 'A bridge over troubled water: Bridging together coaching and counselling'. *The International Journal of Mentoring and Coaching,* 2(1), 1–10.

Bergals, S. (2002). 'The very real dangers of executive coaching'. *Harvard Business Review,* 80(6), 86–92.

Bishop, L. (2018). 'A coping review of mental health coaching'. *The Coaching Psychologist,* 14(1), 24–31.

Bora, R., Leaning, S., Moores, A. & Roberts, G. (2010). 'Life coaching for mental health recovery: The emerging practice of recovery coaching'. *Advances in Psychiatric Treatment,* 16(6), 459–467.

Brookfield, S. (1995). *Becoming a critically reflective teacher.* San Francisco, CA: Jossey-Bass.

Burr, V. (2003). *Social construction,* 2nd edn. London: Routledge.

Campone, F. (2014). 'At the border: Coaching a client with dissociative identity disorder'. *International Journal of Evidence Based Coaching and Mentoring,* 12(1).

Cavanagh, M. (2005). 'Mental-health issues and challenging clients in executive coaching'. In M. Cavanagh, A.M. Grant & T. Kemp (eds.), *Evidence-based coaching, Volume 1: Theory, research and practice from behavioural science.* Bowen Hill, Australia: Australian Academic Press.

Chatham-Carpenter, A. (2010). '"Do thyself no harm": Protecting ourselves as Autoethnographers'. *Journal of Research Practice,* 6(1), 1–13.

Dall'Alba, G. & Sandberg, J. (2006). 'Unveiling professional development: A critical review of stage models'. *Review of Education Research,* 76(3), 383–412.

Dashper, K. (2015). 'Revise, resubmit and reveal? An autoethnographer's story of facing the challenges of revealing the self through publication'. *Current Sociology,* 63(4), 511–527. https://doi.org/10.1177/0011392115583879

Dryden, W. (2011). *Dealing with clients' emotional problems in life coaching: A rational-emotive and cognitive behavioural therapy (RECBT) approach.* Hove: Routledge.

Einzig, H. (2011). 'The beast within'. *Coaching at Work,* 6(3).

Foucault, M. (1972). *The archaeology of knowledge.* London: Tavistock.

Foucault, M. (1982). *Madness and civilization: A history of insanity in the age of reason.* London: Tavistock.

Foucault, M. (1997). *Ethics: Essential works of Foucault 1954–1984, Volume 1* (ed. P. Rabinow). London: Penguin.

Grant, A.M. (2007). 'A languishing-flourishing model of goal striving and mental health for coaching populations'. *International Coaching Psychology Review* 2(3).

Grant, A.M. (2008). 'Past, present and future: the evolution of professional coaching and coaching psychology'. In S. Palmer & A. Whybrow (eds.), *Handbook of coaching psychology: A guide for practitioners.* Hove: Routledge.

Grant, A.M. (2017). 'Solution-focused cognitive-behavioural coaching for sustainable high performance and circumventing stress, fatigue and burnout'. *Consulting Psychology Journal: Practice and Research,* 69(2), 203–217.

Higgins, A. & McBennett, P. (2007). 'The petals of recovery in a mental health context'. *British Journal of Nursing,* 16.

Jenner, N. (2014). 'Life coaching and mental illness: A potential minefield?' *The Online Therapist.* Available at: https://boundariesofthesoul.com/2014/02/26/life-coaching-and-mental-illness-a-potential-minefield (Accessed: August 2018).

Kearns, H., Gardiner, M. & Marshall, K. (2008). 'Innovation in PhD completion: The hardy shall succeed (and be happy!)'. *Higher Education Research & Development,* 27(1), 77–99.

Keyes, C.I.M. (2003). 'Complete mental health: An agenda for the 21st century'. In C.I.M. Keyes & J. Haidt (eds.), *Flourishing: Positive psychology and the life well-lived.* Washington, DC: American Psychological Association.

Krabbendam, L., Myin-Germeys, I., de Graaf, R., Vollerbergh, W., Nolen, W.A., Ledema, J. & Van Os, J. (2004). 'Dimensions of depression, mania and psychosis in general populations'. *Psychology Medicine,* 34(8), 1177–1186.

Lakoff, G. (1992). 'The contemporary theory of metaphor'. In A. Ortony (ed.), *Metaphor and thought* (2nd edn.). Cambridge: Cambridge University Press.

Neenan, M. & Dryden, W. (2002). *Life coaching: A cognitive behavioural approach.* Hove: Brunner-Routledge.

Palmer, S. & Cooper, C. (2010). *How to deal with stress.* London: Kogan Page.

Palmer, S. & Cooper, C. (2013). *How to deal with stress: Creating success.* London: Kogan Page.

Palmer, S., Cooper, C. & Thomas, K. (2003). *Creating a balance: Managing stress.* London: British Library.

Palmer, S. & Dryden, W. (1995). *Counselling for stress problems.* London: Sage.

Palmer, S. & Neenan, M. (2005). *Cognitive-behavioural coaching.* Paper presented at Cognitive Therapy Conference, Gothenburg, Sweden.

Palmer, S. & Whybrow, A. (2008). *Handbook of coaching Psychology: A guide for practitioners.* Hove: Routledge.

Parker, I. (1992). *Discourse dynamics: Critical analysis for social and individual psychology.* London: Routledge.

Rose, N. (1999). *Governing the soul: The shaping of the private self,* 2nd edn. London: Free Association Books.

Sanderson, C., 2015. *Counselling skills for working with shame.* Jessica Kingsley Publishers.

Sherman, S. & Freas, A. (2004). 'The Wild West of executive coaching'. *Harvard Business Review,* 82–90.

Snyder, C.R., Cheavens, J.S., Michael, S.T. (1999). 'Hoping'. In C.R. Snyder (ed.), *Coping: The psychology of what works*. New York: Oxford University Press.

Theeboom, T., Beersma, B. & Van Vianen, A. (2013). 'Does coaching work? A meta-analysis on the effects of coaching on individual level outcomes in an organizational context'. *The Journal of Positive Psychology*, 9(1), 00–00.

Walker. J. (2004). 'Business-class coaches'. *Business Review Weekly*, 15–18.

Willig, C. (1999). 'Discourse analysis and sex education'. In C. Willig (ed.), *Applied discourse analysis: Social and psychological interventions*. Buckingham: Open University Press.

Winkler, I. (2018). 'Doing autoethnography: Facing challenges, taking choices, accepting Responsibilities'. *Qualitative Inquiry*. https://doi.org/10.1177/1077800417728956

How and when we may encounter the grey space

This chapter gives a brief overview of how and when we may encounter the grey space in our coaching practices, drawing on illustrative case examples. This chapter focuses on examples in areas related to stress management, resilience, health and well-being, and how these areas of coaching may bump up against themes of trauma and therefore coaches need to be informed. A case is presented for stress being a "wicked problem" (Brown, 2010), viewing coaching psychology and coaching as being well positioned as practice because it may hold an ameliorative essence when it comes to mental health illness, such as depression and anxiety resulting from long-term chronic stress. The need to consider how and when we may encounter and then navigate this grey space terrain is therefore discussed here.

Health and well-being: stress as a 'wicked problem'

Palmer and Cooper (2013) define stress as something that "occurs when pressure exceeds your *perceived ability* to cope" (p.00, emphasis in original).

My situation is affected by several systems, with a complex range of knowledge landscapes at play throughout my coaching work: specifically, health and well-being (such as stress management) and the prevention and development of resilience. This is in addition to navigating what I have experienced as a grey space, where the boundaries between therapy[1] and coaching may become blurred, as described below.

Brown (2010) puts forward the notion that each decision-maker draws on their breadth of knowledge when making decisions. This knowledge ranges from personal experience, as a member of their community, holding a skillset or specialism from the world of work, through to their own imagination.

Within my own working situation, there are many knowledge cultures operating. At the individual knowledge level, there is the interplay between the client's/coachee's 'individual knowledge'. Here, the client brings both their explicit and tacit knowledge and, through the coaching process, can reflect on their experience to allow the dynamics of change to occur. I, as the coach, also bring my own set of individual knowledge, as mentioned above. When entering coaching work, in order

DOI: 10.4324/9781003509776-4

for my coaching to be effective, I need be aware of my own 'knowledge landscape' and, through reflection and reflexivity, evaluate how these interplay with my client's individual knowledge.

In addition, there is a shared knowledge around what stress is and what impacts it has, through 'community knowledge'. A few examples of campaigns from mental health bodies, as well as local and regional organisational bodies, include: 'Stress: are we coping?'; 'organisational knowledge', through which policies and practices are shaped, and 'A little more conversation', which was launched to raise awareness and to inform communities.

I see myself and my practice as "belonging to, sharing in, in partnership with, an employee of, and an observer within" the "community knowledge" (Brown, 2010, p.27) of the impacts of stress and the need to have processes in place to mitigate it.

Furthermore, 'specialised knowledge' within the coaching area of managing stress has become a growing body of knowledge, which draws on specialised disciplines such as psychology, sports sciences, philosophy and business. I view our understanding of stress and how to deal with it (or not) as one that sits within a 'holistic knowledge': a connected synergistic pattern, where each knowledge space or system has an impact on the whole rather than being isolated within itself. I suggest that our understanding and management of stress in one knowledge landscape has a ripple effect on the rest. Therefore, I propose that stress is a 'wicked problem'. Brown sets out what constitutes a wicked problem, based on Rittel and Webber's original characteristics of wicked problems, as follows:

- Wicked problems evade clear definition. They have multiple interpretations from multiple interests, with no one version verifiable as right or wrong.
- Wicked problems are multi-causal with many interdependencies; thereby involving trade-offs between conflicting goals.
- Wicked problems are often not stable. Problem-solvers are forced to focus on a moving target.
- Wicked problems are socially complex. Their social complexity baffles many management approaches.
- Wicked problems rarely sit conveniently within any one person, discipline or organisation, making it difficult to position responsibility.
- Resolution of wicked problems necessarily involves change in personal and social behaviour; change that may be strongly resisted or encouraged, according to circumstance.

(Brown, 2010, pp.62–63)

"An entry point for an enquiry into a wicked problem is usually some wake-up call, crisis event, a new idea, or shift in social expectation" (Brown, 2010, p.63). I propose that now is the time when we may be seeing such an entry point.

Stress in the UK

According to research, stress is currently at an all-time high in the UK, affecting all social spheres.

> Research has shown that 16 million people experience a mental health problem each year and stress is a key factor in this. By tackling stress, we can go a long way to tackle mental health problems, such as anxiety and depression.
>
> (Mental Health Foundation, 2018)

Stress has an extensive range of negative implications, from the mental health factors mentioned above through to physical health problems, such as impaired immune function, high blood pressure, cardiovascular disease, digestive issues, back pain and sleep disturbance. These conditions can become chronic debilitating conditions adversely affecting individuals' quality of life, sense of self and their relationships on every level.

Every area of our society is being affected by stress, from children and adults of all ages through to the business and corporate sphere. This situation is compounded by underfunding in the NHS for mental health services. Budgets have been – and are still being – cut, yet stress is rising.

Mental health is still seen as a taboo subject by some sectors of the population, despite the creation of large organisations – such as Heads Together, a coalition of eight mental health charities – to tackle stigma and to change the conversation on mental health.

Culturally, we live in a time when being busy and 'switched on' is seen as a medal of achievement. We are more connected now than ever because of technology, never able to switch off and disconnect from business, which has a direct impact on our ability to cope with stress. One could argue that we are living in, and creating, a culture of burnout, with more pressure on our young people to succeed in the schooling system; an age of social media that creates a need to achieve a state of perfectionism and ever-increasing pressure to work faster, harder and longer than in previous generations. Our professional environment has changed more in the last 50 years than in the previous 2,000, and it could be suggested that this will increasingly be the case for 20 years on from the time of this research.

Additionally, with regard to our everyday stressors, the world recently underwent an unprecedented experience, which we are still coming to terms with. The impact and implications of the global COVID-19 pandemic on stress and mental health have been seismic. In 2020, the mental health charity Mind conducted research called 'The mental health emergency: how has Coronavirus impacted our mental health?' demonstrating the scale of the effects, with individuals with prior mental health problems reporting declining mental health (65 per cent of adults over 25, and 75 per cent of young people [aged 13–24]). An article by BBC News (2021) suggests that the issues impacting our mental health were "fuelled by feelings of loneliness, anxiety and fears for the future". In addition there are reports of greater risks of suicidal ideation during the pandemic due to lack of social connection and loneliness.

Once lockdown had been lifted and workers returned to work, Bupa reported that 65 per cent of British workers experienced anxiety regarding their future and the impact of schemes such as furlough and mortgage holidays ending. Research conducted by Orestis et al. (2021) highlighted "an increased burden on mental ill-health in the UK" due to financial stressors (p.3832), concluding that economic worries have implications for the nation's mental health.

In July 2021, Mind conducted further research 'Coronavirus: the consequences for mental health', with key findings being: individuals who had previously struggled with mental health are struggling more; anxieties remain high; COVID-19 has heightened inequalities; more young people are finding it hard to cope; and there is an urgent call for more support – in particular, high-quality trauma-informed support. Furthermore, it was found that "higher COVID-related stress predicted increased risk in Generalized Anxiety Disorder and Major Depressive Disorder" (Monistrol-Mula et al., 2022, p.4, cited in Mind, 2021).Moreover, post-lockdown, there was the following call from Jagan Chapagain, Secretary General of the International Federation of Red Cross and Red Crescent Societies (IFRC): "Now more than ever we must invest in mental health and psychosocial support for everyone—communities and carers alike—to help people cope, rebuild their lives and thrive through this crisis" (IFRC, 2020).

The American Psychological Association reported in 2023 (Ortlund et al., 2025) that two out of three Americans indicated feeling stressed about the future of the U.S., with significant sources of stress including social divisiveness, healthcare, national debt and the economy.

It is fair to say that the world in which we currently live has many factors contributing to our stress and our ways of coping. As discussed, chronic stress and the long-term impacts it can have – such as creating anxiety and depression – are vast. This situation has implications for commerce, our health services, communities, family lives and the individuals who are dealing with chronic stress. In the last few years there have been drives by the Institute of Directors, Mind and the Mental Health Foundation – to name but a few – to raise awareness and encourage society to understand the implications of stress, and to incorporate strategies to help manage it alongside global factors such as COVID-19 and the current war in Ukraine.

Coaching, health, well-being and stress

Gherardi (2009) proposes that, once we deem activities to be practices, such as strategies for the management of stress, this legitimises and normalises the accountability of various conducts. Moreover, what one "produces in their sustained practice is not only work, but also the (re)production of society" (p.536). This brings with it a huge responsibility for what we regard as practices that are ethical and best practice. As Gherardi (2009) further states: "practice is an analytic concept that enables interpretation of how people achieve active being-in-the-world" (p.536). I view coaching as such a practice; one that can support the (re)production of society in mitigating and managing stress, and in the development of resilience.

Specifically, I see myself as being part of the experience of, creation of and solution to stress – on several levels in relation to the 'knowledge cultures', as discussed above. I see myself being both subjected to, and part of, the issue of stress creation. This comes from the position that we, in this space and time, are all subjects of our 'cultural values' and 'social expectations', which both influence and shape us. That said, we can learn and develop tools (such as those used in coaching) to challenge and resist such power structures of cultural values and social expectations. This then impacts how stress is produced and managed. I see this as being achieved by 'cultivating' myself and encouraging others to do the same, through the coaching work that I do. Foucault (1978) further argues that one cannot escape or move beyond the cultural values and social expectations; rather, one can learn which to accept or resist, which he referred to as the "art of existence".

Coaching psychology has already created interventions for the non-clinical population by drawing on existing psychological theories and techniques. However, I view my work as presenting a discourse that may not have been accessible previously. Willig (1999) proposes that "individuals are constrained by available discourses because discursive positions pre-exist the individual whose sense of 'self' (subjectivity) and range of experiences are circumscribed by available discourses" (p.114). Therefore, by eliciting from the discourses that are now available, the client can re-author the self, through crafting and reconstructing how they produce their story – and ultimately their identity – in relation to stress.

I view my professional self as being positioned within and having influence on the situation. Foucault (1982) suggests that madness through our cultural perspective is 'owned' by, or belongs to, the disciplines of psychology/psychoanalysis and psychiatry. It is here that these disciplines assume an expert position of power; where another's behaviour is assessed and determined with significant consequences. It may be argued that there is still caution within our culture and society, resulting from these positions of power, causing a dynamic between patient and therapist/psychologist, where the power is distributed towards the expert. I suggest that this may impact individuals seeking support when it comes to stress-related issues. So, it is here that I see myself as a coach being located within this situation in an alternative position, regardless of the ontology of the coaching tools and processes used. The discourses that are now made available through the coaching process but previously were not enable coachees to re-author the self in relation to stress, thus offering up new ways in which to construct, produce, formulate and perform ways of coping.

Empowering the client

As a coaching psychologist, I relate to my clients on an equal footing, while still offering expertise. This is unlike the attitude of a clinical/counselling psychologist who assumes a position of 'expert'. The relationship developed during coaching between the coach and the client is one of full transparency and equality. "Coaching requires a sophisticated set of skills and the ability to draw on expert knowledge, whilst at the same time facilitating the self-directed learning which lies at the core of the coaching enterprise", such as drawing on Grant's (2007) Engagement/Well-being Matrix and Proposed Model of Goal Striving and Mental Health, with stress as one example of health and well-being (see p.24); ultimately empowering the client to become their own self-coach. It is suggested that this results in less perceived stigma because coaching is seen in a more positive light than therapy/counselling. Consequently, individuals may see coaching as being more approachable and therefore may be amenable to facing challenges and concerns earlier, prior to the difficulties becoming clinical. However, it is here that the boundaries between therapy and coaching may become blurred, entering a grey space, which will be discussed later. I have often found myself grappling in this grey space within my practice; these experiences resulting in the development of this research (see e.g. p.20, Case Study 2 – Client A2).

Setting and recognising boundaries

On reviewing the literature relating to the boundaries between therapy and coaching and what the ethical procedures are, some guidelines have been set. However, there are no clear-cut lines of demarcation, but more vague, generic guidance, which is, at times, conflicting (see pp.20).

Grant (2007) suggests a "discrepancy between the espoused ideas of what coaching 'should' be and the reality of what happens in real-life coaching practice" (p.177); indicating that the boundary between the practice of coaching and that of therapy may be blurred. Bachkirova and Cox (2004) argue that the differences of concern within client-therapy and client-coaching are not necessarily clear-cut. Moreover, studies suggest that clients who voluntarily seek life coaching have higher levels of psychopathology, with 25–50 per cent more people meeting clinical mental health criteria (Green, Oades & Grant, 2005; Spencer & Grant, 2005) than those who enter coaching through workplace coaching programmes (Grant, 2007). As a result, Grant (2007) has presented questions such as:

> Given that a proportion of clients presenting for coaching will have mental health problems, do such issues exclude them from coaching? Can a professional coach ethically coach someone with an anxiety disorder when the goal of the coaching engagement is about a work or leadership development related issue, or if a client becomes depressed during the coaching engagement?
>
> (p.253)

I would go further and ask such questions as: 'How do we understand and manage boundaries around such mental health issues in relationship to goal attainment, which emerges from within the context of personal development or stress management?'

Furthermore, as stress may be seen as a "continuum of stress" (Krupnik, 2020. p.2), this is particularly relevant to the grey space: whilst on one side of the continuum we may see 'normative stress' responses, further along the continuum we move towards 'traumatic stress responses'. "Trauma is defined not as an event but the subjective experience of *stress*, that is, stress response" (Krupnik, 2020. p.2, emphasis in original). Therefore, I propose that, as coaches working with clients to manage stress and create greater resilience, it is more likely that we will encounter clients on the continuum of stress precisely because these are the people who are in need of assistance. The hybrid model Figure 3.1 defines the stress continuum along two axes: severity of stressors and strength of self-regulation functions. Their ratio determines the nature of stress response; that is, its place on the continuum (Krupnik, 2019). "The continuum is divided into three categories: normative stress response (NSR), pathogenic stress (PSR) and traumatic stress (TSR)" (Krupnik, 2020, p.2). This model highlights that all three aspects of stress sit on a continuum. Therefore, I propose that, as coaches working within the sphere of stress management, we may face a range of 'stresses', not only NSR; once again opening up the possibility of encountering the grey space.

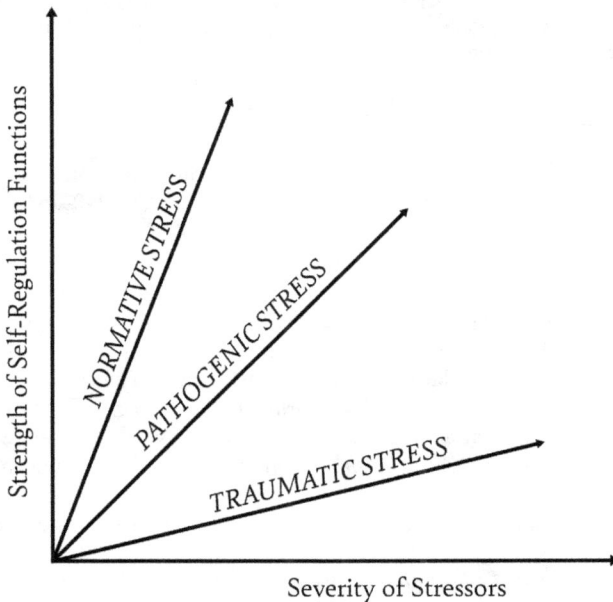

Figure 3.1 Hybrid Categorical-Dimensional Model of Stress
Source: Krupnik, 2019, p.2.

Summary

Chapter 3 used case study examples to give a brief overview of how and when we may encounter the grey space as practitioners. The chapter investigates stress as a 'wicked problem' and situates my research topic within real-world examples. The importance of setting and recognising boundaries is also briefly reflected upon, to be further explored in later chapters.

Discussion points

1. Consider the impact that the COVID-19 pandemic had on the meaning of stress in your practice using Rittel and Webber's characteristics of a 'wicked problem' as a reference.
2. How does stress show up in your practice?
3. In which ways do/are you able to distinguish the severity of stress in your practice?

Note

1 Throughout this chapter the terms 'therapy' and 'counselling' are used interchangeably to encompass all terms referring to therapy, counselling, psychotherapy and counselling/ clinical psychological interventions.

Suggested reading

Grant, A.M. (2007). 'A languishing-flourishing model of goal striving and mental health for coaching populations'. *International Coaching Psychology Review* 2(3), 250–264.

References

BBC News (2021). 'How has coronavirus affected mental health?'. Available at: How has coronavirus affected mental health? - BBC News (Accessed: May 2023).

Bachkirova, T. & Cox, E. (2004). 'A bridge over troubled water: Bridging together coaching and counselling'. *The International Journal of Mentoring and Coaching,* 2(1), 35–45.

Brown, V. (2010). 'Collective enquiry and its wicked problems'. In V. Brown, J.A. Harris & Y. Russell (eds.), *Tackling wicked problems through the transdisciplinary imagination.* London: Earthscan.

Foucault, M. (1978). *The history of sexuality, Volume 1: An introduction.* New York, NY: Vintage.

Foucault, M. (1982). *Madness and civilization: A history of insanity in the age of reason.* London: Tavistock.

Gherardi, S. (2009). 'Practice? It's a matter of taste!' *Management Learning,* 40(5), 535–550.

Grant, A.M. (2007). 'A languishing-flourishing model of goal striving and mental health for coaching populations'. *International Coaching Psychology Review* 2(3), 250–264.

Green, S., Oades, L.G. & Grant, A.M. (2005). 'An evaluation of a life-coaching group programme: initial findings from a waitlisted control study'. In M. Cavanagh, A.M. Grant & T. Kemp (eds.), *Evidence based coaching, Volume 1: Theory, research and practice from the behavioural science.* Bowen Hills, Australia: Australian Academic Press.

International Federation of Red Cross and Red Crescent Societies (IFRC). (n.d.). 'World Mental Health Day: New Red Cross survey shows COVID-19 affecting mental health of one in two people'. Available at: World Mental Health Day: New Red Cross survey shows COVID-19 affecting mental health of one in two people | IFRC (Accessed: May 2023).

Krupnik, V. (2019). 'Trauma or adversity?' *Traumatology*, 25(4), 256–261.

Krupnik, V. (2020). 'Trauma or drama: A predictive processing perspective on the continuum of stress'. *Frontiers in Psychology*, 11, 1248–1248.

Mental Health Foundation. (2018). 'Stress: are we coping?' Available at: https://www.menta lhealth.org.uk/publications/stress-are-we-coping (Accessed: October 2018).

Mind (2021). 'Coronavirus: the consequences for mental health. The ongoing impact of coronavirus pandemic on people with mental health problems across England and Wales'. Available at: the-consequences-of-coronavirus-for-mental-health-final-report.pdf (mind. org.uk) (Accessed: May 2023).

Mind (2020). 'The mental health emergency: How has the coronavirus pandemic impacted our mental health?'. Available at: https://www.mind.org.uk/media-a/5929/the-mental-hea lth-emergency_a4_final.pdf (Accessed: August 2020).

Orestis, Z., Butter, S., Bennett, K., Hartman. T.K., Hyland, P., Mason, L., McBride, O., Murphy, J., Gibson-Miller, J., Levita, L., Martinez, A.P., Shevlin, M., Stocks, T.V.A., Vallieres, F. & Bental, R.P. (2021) 'How does the COVID-19 pandemic impact on population mental health? A network analysis of COVID influences on depression, anxiety and traumatic stress in the UK population', *Psychological medicine*, 52(16), 3825–3833.

Ortlund, K., Chandler, M., Lin, B., Anastario, M., & Eick, S. M. (2025). 'Politics negatively impacts women's mental health in Georgia: Depression, anxiety, and perceived stress from 2023 to 2024'. *Social Science & Medicine*, 368, 117800. https://doi.org/10.1016/ j.socscimed.2025.117800

Palmer, S. & Cooper, C. (2013). *How to deal with stress: Creating success.* London: Kogan Page.

Rittel, H. & Webber, M. (1973). 'Dilemmas in a general theory of planning'. *Policy Science*, 4, 155–169.

Spencer, G.B. & Grant, A.M. (2005). 'Individual and group life coaching: Initial findings from a randomised, controlled trial'. In M. Cavanagh, A.M. Grant & T. Kemp (eds.), *Evidence based coaching, Volume 1: Theory, Research and practice from the behavioural science.* Bowen Hills, Australia: Australian Academic Press.

Willig, C. (1999). 'Discourse analysis and sex education'. In C. Willig (ed.), *Applied discourse analysis: Social and psychological interventions.* Buckingham: Open University Press.

YouGov (March, 2022). 'War in Ukraine leads to spiking stress, fear, and sadness among Britons'. Available at: War in Ukraine leads to spiking stress, fear and sadness among Britons | YouGov (Accessed: May 2023).

Chapter 4

Navigating the grey space Part I

The grey space compass: the process of how coaches explore and plot this territory

This chapter aims to review previous guidance, which provided the purpose of this research. In doing so, we as coaches can manage the complexities of the grey space while staying ethical. This chapter then plots the terrain offering a recalibration of our compass as coaches, by charting and mapping how coaches explore and navigate this grey space. It includes exploring when and how coaching continues and when to signpost to other professional interventions, such as therapy. It can be surmised that this is not a one-size-fits-all approach. Questions are contemplated such as: What are the similarities and differences of various coaches when managing and approaching the grey space with their clients?, How and when do coaches signpost? The extracts presented are representative of the collaborative enquiry group workshops and cross-boundary experts' one-to-one conversations, exploring the lived experiences of coaches navigating this terrain.

Defining trauma and its impacts

Maté (2022) suggests that there is a continuum that we all sit on regarding being affected by trauma, rather than a distinction between those who are traumatised and those who are unaffected. Vaughan-Smith (2019) further advises that "working with trauma in clients and us is the 'norm' for coaching, not the exception" (p.15). She adds that, by understanding trauma, we as coaches can retain a coaching position with our clients; not becoming activated by our own "survival defences". This is not only important for us as coaches but also for our clients.

> The expression of trauma symptoms may not be so dramatic, but we meet them regularly in our work. These symptoms can get in the way of effective coaching and of personal development. It is for this reason that coaches need to learn about trauma, so they can apply that learning to their own mode of working.
>
> (Maté, 2022, p.3)

Furthermore, in Vaughan-Smith's (2019) book, *Coaching and Trauma*, a table is presented (see Table 4.1) on the skills, techniques and attitudes relating to working

DOI: 10.4324/9781003509776-5

Table 4.1 Core skills, techniques and attitudes coaches require when trauma is present in coaching

Principle	Application
Attentive listening without the chatter in our heads; instead, listening to words, observing emotions, body language and what is not being said	Asking powerful questions: used effectively. These are aimed at the non- traumatised resources
Coaches' capacity for being fully present and grounded in contact with themselves and their body	Reflecting, sharing feedback and observations in a way that is useful to the client
Asking permission	Self-awareness, authenticity, curiosity
Clarifying, acknowledging, validating	Acceptance, non-judgemental

Source: Adapted from Vaughan-Smith (2019, p.100).

with clients when trauma is present. The themes that are presented are similar to the themes that emerged in my own research.

There are various types of trauma. Currently, they are described as follows:

- **Single-incident or acute stress disorder**, which results from a single traumatic event, such as a robbery, physical assault or acute medical illness. Symptoms such as re-experiencing, avoidance/numbing and hyperarousal may occur. Symptoms resolve within one month.
- **Post-traumatic stress disorder** (PTSD) or **chronic trauma**, which can result from a variety of different traumas and "can result from a single acute event that turns chronic, or it can occur after several related events", such as a car collision, rape, loss of a loved one or witnessing another's trauma (Anderson, 2021, p.13). Symptoms such as intrusive images, avoidance, negative beliefs, increased arousal and reactivity with symptoms persist beyond one month.
- **Complex PTSD** or **relational trauma** is relational in nature, where trauma is repetitive. Herman (1992) proposes that complex PTSD results from exposure to extended or recurrent occurrences or multiple forms of interpersonal trauma "often occurring under circumstances where escape is not possible due to physical, psychological, maturational, family, environmental or social constraints" (cited in Anderson, 2021, p.13). Symptoms include core PTSD symptoms as well as difficulty with emotional regulation, relational difficulties, alterations in attention and consciousness, negative beliefs and somatic distress.
- **Developmental trauma** may be viewed from two perspectives. The first considers this as complex and relational trauma in childhood, also known as developmental trauma disorder (van der Kolk, 2005). The other considers the developmental stage the individual was at when the trauma occurred, impacting brain development, with different parts of the brain being affected at different ages and by different traumas (Teicher & Samson, 2016).

- **Extreme** or **dissociative trauma** may be viewed as a spectrum disorder ranging from dissociative parts on the benign scale of spacing out, to the most extreme dissociative identity disorder. This forms when the individual believes they are in a life-or-death situation and so this becomes a survival mechanism.

(Anderson, 2021, p.13)

In Taylor's (2022) trauma-informed model, she "rejects biomedical models, psychiatric theory and diagnosis, labelling and treatment", and instead seeks to work with "people as humans who have been subjected to different forms of stress, trauma, oppression, pressure, inequality, injury and abuse (both acute and chronic)" (p.14). Rather than discussing symptoms and illness when talking about trauma, "we talk about responses and coping mechanisms", with behaviours, thoughts or feelings after trauma or distress viewed as responses or coping mechanisms, rather than categorising this as mental disorder, symptom or illness (Taylor, 2022, p.14).

What is trauma-informed/sensitive practice?

Heller and Kammer (2022) suggest that there has been growing recognition that trauma has changed our understanding and approach to treating mental health to a considerable extent +over the past 40-plus years. Additionally, a trauma-informed approach is being used beyond the field of psychology, from health care, education, public policy and law enforcement all the way through to yoga, meditation and coaching, to name but a few. "Trauma-informed care is a broad set of principles that shape how services are delivered and how individuals and communities are supported" (Heller & Kammer, 2022, p.23). The authors draw on an example from the documentary film *Paper Tigers* (2015). It is about a school where all the 'troubled kids' were sent, where high rates of absenteeism, substance abuse, fighting, teen pregnancy, gangs and criminal behaviour are common. The principal, having been introduced to cutting-edge research of adverse childhood experiences (ACEs) and complex trauma, was inspired to implement a trauma-informed approach, recognising that the children had unresolved trauma. He changed the way in which teachers taught and related to the children, moving from a punitive approach to one of curiosity and compassion. "The trauma-informed movement is striving to change these often-dehumanising systems to become more humane, supportive, and life-affirming" (Heller & Kammer, 2022, p.25).

Table 4.2 details the differences between the conventional perspective and the neuro affective relational model (NARM) based on trauma-informed care, and former ways of focusing on client care (Heller & Kammer, 2022, p.25).

What is particularly interesting to me is that trauma-informed/sensitive training was not a standard training within my psychology degrees, with the British Psychological Society (BPS) only recently offering training on trauma-sensitive

Table 4.2 Differences between the conventional perspective and NARM-based trauma-informed perspective of focusing on client care

Conventional Perspective	NARM-based Trauma-informed Perspective
"What's wrong with you?"	"What happened to you? And how have you adapted to what happened to you?"
Treatment focused on individual symptoms and behaviours	Treatment focused on the whole person, recognising that they are living within families, communities and the systems that impact them
Symptoms/problems are pathological; clients are sick, ill or bad	Symptoms/problems are survival strategies clients use to deal with unresolved trauma; clients are generally doing the best they can, given their circumstances
Use labels to describe client pathology	Humanise clients by describing the impact of trauma on individuals, families and communities
Helping professionals are the experts providing services to broken survivors	Helping professionals collaborate with clients, supporting agency, choice and control in the healing process
Goals are defined by helping professionals, and focus on symptom reduction	Goals are defined by clients and focus on recovery, self-efficacy, growth and healing
Help is provided reactively, generally focused on managing crises	Help is provided proactively, generally focused on preventing further crises and strengthening resilience
Treatment aimed at managing or eliminating symptoms and behaviours	Treatment aimed at resolving underlying trauma and supporting greater connection to self and others

Source: From *The Practical Guide for Healing Developmental Trauma: Using the Neuro-Affective Relational Model to Address Adverse Childhood Experiences and Resolve Complex Trauma* by Laurence Heller and Brad Kammer, published by North Atlantic Books, copyright © 2022 by Laurence Heller and Brad Kammer. Reprinted by permission of North Atlantic Books.

practice. I would argue that this should be standard training across all fields and helping professions.

Boundaries and ethics

Figure 4.1 illustrates that the boundaries between therapeutic and coaching work are not clear.

Boundaries within coaching act to serve the coach and client on several levels: providing clarity to the coach as to what is acceptable practice, as well as

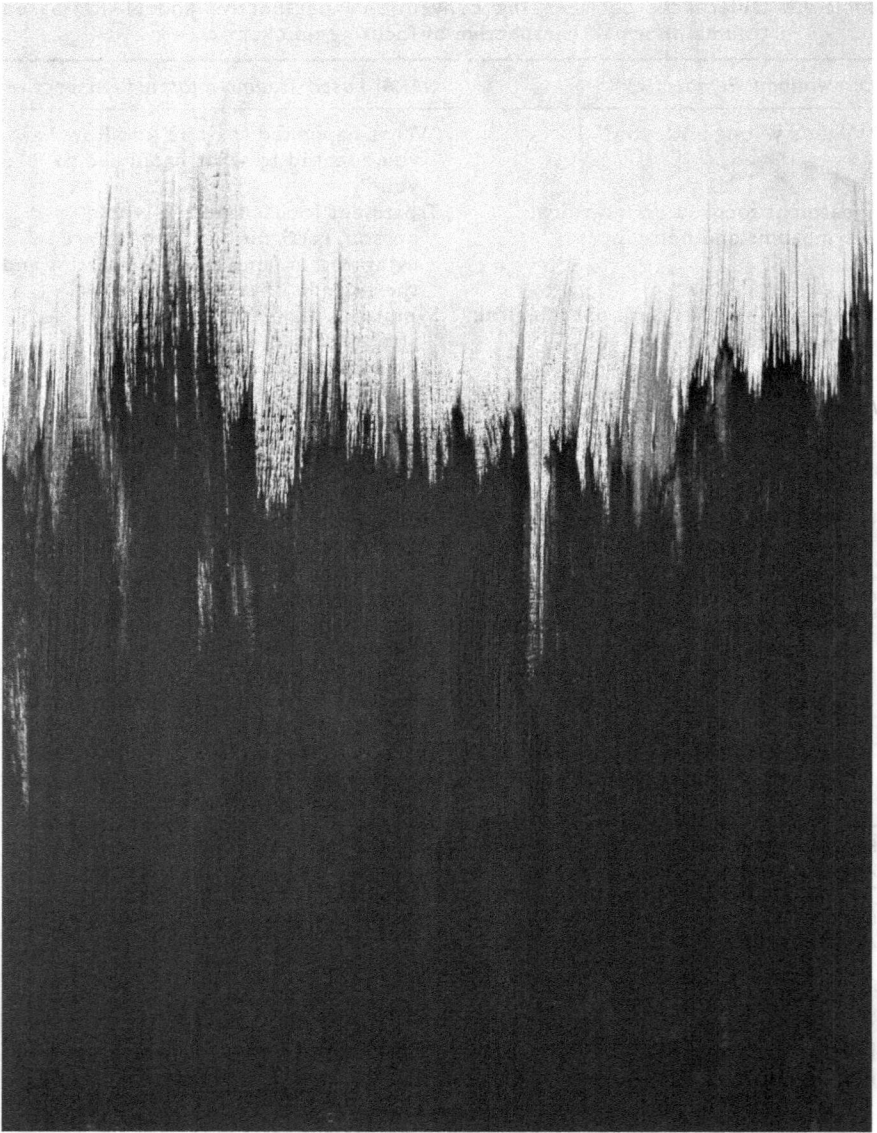

Figure 4.1 Conceptual overlap of therapeutic and coaching practices
Source: https://danslelakehouse.com/2012/02/simple-but-striking-diy-painting.html

a yardstick against which they can discern what is expected (Popovic & Jinks, 2014). Boundaries create structure, expectations, trust and safety, as well as out-lining the responsibility of both client and coach, thus providing a supportive environment.

Some guidance on how to manage the situation of a coachee, who may be presenting a mental health issue, is available. Grant (2007) suggests that the task of the coach is not to diagnose whether a client has a mental health issue, but rather to ask: "Can my coaching help? What are my limitations with this issue? What is in the best interest of the client?" Cavanagh (2005) suggests five questions one should ask oneself when considering whether to refer on a coachee if one has concerns about some of their behaviours or thinking. These are: 1) How long has the distress been going on? 2) How extreme are the behaviours and responses? 3) How pervasive are the distress and dysfunctional behaviours? 4) How defensive is the person? and 5) How resistant to change are they? The answers assist in helping the coach gain a bigger picture of what the coachee may be experiencing. However, what this may mean for the continuation of coaching depends on several other factors, such as the coaching context, the contract, the skill set of the coach and the desires of the coachee.

There are several factors to be taken into consideration, such as the coachees' ability to process their adult selves, while displaying openness to implementing new behaviours in order to achieve the coaching goals. Other points to be considered are the context and content for which the coachee seeks support, whether the coach has a broad ability and whether the coachee is not directly seeking therapy and is able to manage change (Joseph, 2006; Popovic & Jinks, 2014).

Rutkowski (2014) acknowledges that understanding the difference between coaching and therapy with precision is a complex task. Definitions of coaching offer modest distinction or clarity; suggesting that it is of substantial interest to both professions to understand how coaching and therapeutic practices vary in action.

An acceptance of an overlap or "fuzzy space" (Joplin, 2007) between therapy and coaching in general has featured within the coaching literature, acknowledging the complexity of this space (Hart & Leipsic, 2001; Maxwell, 2009; Price, 2009; Rutkowski, 2014). Maxwell (2009) proposes that the boundary distinctions do not lie within the fields of coaching or therapy, but rather within the practitioner, with the "willingness and ability of both coach and client to work with personal/psychological material" (p.82).

Ethics, on the other hand, is viewed as a "moral philosophy in which issues of good and evil, right and wrong, justice and injustice are considered" (Garvey & Stokes, 2022, p.282). The difficulty is that what one individual considers wrong another may consider right. Furthermore, Garvey and Stokes (2022) pose that due to the structure of most professional associations' ethical frameworks, which are created in a normative, punitive and prescriptive manner, it is inevitable that individuals will find themselves sweeping genuine ethical dilemmas under the carpet, as they will certainly be either right or wrong at some point, as a result of the structure of these ethical frameworks. In addition, ethics is viewed as time and context bound, with ethics being socially defined to satisfy specific prevailing conditions. It is suggested that what was once relevant may not remain relevant at a future point in time, due to contextual changes, and so ethics should rather be viewed as dynamic (Garvey & Stokes, 2022, p.282). Research undertaken by Faiten Diochon and Nizet (2015), investigating how coaches applied codes when faced with ethical dilemmas, identified three main categories: 1) the code was not relevant; 2) the code has 'shortcomings' itself; and 3) the code was an 'obstacle' to the ethics of the coach. When considering the management of boundaries, particularly the intersection of therapy and coaching as discussed above, I would argue that if a practitioner turns to the ethics and codes of conduct of whichever body or association the coach is associated with, they will be met with standardised, normative and prescriptive codes of conduct that do not shine a light on the best way to move forward.

Moreover, arguments may be put forward by some professional bodies that "these codes offer '*protection from harm*' but do not consider the potential benefits of actions that a code might deem as unethical" (Garvey & Stokes, 2023, p.39, emphasis in original). Finally, it could be said that the rhetoric from all professional bodies is rather "unsophisticated in terms of ethical theory. Ethical theory and definitions on ethical stance approach and impact are vague, broad and lack support from empirical data" (Garvey & Stokes, 2023, p.48).

The role of the coach

Sime and Jocob (2018) suggest that detailed and robust research surrounding the experience of "how coaches work, the roles they adopt, how they experience boundaries and where they actually lie within the professional practices does not currently exist" (p.49); further proposing that the foundation of key theories that could shape the conversation surrounding coaching should be practical information such as this. In their study to explore the coaches' perceptions of roles, borders and boundaries, Sime and Jocob (2018) concluded that this resulted in more questions being raised regarding the boundary between coaching and therapy; calling for acceptance from both professions to acknowledge the overlap and suggesting that the focus should be on continued, transparent and judgement-free dialogues between the two professions. "Focusing on what benefits the client more than how to support the development of the profession and its practice is far more important than continuing the attempts to draw a clean line in the sand" (p.60). Giraldez-Hayes' (2021) study explored how coaches and therapists perceive similarities and differences and how they set boundaries, concluding that "although therapy and coaching are recognized as distinct fields, professionals acknowledge a 'grey area' or overlap between their practices" (p.26).

As discussed, an argument has been presented that there is a fine line and even a fuzzy space (Joplin, 2007) between what signifies coaching and what gradually starts to become therapeutic territory. Grant (2007) proposes that one of the principal distinctions is that of working towards the client's goals, where coaching goal striving and mental health/mental illness sit side by side (Keyes, 2003). Grant

(2007) also suggests that, while remaining in the bounds of coaching, the "primary focus is not explicitly on alleviating psychopathology or primarily dealing with distress; rather it is about assisting clients in articulating goals and helping them systematically strive towards goal attainment" (p.252).

When coachees enter coaching, they bring all of themselves. Therefore, it is important that we, as practitioners, are able to navigate this terrain; not to be fearful but, rather, to be able to be courageous and face challenging emotions, so as not to conspire with the "tyranny of the positive" (Einzig, 2011). At the same time, we must remain within the ethical considerations of what it is to be a coach, knowing one's own limits and boundaries, while ensuring a basic awareness of psychological and personality disorder, and employing the ability to recognise disorders (Einzig, 2011).

The purpose of my work has been to learn more about how I and other coaches manage this murky grey space, while remaining ethical. Personally, I draw on supervision; my supervisor being Dr S. O'Riordan, who is a chartered psychologist and chartered coaching psychologist, as well as being a leading figure within coaching psychology as a founder chair and fellow of the International Society for Coaching (ISCP), and course co-director/trainer on coaching and coaching psychology at the Centre for Coaching and Centre for Stress Management (UK). She is also registered as a supervisor with both BPS and Applied Psychology Practice Supervisors and is an ISCP accredited supervisor. In addition to supervision, I maintain CPD from my professional communities. In other words, I am a member of the BPS, the Division of Coaching Psychology-BPS, the ISCP and the Association for Coaching (AC), who publish ethical guidelines and codes of conduct.

One example of ethically navigating the grey space is Client A2, the subject of Case Study 2 (see p. 20).

Approach and method

Little is known about how of coaches with various levels of expertise and competency manage and deal with ethical and boundary issues on a practical level, for example, when a coachee presents that they have or may be having mental health issues during the process of coaching work. As discussed, there are frameworks, models and matrices (Grant, 2007; 2017) available that help set out guidance for boundary management. These include when and how coaching can continue by drawing on tools, for example, the use of action plans and goal attainment, or when to signpost to other professional interventions, such as therapy. This scenario is not a one-size-fits-all approach, with much being left to the coach's discernment. This may push coaches into one of two spaces: first, that of being narrowly focused and not acknowledging the client as a whole, with coaches – due to these complexities, such as trauma or mental health illness being disclosed – possibly not being brave enough (Einzig, 2011) to step into the grey space; or, second, coaches stepping far beyond their own abilities and capabilities. Both of these spaces result in the client's progress being hindered. Yet, there may be a third space, where coaches can navigate these complexities while remaining within the boundaries of coaching. This is what I am particularly interested in.

Due to my curiosity, questions began to emerge in my own practice, such as: Do other coaches experience, manage and approach the grey space as I do? What are the differences and similarities in the meaning of the grey space for other coaches? Do they share a similar sense of self-examination, isolation and questions surrounding improvement of practice? What practices do other coaches use to develop their own 'knowledge landscape' (Brown, 2010). These gave rise to my research questions and focus.

At the heart of this research is collaborative enquiry, which aims to explore the differences and similarities between how coaches negotiate the grey space, in order to better understand how we can navigate this complex terrain and improve the management of boundaries and ethics both for coaches within practice and to safeguard clients. The aim of this study is threefold: 1) for me: research contributes to my personal development; 2) for us: research is a cooperative endeavour, which enables us to act effectively in the world; and 3) for others: research contributes to the fund of knowledge (Reason & Marshal, 1987, p.113).

I address these three aspects in this research/enquiry to improve my own practice and navigation of the grey space; through taking part the co-enquirers gain reflective and reflexive practice to improve their navigation of the grey space. And as a result of my research the coaching profession receives a body of knowledge that adds insights into how we may improve navigating the grey space ethically.

This research contributes to the field of coaching by combining action research and reflexive personal narrative informed by autoethnography, with constructive thematic analysis (CTA) in post-positivist qualitative research. Furthermore, my research aims to gain an insight and understanding into how I and other coaches retain ethical and boundary considerations and help the client to meet their objectives, while walking the tightrope of the grey space when working with stress management, resilience and personal development coaching, as it straddles the boundaries of coaching and therapy. This assists in supporting and informing best practice for coaches, as well as developing an understanding of how the coaching process may influence the client.

I drew from the work of Coghlan and Brannick and McNiff and Whitehead, generally dividing this study into action research using second-person research with others as a collaborative endeavour, and first-person self-study action research, with a sequence of actions taking place using first-person research to second-person research and then back to first-person research.

The work of Coghlan and Brannick (2014) influenced my collaborative enquiry groups and the one-to-one interviews/conversations I had with cross-boundary experts, who straddle the therapy and coaching worlds. Because their work was designed to undertake action research in an organisational context, the enquiry groups and one-to-one conversations were akin to doing research within an

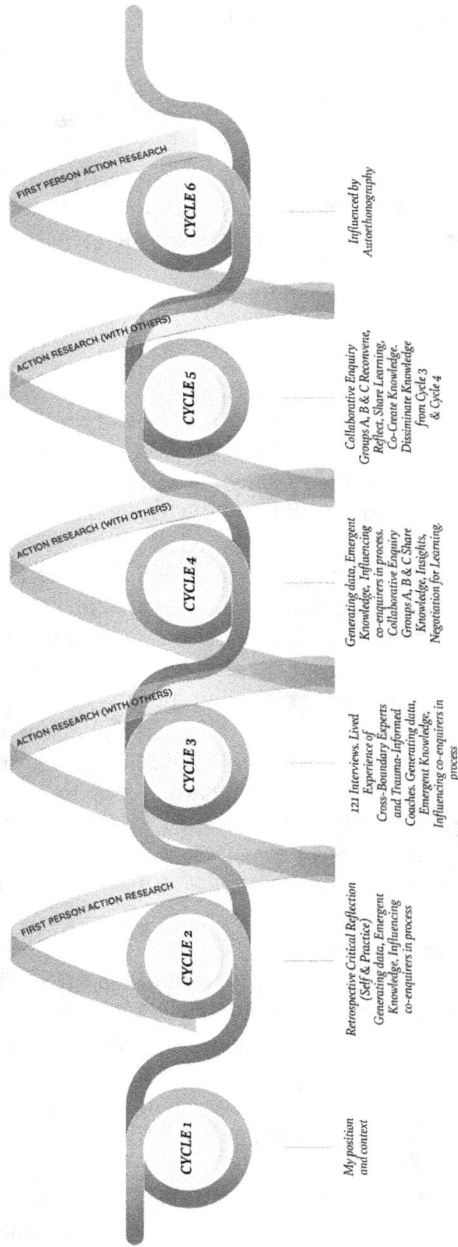

Figure 4.2 Action research design cycles

organisation as the one-to-one conversations and groups were made up of professionals. In the context of my first-person self-study action research, I drew from the work of McNiff and Whitehead (2010) including being informed by autoethnography approaches and retrospective critical reflection narrative enquiry. However, there have been moments when I have drawn on this body of work across second-person research with others and first-person self-study using aspects of the principles of action research interchangeably.

Sitting within the action research framework, a mix of qualitative approaches was adopted, combining critical reflection, narrative enquiry informed by autoethnography, retrospective critical reflection narrative and inductive CTA. Figure 4.2 shows the research design cycles.

Action research

Action research provided the overarching framework for this enquiry because the principal purpose of action research is to facilitate social change and improvement (Coghlan, 2006). Action research takes place within cycles of enquiry. Cycles of enquiry 'with others' and my own self-study ran parallel throughout the enquiry as the principal researcher and author of this book. This enabled the generation of data to identify core themes for knowledge and practice.

Action research is seen as a practical way in which a practitioner can enquire into their own work to examine if all is as they would like it to be (McNiff, 2002), because the researcher is considered to be situated within and part of the research. It has the capacity to assist the practitioner to make sense of their life because it moves beyond the surface structure of method (while still regarding it as important) to look deeply at the underlying configuration of our values and intentions of our lived experience (McNiff, 2002). Overall, action research is a flowing set of principles used for everyday practice to: 1) understand what has happened; 2) plan for actions for the future; 3) perform those actions; and 4) reflect on what has occurred post-implementation. These steps form multiple cycles, which often overlap and do not always follow a neat and tidy sequence (Githens, 2015).

Action research is also about helping others find ways to investigate their own practices, with the principal researcher in a relationship of collaborative enquiry. In the spirit of collaborative enquiry, the principal researcher does this by taking action on others' own thinking, to help them discover ways in which this can influence thinking and learning, so that they can, in turn, investigate their own practices; the point being how learning informs action and how the researcher's learning can inform their own and others' learning (McNiff & Whitehead, 2010). In this case, myself and other coaches.

I have chosen action research as my overarching approach, within which my research activities sit, because of its goal of creating "actionable knowledge" (Argyris, 2003), which benefits both practitioners and academia through an emergent enquiry process (Adler & Shani, 2001). It is a process that is collaborative, with the objective of involving individuals in the creation of actionable know-ledge regarding themselves, the actions taken and their work. Actionable know-ledge arises through maintaining a sense of curiosity as a collective. In doing so, a dynamic space is created, allowing for a wealth of knowledge to emerge. Action research views the co-enquirer as being rooted within and forming part of the research, rather than a detached observer. It, therefore, enabled other coaches and myself to explore ourselves as coaches, how we work and how we manage the grey space, with the objective of creating actionable knowledge through shared learning and exploration. Moreover, action research positions itself as not being "grounded in formal propositions but … a human activity which draws on different forms of knowing" (Coghlan, 2006, p.295).

Consequently, action research is the principal approach on which this research was designed and it acted as the 'container' for engaging in the process of asking and addressing the research question.

In addition, action research lends itself to cycles that are central to the develop-ment of actionable knowledge, drawing from the following methodologies to help inform it. I used critical reflection, autoethnography and CTA to inform the action research cycles and to support the analysis process. Furthermore, research cycles are central to the development of actionable knowledge due to the "reflection on reflection" (Argyris, 2003): a process of stepping back at every cycle to evaluate the process, the meanings and the experience; all of which then inform further planning for action. It is through this process that insider action research gains its quality, and why the knowledge that emerges has the capacity to become actionable (Coghlan, 2006).

My rationale for drawing on forms of narrative enquiry throughout the research design was because in action research "doing research and writing on research are intermingled" (Heikkinen et al., 2012, p.11). Through the narrative accounts of action research, there is a collaboration with the participant-storyteller. "We think that narratives are a means to not only report action research, but also to provide a fundamental connection for action research and narrative enquiry. We think both action research and narrative enquiry are participatory approaches by nature" (Heikkinen et al., 2012, p.18). As a result the stories told represent the co-enquirers' meaning-making of their experiences of all aspects of their lives. These narratives and accounts are constructed and arranged from 'messy' internal experiences, which are likely to be multivocal and dialogical facets of the self that emerge in conversation, without any sign of self-representation Consequently the story constructed reflects the internal as well as the social world of the participant-storyteller, rather than the researcher just describing and classifying themes (Josselson, 2011). Furthermore, Brody (2002, p.186) states that "narrative is not just an explanatory device, but is actually constitutive of the way we experience things".

I believe that this approach is well suited to enabling me to gain further under-standing of the dilemmas that I and other coaches face from a boundary and ethical perspective when negotiating the grey space.

Research in the right direction

I pivoted from wanting to research what the effects were on individuals' post 'stress management coaching' to an exploration of how coaches manage the boundaries between the therapeutic and coaching terrain. As a result, my research design also needed to change. I moved from a design that was familiar (semi-structured interviews, drawing on discourse analysis) to exploring action research. I believe that this is the best design for the aims of my research, which is to understand how other coaches navigate and experience the grey space. Another aim is to enhance coaching as a practice for myself and others so that we might better understand these boundaries, become better equipped as practitioners and ensure that coaching is conducted ethically.

McNiff argues that action research is based on principles, which include the

> need for justice and democracy, the right for all people to speak and be heard, the right of each individual to show how and why they have given extra attention to their learning in order to improve their work ... to experience truth and beauty in our personal and professional lives.
>
> (McNiff, 2002, p.5)

Within these principles, action research offers the possibility to share learning. In this way change can take place immediately. The quote above resonates with me as both a practitioner and an individual, with the belief that everyone has the right to gain the knowledge to become empowered and improve their lives, both personally and professionally. These core principles within action research resonate with my own ontological views, which constitute a transformative ontology concerned with giving voice to the disenfranchised and the creation of social change through addressing issues of power, social justice, discrimination and oppression. I view it as my role as researcher to facilitate voice to the lived experiences of co-enquirers and their clients, who may not otherwise have the opportunity.

I hold a social constructionist position:

> social constructionism insists that we take a critical stance towards our taken-for-granted ways of understanding the world, including ourselves. It invites us to be critical to the idea that our observations of the world unproblematically yield its nature to us, to challenge the view that a conventional knowledge is based on objective, unbiased observations of the world. It is therefore in opposition to positivism and empiricism in traditional science – the assumption that the natural world can be revealed by observation, and that what exists is what we perceive to exist.
>
> (Burr, 1995, pp.2–3)

Rather, reality is seen as moment-by-moment representations that are constructed within an immediate contextual framework. Therefore, individuals' accounts are viewed as meaningful situational statements rather than objects of reference (Antaki,

2004; Edwards, Ashmore & Potter, 1995; Jost & Kuklinski, 2002; Mallon, 2007) (as discussed on pp.00–00).

Brenè Brown's idea that "a surefooted and confident mapmaker does not a swift traveller make" (Brown, 2012, pp.15–16) not only reflects my personal experience but also the way in which I expect the research itself to evolve. I find that even in my own journey "there are times when frustration and self-doubt take over" (Brown, 2012). Using these ideas, when drawing on an action research approach, one needs to hold a space for managing uncertainty and the frustration that this may bring. Not only was the data generative but so too was the process of conducting the research, as well as the way I and the co-enquirers agreed and co-created this enquiry.

Cycles and workshops

Cycle 1: First-person action research: my position and context

The starting point for any action research enquiry is the exploration of values. To be a self-reflexive practitioner, one needs to be aware of what propels us in our life as well as in our work. This enables one to be clearer about what one is doing and why (McNiff, 2002).

Therefore, acknowledging my positionality is imperative as a researcher conducting a Doctorate of Professional Studies. Holmes (2014) poses that positionality is context, situation-specific and flexible not fixed. Furthermore, from this stance, the research design and process are shaped by the views and positions of the researcher, which are coloured by values, beliefs, demographics, social and political standing, perception, etc. (Holmes, 2014). Therefore, taking the researcher's worldview into consideration is vital. This is why my position and context were explored in Chapter 2.

Cycle 2: First-person action research: retrospective critical reflection

I conducted a retrospective critical reflection to clarify my values, evaluating how these elements play out in my practice and within my coaching relationship, forming the basis for my action research as well as informing the first cycle of actionable knowledge.

Cycle 2 was a retrospective critical reflection on how I had encountered and navigated the grey space with clients in the past (see Chapter 2). This created a starting point for discussion and sharing, based on my own experience of difficulties relating to boundary negotiation, ethics, values and the personal and professional positions that I hold and how I navigated them.

My self-reflection provided a way of opening discussions, which was shared in order to begin the collaborative discussion of the dis/similarities with both the cross-boundary experts and the collaborative enquiry groups. My objective was to set the tone, as well as create shared learning immediately, I wanted to create a space for reflecting on the practice of others as well as gaining insight by hearing their stories, so by sharing my own story I hoped to encourage the co-enquirers to share theirs. This would result in learning through hearing how others navigate this terrain as well as moving through a cycle of reflecting, refining and improving practice. In addition to this, it was important that I set a respectful tone and acknowledged the diversity of each co-enquirer, what shaped their stories and their accounts. Forces that shape our sense of self include nationality, religion, gender, education, ethnicity, socio-economic class and geography (Chang, 2005). Respect for differences was a vital core value to maintain throughout the study (Haydon, 2006; Wilson, 2009) as it shapes the way we narrate the self. For us to become cross-culturally sensitive to diverse cultural backgrounds, self-reflection and self-examination were essential keys (Florio-Ruane, 2001; Nieto, 2003). Therefore, at the beginning of the first cycle (see p.57–60, Cycle 4) of the collaborative enquiry groups, explicit boundaries were co-created, with each group acknowledging and agreeing to respect each other's differences, with a reminder about the agreed boundaries at the start of the second cycle (see p.60–62, Cycle 5) and the collaborative enquiry groups.

Cycle 3: Co-enquirer/researcher

Having gained this knowledge, I was able to move forward through the next cycles, each time adding further actionable knowledge and shared learning because this created the context for "critical conversations" (McNiff, 2002). Critical conversations were those in which co-enquirers in this research (coaches and myself) were there to learn more about themselves and the ways in which they could practise as equals. The reason for using collaborative enquiry groups was to create a collaborative and shared learning space; investigating how everyone manages boundaries and ethics when working with clients in the grey space. Once the structure of the workshops had been set up, I adopted the position of co-enquirer within the workshop space and so my voice became that of one of the co-enquirers.

The action enquiry begins by reflecting on an individual's practice; in this context, mine. When this is shared with other individuals who wish to be involved, through critiquing, to implement something similar by offering ideas, there is a shift to the question of 'we' – and collaborative learning takes place (McNiff, 2002). I started the enquiry with: "How can I, as a coach, improve the practice of dealing with ethics and managing boundaries in the grey space when working with clients experiencing stress?" in anticipation of it becoming "How can *we* as coaches improve the practice of dealing with ethics and managing boundaries in the grey space, when working with clients experiencing stress?" At this juncture I offered my perspective, which was developed through my own critical reflection process and shared with the various collaborative enquiry groups to be tested against their lived experiences as coaches. The research then moved from my enquiry to a more collaborative process (see pp.57–61). As my perspective was given to spark discussion and debate, stepping into the role of practitioner researcher, I bracketed my own experience to explore the experiences of my co-enquirers; moving the research from *my* enquiry to *our* enquiry.

Co-enquiry and critical friends

Furthermore, co-enquirers were recruited on the basis that they were willing to engage in critical reflection throughout the research process so that they too could identify their 'professional identity' and how they went about 'practice', to reveal the shared commonalities and the differences we bring to the profession. Professional identity can be viewed as a culmination of professional judgement and reasoning, critical self-evaluation and learning (Paterson et al., 2002) how one makes sense of practice (Trede, Macklin & Bridges, 2012) and exploring the self-construction of one's professional identity. Researching the self, using reflective and reflexive practice, offers an opportunity to create and make sense of one's professional identity. Critical reflection is of great importance as a practitioner because it creates a process for gaining awareness, through exploration of the "everyday taken-for granted" (Schön, 1983). By obtaining a new awareness, we may confirm or reconstruct our identities as practitioners (Fook, 2010).

In addition, I engaged in critical conversations with 'critical friends'. A critical friend is someone whose opinion is valued, and their role is to critique and reflect my work back to me as I go through the research process, offering me new ways of viewing my work (McNiff & Whitehead, 2010). Dr Mary Hortog, Dr George Sandamas (my university supervisor), Dr Siobhain O'Riordan (my coaching supervisor), Professor Sarah Corrie, Andrew Meeker (Executive Coach in Applied Positive Psychology) and Barbara Babcock MA (Coaching Psychologist) acted as my critical friends throughout this project.

Several cycles of critical conversation in the form of collaborative enquiry groups, cross-boundary, trauma-informed coaches' conversation/interviews and collaborative discussions with critical friends took place through Cycles 3, 4 and 5 as detailed below.

Cycle 3: Second-person action research with others: one-to-one conversations

On completing my retrospective critical reflection, I revealed how I had encountered and negotiated the grey space with past clients, and examined how different elements played out in my practice and within my coaching relationships.

Parallel to collaborative enquiry, I opened up one-to-one critical conversations (McNiff, 2002) with several cross-boundary experts to discuss, compare and contrast our lived experiences of the grey space and the navigation of it. I define cross-boundary experts as individuals who have had a significant influence on the progression of the field of coaching psychology, in addition to beginning their careers as clinical psychologists, counselling psychologists or psychotherapists.

They are established experts in the field of coaching/coaching psychology, who have a foot in both camps; their other foot being in clinical, counselling psychology, psychotherapy and therapy. This enquiry looked to explore their lived experience of the grey space, how it has informed their practice, thinking, research and writing and create shared learning. By disclosing my lived experience, I hoped to also explore whether the cross-boundary experts held similar or contrasting positions.

The purpose of these interviews was to create actionable knowledge (Argyris, 2003), which could be disseminated within my own practice as well as in the collaborative enquiry groups. The sharing of stories offered insight into how these cross-boundary experts navigated this terrain, which I hoped would offer ways of improving our coaching practices. These semi-structured interviews were recorded and transcribed, using the same six-step process for thematic analysis as suggested by Braun and Clarke (2006i). Codes and themes were given to the collaborative enquiry groups at the end of the groups' second cycle (Cycle 5) (see p.60), so as not to unintentionally influence the groups, or for these experiences to act as doctrine, because of the status that some of these experts have, i.e. coaching gurus.

In addition to a co-enquiry role within the collaborative enquiry groups – and semi-structured conversations with the cross-boundary experts – I created the opportunity to interview trauma-informed coaches as active critical friends to my research. Ten individuals agreed to engage in these conversations. I would like to especially acknowledge Hetty Enzig for her contribution to knowledge through participating as a cross-boundary expert.

As a result of the process of my own reflexive enquiry, I attended trauma-related coaching training. Trauma can be seen to sit under the umbrella of a stress response (see Table 4.2). Therefore, it felt relevant to explore not only how trauma may present in coaching but also in particular how it may present in the grey space, because of the precarious nature of this space. Consequently, I interviewed coaches who were training coaches to become trauma-informed coaches as well as working within this trauma-informed space as coaches.

The conversations with both the cross-boundary experts and the trauma-informed coaches were held on a one-to-one basis, either via Zoom or face to face. In line with the values of action research, explicit permission was obtained for the following: collaborative conversations to be recorded and transcribed furthermore individuals were given the option of being named or remaining anonymous and credited in my report or when sharing knowledge. Once recordings had been transcribed, CTA was used to analyse the transcripts.

The following questions were presented in a semi-structured interview form. Interviews began with my explanation of the grey space, as well as my lived experience of navigating this terrain in order to set the scene.

Cross-boundary experts' questions

- What type of coaching do you do?
- What drew you to coaching?

- How does the grey space show itself in your type of coaching?
- How do you know you are in the grey space (signs, warnings, signals, etc.)?
- How do you currently manage boundaries between therapy and coaching?
- What does the grey space mean to you?
- What do you do when you find yourself in the grey space?
- How comfortable are you in the grey space?
- What is most challenging about the grey space?
- What is your guidance system/guiding star in navigating this space?
- When do you refer on (if you do)?
- How do you manage the process of referring on (if you do)?
- What would you suggest to another coach about how to manage this grey space?
- What do you do when a client discloses they have a mental health issue or they self-diagnose during the course of coaching?
- Please could you give me an example(s) of a coachee you have worked with who was in the grey space? What was the situation? How did you know it was grey space? What did you do? What was the outcome?

Additional questions for those who were supervisors

- Do the coaches you supervise experience the grey space?
- If so, what do they wrestle with? Any themes that keep coming up?
- How do you support them in the grey space?

Trauma-informed experts' questions

- What drew you to coaching?
- What drew you to trauma-informed coaching?
- What role do you see coaching playing when it comes to trauma?
- How would you advise a trauma-informed coach to manage boundaries?
- Your thoughts on the grey space?
- How do you navigate the boundaries between therapy and coaching?
- What do you see is different about coaching in comparison to therapy/psychotherapy/counselling?

Cycle 4: Second-person action research with others: collaborative enquiry groups – Workshop 1

Concurrent with Cycle 3, three collaborative enquiry group workshops were run with a range of coaches as co-enquirers exploring our lived experience of the grey space. This was achieved through facilitating parallel face-to-face workshops held in London, consisting of three groups, each ranging from four to ten people, with coaches from various backgrounds as well as coaching psychologists. Co-enquirers/participants (these terms will be used interchangeably) were invited to participate through Middlesex University and other organisations, such as the ICF and Ashridge

Executive Education, as well as through networks, such as the ISCP, LinkedIn and the BPS – Special Group for Coaching Psychology. The aim was to invite a range of coaches from various positions, with a lot of experience and expertise.

In order to participate coaches had to: have three years' practice as a coach; have worked with the elements of stress, personal development or transformational coaching; and have worked with a range of different clients. Concurrent with Cycle 3, three collaborative enquiry group workshops were run with a range of coaches as co-enquirers exploring our lived experience of the grey space. This was achieved by facilitating parallel face-to-face workshops, which were all held in London, consisting of three groups, each ranging from four to ten people, with coaches from various backgrounds as well as coaching psychologists. Co-enquirers/participants (these terms will be used interchangeably) were invited to participate by Middlesex University and other organisations, such as the International Coaching Federation (ICF) and Ashridge Executive Education, as well as through networks, such as the International Society for Coaching Psychology (ISCP), LinkedIn and thenal development or transformational coaching. They had all worked with a range of different clients and held training to an equivalent level or were part of an association, such as ISCP, European Mentoring and Coaching Council (EMCC), AC and ICF.

Co-enquirers

Each of the three groups took part in the action research process, which consisted of two cycles (see Figure 4.3). In total, there were 15 co-enquirers (as a result of COVID-19 and for health reasons). Unfortunately, three of those co-enquirers had to remove themselves or withdraw from the research at various stages. We met twice, with a six-month space between meetings. The first workshop was conducted face-to-face as a group. However, because of lockdown, the second cycle of collaborative enquiry workshops was held online via Zoom.

The first collaborative enquiry group consisted of coaches with a variety of training backgrounds from a number of associations. The second group consisted of coaching psychologists or psychologically informed coaches. I define psychologically informed coaches as those who have received formal training in psychology and/ or therapy/counselling. The third group was a mix of coaching psychologists/psychologically informed coaches and coaches from a variety of training backgrounds and associations. Initially, two groups were formed consisting of coaches from various backgrounds and coaching psychologists/psychologically informed coaches in order to compare and contrast how they may be traversing this space. However, the third group was then created to provide a broad range of knowledge, the potential for knowledge formulation and information on how this may impact co-enquirers' practices.

Workshop 1

In line with Cycle 3, the aim of the workshop was to use the actionable knowledge gained from my retrospective critical reflection as the opening to a conversation

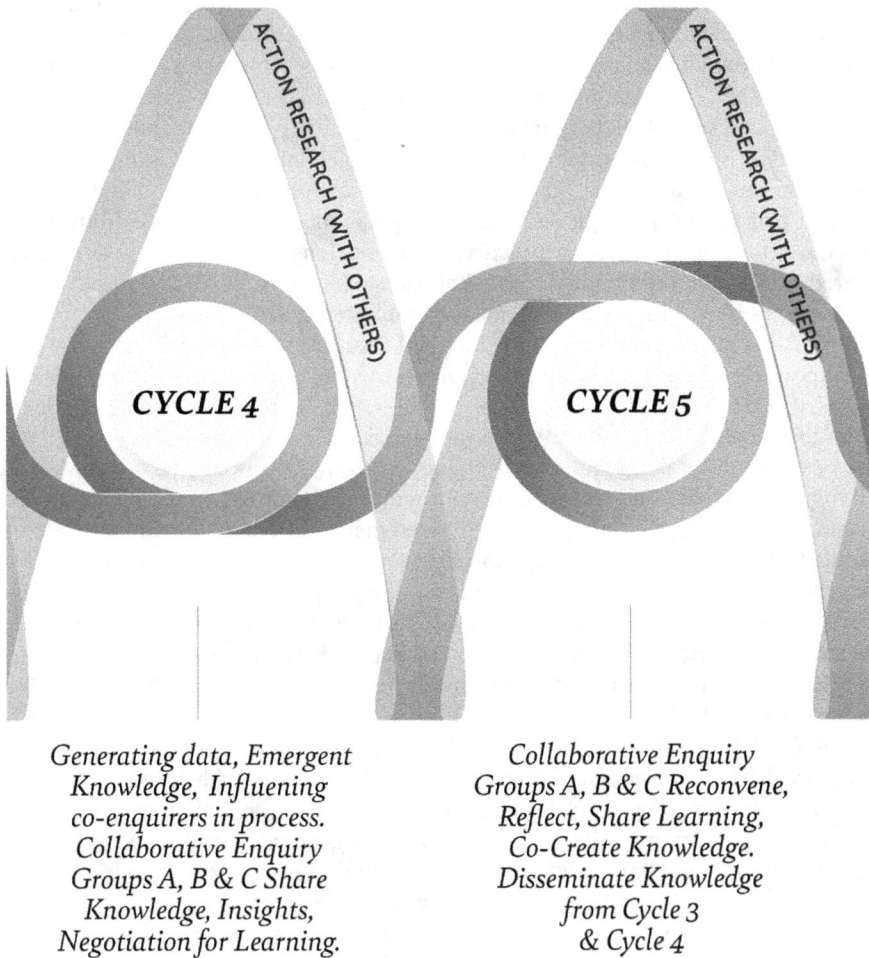

Generating data, Emergent Knowledge, Influening co-enquirers in process. Collaborative Enquiry Groups A, B & C Share Knowledge, Insights, Negotiation for Learning.

Collaborative Enquiry Groups A, B & C Reconvene, Reflect, Share Learning, Co-Create Knowledge. Disseminate Knowledge from Cycle 3 & Cycle 4

Figure 4.3 Collaborative enquiry group cycles

relating to my lived experience of the grey space (as discussed in Cycle 2). Once again, this acted to set the tone, as well as create immediate shared learning. At this juncture I shared my perspective, which was developed through my own critical reflection process, with the various collaborative enquiry groups in order for them to test it against their lived experiences as coaches. The research then moved from my enquiry to a more collaborative process. As my perspective was being used to spark discussion and debate, stepping into the role of practitioner researcher, I bracketed my own experience so as to explore what the experiences of my co-enquirers had been; moving the research from *my* enquiry to *our* enquiry. From this perspective, co-enquirers were invited to share their stories, and a space was created for reflection on each of them. Through this process, each co-enquirer was able to explore their practice, bringing to light "everyday taken-for granted" (Schön, 1983). Thus, gaining insight and learning from themselves, as well as from hearing shared stories relating to how others navigate this terrain. Schön (1983) put forward the concept of "reflection in action", suggesting that in making decisions in the process of their work, there is a continued interplay between a practitioner's thought and action. Through reflection, one gains the ability to move from being reactive to being proactive in practice. Conversations held in this cycle created shared learning and further actionable knowledge (Argyris, 2003) and insights into each other's lived experiences when navigating grey space.

From an action research position, the role I assumed was that of facilitator – one of empowering co-enquirers to learn in an experiential group (Heron, 1999) – drawing further on the 'co-operative mode of facilitation' as well as deriving elements from the 'hierarchical mode'. Within the hierarchical mode, the facilitator adopts the position of directing and exercising power over the process, taking charge of all major decisions, such as objectives, structure of the programme, managing the group, how and what is interpreted and given meaning. The co-operative mode of facilitation, however, is one where power and management of different dimensions are shared; enabling, encouraging and guiding the group to become more self-directing; working with co-enquirers to decide on what confronts, resists and gives meaning to. As the facilitator, my view was shared. However, it was considered as one view of many; a collaborative stance where outcomes are negotiated by the group (Heron, 1999).

Initially I adopted a hierarchical mode stance to frame the research and create structure, such as the boundaries and conduct of the group, addressing confidentiality and informing the group regarding the practicalities, as well as beginning the discussion by sharing my lived experience of the grey space and reflections from my retrospective critical reflection; my perspective. However, once the framework had been created, an explicit explanation of my role as co-enquirer was given to the group, as well as an invitation for this focus to be the lived experience of each co-enquirer in whatever form that may be. I then transitioned into a co-operative mode of facilitation, stepping into the role of co-enquirer, so my voice became one of the co-enquirers, contributing to the themes and sub-themes produced.

In addition, I invited several research actions from the other co-enquirers to facilitate the process of collaborative enquiry:

- Pre-Workshop 1 reflection
  Write 500 words (this was brought and read out in Workshop 1, which formed part of the themes for this cycle to share with the group, drawing on the Patchwork Text Model (Winters, 2003)).
  Consider the following questions:
  - How do you currently manage boundaries between therapy and coaching (grey space)?

- How do you know you're in the grey space (signs/warning signals/ etc.)?
- What do you do when you find yourself in the grey space?
- What is most challenging about the grey space?
- What is your guidance system/guiding star in navigating this space?
- When do you refer on (if you do)?
- How do you manage the process of referring on (if you do)?
- Any other reflections on the grey space?

- Carry out a reflective enquiry by keeping a diary of your experience in the grey space, detailing any dilemmas and tensions you may face throughout the enquiry, including reflecting on how the shared learning and actionable knowledge through these critical conversations influences your practice.

I recorded the conversation during the collaborative enquiry workshop to be transcribed, conducting CTA on the transcripts for analysis.

Alongside these actions, using elements from the co-operative mode (Heron, 1999), my intention was to facilitate the group in much the same way as a coaching conversation, allowing the emergent nature of this approach. Furthermore, there was joint negotiation about how to capture data that was generated during group sessions and how to gather data during the group sessions and in-between sessions, with each co-enquirer deciding how they may do so individually, for example, in the form of:

- Reflective pieces during coaching work with clients
- Extracts of journals and transcripts of coaching sessions being provided for analysis
- Poems
- Artwork.

As a result, each group differed slightly in the way it was facilitated, as well as in the dynamics and culture of the group. I did, however, create a framework for the facilitation of each group, using a PowerPoint presentation for each cycle which was carried out in the same manner as a semi-structured interview or a coaching conversation which is client led, in keeping with Heron's (1999) co-operative mode of facilitating a group, which was drawn from Heron's dimensions .

Critical conversations (McNiff, 2002) within groups were facilitated in line with the values of action research. Explicit permission was obtained for collaborative conversations to be recorded and transcribed, in addition to negotiation as to whether individuals would like to be named or remain anonymous and be credited in my report or when sharing knowledge. Where individuals preferred to remain anonymous, fictitious names were assigned.

Due to the co-enquiry nature of the action research (Coghlan, 2006; Heron, 1999), once recordings had been transcribed – and CTA of the transcripts conducted

– the findings were shared with all the co-enquirers within the groups to ensure that I had represented the essence of their experience. The alteration of themes and sub-themes was negotiated; all themes presented having been agreed on. This same process was implemented for Cycle 5.

Cycle 5: Second-person action research with others: collaborative enquiry groups – Workshop 2

Each group agreed on a time to reconvene for the final group workshop. This was roughly six months after Cycle 4. Because of COVID-19 restrictions, workshops had to be held remotely, via Zoom. They were run as though they were face-to-face regarding timings and the ability to present PowerPoint presentations. The groups adapted well to this format. As previously, my role within the groups was as a facilitator, drawing on Heron's (1999) co-operative mode blended with the hierarchical mode. However, once the framework had been created, an explicit explanation of my role as co-enquirer was given to the group, as well as an invitation for this focus to be the lived experience of each co-enquirer in whatever form that may be. I then transitioned into the co-operative mode of facilitation, stepping into the role of co-enquirer, with my voice becoming one of the co-enquirers. My objective was to work with my co-enquirers to decide on what to confront, resist and give meaning to.

Once the workshops were complete and the data was analysed, themes were presented to each group and then discussed and negotiated, with a majority vote being utilised when required.

This was particular to the development of the workshops and research questions asked, again to facilitate critical conversation (McNiff, 2002). The aim was to share reflections, possible insights, implementation of any actionable knowledge (Argyris, 2003) and alternative ways of thinking that may have taken place in practice regarding the grey space during the six months between Cycles 4 and 5 as a result of participating in Cycle 4, as well as shared discussions with co-enquirers' critical conversations, shared learning and the in-between workshop reflective practices. In line with the iterative process of action research, each cycle aimed to reflect, review and implement gained actionable knowledge (Argyris, 2003) as it moved through the cycle again. The workshops were brought to a close by sharing with the groups the CTA themes generated from Workshop 1/Cycle 4 and the cross-boundary experts and trauma-informed coaches Workshop1/Cycle 3; generating further shared learning and actionable knowledge so that the cycle of knowledge creation (Argyris, 2003) and insight into our lived experiences as coaches navigating the grey space, continued.

With regard to this research, the action research cycle ended there. However, the potential to continue it, whereby each cycle would bring with it deeper understanding, learning and new actionable knowledge, is always present.

Adhering to prior agreements, anonymity and credits were reported as requested, and data handled, as outlined in Cycle 4.

Cycle 6: First-person action research: narrative enquiry informed by autoethnography

As a practitioner researcher conducting a self-study, first-person action enquiry reflecting on one's motivations to conduct research is imperative. Reason and Marshall (1987) propose that the topics chosen by the researcher are chosen consciously or unconsciously, driven by "a bid for personal development" (p.115). My self-study was informed by an autoethnographic approach because it lent itself as a way of exploring my experience as a practitioner and researcher in the grey space. Furthermore, through this self-study, using first-person action enquiry informed by an autoethnographic approach, I intended to offer insight into how and why I conduct my practice in the grey space as I do, in the hope that a glimpse into my lived experience as a person, practitioner and researcher (McIlveen, 2008) may benefit the wider coaching practice. Hartog (2018) suggests that we attempt to find coherence and meaning through the stories we tell ourselves, and through a narrative enquiry of these stories we can illuminate "assumptions that underlie our thinking and practice" (p. 232).

Limitations

As an insider action researcher – in a project designed around collaborating with other individuals, who act as co-enquirers within the coaching context – it could be argued that there is a closeness to the data that creates a limitation (Coghlan, 2006). Recognising this, I needed to be vigilant that I didn't presume that each co-enquirer had the same understanding of lived experiences, jargon and insider knowledge, because this would hinder the ability to uncover current ways of thinking or alternative ways of thinking. A reflective approach was adopted in order to minimise the possibility of this in addition to drawing on my critical friends to maintain my awareness. However, one cannot account for the experiences of everyone participating in this co-enquiry. Furthermore, due to the size of the groups, this was only a representation of what the lived experience of the grey space is for a coach. Therefore, this is only the beginning of understanding the grey space. The need for further research on what emerges is further considered.

I acknowledge the need for reflexivity during the research process, and consideration of my position, which is non-neutral and reflects a "particular world-view and set of interests" (Wetherell, Taylor & Yates, 2001). To manage my position as practitioner-researcher (principal researcher), questions posed were as open and non-directive as possible, and my role was one of facilitation through the course of discussion and knowledge production, rather than to direct or lead. Additionally, during the analysis process, I was mindful of my role as a practitioner-researcher paying attention to what was my experience and what emerged in the group – by attempting to recognise my role as facilitator and enable the voice of others and not focus only on my own objective voice while undertaking a reflexive analysis of the texts. It was essential that throughout this process an awareness was cultivated of the shift between the roles of researcher and practitioner and any tensions that arose in consequence. Tensions may result from holding a value and viewpoint as a practitioner and what that lived experience may be, as well as critically disseminating these experiences as the researcher. I believe that awareness of potential tensions was key in relation to personal values and ethical dilemmas that could have taken place as I navigated these two roles. At this stage of the process, I was not aware of what these dilemmas might be. Therefore, I proposed the following to aid me.

To retain a position of reflexivity, I kept a diary, noting down my thoughts and reflections of each group co-enquiry and critical friend conversation, as well as how I navigated my own coaching through the grey space with my clients and during the analysis process. Furthermore, this diary acted to inform my self-study, using first-person action enquiry informed by an autoethnography, in addition to maintaining regular contact with my research supervisors and firmly grounding my analysis in past research, as well as giving myself ample time to ensure reflexive and relevant analysis.

Ethical considerations

Questions were put to me during my mock Preliminary Academic Paper

(PAP) regarding coaching raising the issue of whether coaching brings with it its own discourses, and whether research into coaching may be reinforcing the discourses surrounding coaching.

Diary extract

The mock PAP has left me with these fundamental questions that have kept coming up throughout the process of designing and crafting this research proposal.

I do frequently ask myself how this research may be playing into bolstering certain discourses (Burr, 2003). I have been – and am now even more – aware that through my research there were objects of knowledge (Foucault, 1972) offered up. Furthermore, I am aware that as a coaching psychologist and researcher, I hold a privileged position (Foucault, 1982).

What's more, these questions have been raised to me in my mock PAP, that coaching brings with it its own discourses, and that researching into coaching may be reinforcing these discourses..

However, on reflection, I end up in the same position, with the same conviction and the same passion to enquire into the grey space. I believe that, whether one agrees with coaching as a practice or not, it is here for the foreseeable future.

I frequently asked myself how this research might help to bolster certain discourses (Burr, 2003). I have been, and will now be, permanently aware that as a result of my research "objects of knowledge" (Foucault, 1972) may be offered up. Furthermore, I am aware that as a coaching psychologist and researcher I hold a privileged position (Foucault, 1982).

One question I considered from the beginning of the research process was: does coaching play into keeping a societal status quo by placing the onus on the individual to take responsibility for what is a societal issue? (Foucault, 1982; Rose, 1999). For example, an individual who is learning to manage stress at work when the organisational structure is fundamentally flawed, or the young adult who is learning to manage their stress about their future prospects, when there are political and social issues that impact their situation? Furthermore, Brockbank and McGill (2012) posit that performance coaching reinforces the existing system and maintains the status quo by suppressing any challenge or questioning of the existing power structure. I am very aware that coaching could be something that becomes a tool to retain social and cultural influences – and that research carries a great responsibility. Consequently, this is an issue that I have grappled with. I believe that, whether one agrees with coaching as a practice or not, it is here for the foreseeable future. I reiterate that researching coaching – and particularly the grey space – is important. Coaching can offer up objects of knowledge (Foucault, 1972) that were previously retained by the expert (Foucault, 1982). I still view coaching as equipping a client with the basis (even if this is just a starting point) to question and resist knowledge/power structures (Foucault, 1997).

During the phase of developing my research question, after every discussion I had with my cohort and the supervisory staff, I came away with a range of challenging questions that had been offered to me. Forbe's theory that doctoral learning is not defined by the "Aristotelian notion of 'mastery'", but is characterised by "the experience of epistemological uncertainties, ambivalence and oscillations and of constantly remaining reflexively self-aware of that" (Forbes, 2008) is of importance in my practice. These values were vital in the reflection process of how and why I constructed the design of the research and why the research was worth pursuing. Many times, I came away feeling unsettled, but each of these times significantly helped in the development of my argument and my ability to articulate my interest. Working in this group as part of a collaborative co-constructive process helped me to formulate my research design. Additionally, I understand who and what has formed me into the practitioner that I am today.

On a practical note, all critical conversations (McNiff, 2002) were conducted voluntarily. Furthermore, I obtained informed consent (before) and gave each co-enquirer a debrief form (after) explaining the purpose and procedures of the study, which included relevant contact information. In their briefing, co-enquirers were assigned their own unique four-digit code, thereby offering anonymity and enabling them to withdraw their data from the study should they so wish, in accordance with Middlesex University's ethical procedures.

Consent forms and transcripts/recordings were filed separately in secure, locked cabinets for two years to protect the confidentiality of co-enquirers, as well as to comply compliance with the General Data Protection Regulation (GDPR).

The purpose of this chapter was to focus on my overall research design and to focus on my overall research design and to illustrate my approach and methods.

I explore trauma and its impacts, before considering and explaining my research methods, taking into account ethical considerations and limitations.

Discussion points

1. Reflect on the discourses and objective knowledge you bring into your practice as a coach.
2. Are there any discrepancies in your values as a practitioner? If so, how can these be addressed?

Suggested reading

Anderson, F. (2021). *Transcending trauma. Healing complex PTSD with internal family systems therapy*, Vol. 13. Greenwich, CT: PESI Publishing.

Burr, V. (1995). *Social construction.* London: Routledge.

Burr, V. (2003). *Social construction*, 2nd edn. London: Routledge.

Cavanagh, M. (2005). 'Mental-health issues and challenging clients in executive coaching'. In M. Cavanagh, A.M. Grant & T. Kemp (eds.), *Evidence-based coaching, Volume 1: Theory, research and practice from behavioural science.* Bowen Hill, Australia: Australian Academic Press.

Einzig, H. (2011). 'The beast within'. *Coaching at Work,* 6(3), 40–43.

Garvey, B. & Stokes, P. (2022) *Coaching and mentoring: Theory and practice*, 4th edn. London: SAGE.

Garvey, B. & Stokes, P. (2023). 'Ethics and professional coaching bodies'. In W. Smith, J. Passmore, E. Turner, Y. Lai & D. Clutterbuck (eds.), *The ethical coaches' handbook: A guide to developing ethical maturity in practice.* Abingdon: Routledge.

Giraldez-Hayes, A. (2021). 'Different domains or grey areas? Setting boundaries between coaching and therapy: A thematic analysis'. *The Coaching Psychologist*, 17(2), 18–29.

Githens, R.P. (2015). 'Critical action research in human resources development'. *Human Resources Development Review*, 14(2), 185–204.

Hart, V. & Leipsic, S. (2001). 'Coaching versus therapy: A perspective'. *Consulting Psychology Journal: Practice and Research,* 53(4), 229–237.

Joplin, A. (2007). 'Part One: The "fuzzy space": Exploring the experience of space between psychotherapy and executive coaching'. Unpublished MSc dissertation, New School of Psychotherapy and Counselling, London. Available at www.scribd.com/document/17168 879/Research-Thesis-The-Fuzzy-Space-Between-Psychotherapy-and-Executive-Coach ing (Accessed: October 2018).

Maxwell, A. (2009). 'The co-created boundary: Negotiating the limits of coaching'. *International Journal of Evidence Based Coaching and Mentoring,* 4(1), 82–94.

Rutkowski, N. (2014). Coaching and therapy: Finding common ground in gestalt practice'. *Gestalt Review,* 18(2), 146–153.

Schön, D.A. (1983). *The reflective practitioner: How professionals think in action.* New York, NY: Basic Books.

Sime, C. & Jocob, Y. (2018). 'Crossing the line? A qualitative exploration of ICF master certified: coaches' perception of roles, borders and boundaries'. *International Coaching Psychology Review*, 13(2), 112–126.

van der Kolk, B. (2005). 'Developmental trauma disorder: Towards a rational diagnosis for children with complex trauma histories'. *Psychiatric Annals*, 35(5), 401–408.

Vaughan-Smith, J. (2019) *Coaching and trauma. From surviving to thriving*. London: Open University Press.

References

Adler, N. & Shani, A.B. (2001). 'In search of an alternative framework for the creation of actionable knowledge: table-tennis research at Ericsson'. In W. Pasmore & R.W. Woodman (eds.), *Research in organisational change and development*, Vol. 13. Greenwich, CT: Emerald. Group Publishing.

Anderson, F. (2021). *Transcending trauma. Healing complex PTSD with internal family systems therapy*. Eau Claire, WI: PESI Publishing.

Antaki, C. (2004). 'Reading minds or dealing with interaction implications?' *Theory & Psychology*, 14(5), 667–683.

Argyris, C. (2003). 'Actionable knowledge'. In T. Tsoukas & C. Knudsen (eds.), *The Oxford handbook of organizational theory*. Oxford: Oxford University Press.

Braun, V. & Clarke, V. (2006). 'Using thematic analysis in psychology'. *Qualitative Research in Psychology*, 3(2), 77–101.

Brockbank, A. & McGill, I. (2012). *Facilitating reflexive learning: Coaching, mentoring and supervision*, 2nd edn. London: UK Kogan Page.

Brody, H. (2002). *Stories of sickness*, 2nd edn. Oxford: Oxford University Press.

Brown, B. (2012). *Daring greatly*. London: Penguin Books.

Brown, V. (2010). 'Collective enquiry and its wicked problems'. In V. Brown, J.A. Harris & Y. Russell (eds.), *Tackling wicked problems: Through the transdisciplinary imagination*. London: Earthscan.

Burr, V. (1995). *Social construction*. London: Routledge.

Burr, V. (2003). *Social construction*, 2nd edn. London: Routledge.

Cavanagh, M. (2005). 'Mental-health issues and challenging clients in executive coaching'. In M. Cavanagh, A.M. Grant & T. Kemp (eds.), *Evidence-based coaching, Volume 1: Theory, research and practice from behavioural science*. Bowen Hill, Australia: Australian Academic Press.

Chang, H. (2005). 'Cultural autobiography for Christian multicultural educators: A way of understanding self and other'. *A Journal of the International Community of Christians in Teacher Education*, 1(1), 1–18.

Coghlan, D. (2006). 'Insider action research doctorates: Generating actionable knowledge'. *Higher Education*, 54(2), 293–306.

Coghlan, D. & Brannick, T. (2014). *Doing action research in your own organisation*. London: Sage.

Edwards, D., Ashmore, M. & Potter, J. (1995). 'Death and furniture: The rhetoric, politics and theology of bottom-line arguments against relativism'. *History of the Human Sciences*, 8(2), 25–49.

Einzig, H. (2011). 'The beast within'. *Coaching at Work*, 6(3), 40–43.

Faiten Diochon, P. & Nizet, J. (2015). 'Ethical codes and executive coaches: one size does not fit all'. *The Journal of Applied Behavioural Science*, 51(2), 277–301.

Florio-Ruane, S. (2001). *Teacher education and the cultural imagination: Autobiography, conversation and narrative*. London: Routledge.

Fook, J. (2010). 'Beyond reflective practice: reworking the "critical" in critical reflection'. In H. Bradbury, N. Frost, S. Kilminster & M. Zukas (eds.), *Beyond reflective practice: New approaches to professional lifelong learning*. London: Routledge.

Forbes, J. (2008). 'Reflexivity in professional doctoral research'. *Reflexive Practice, 9*(4), 449–460.

Foucault, M. (1972). *The archaeology of knowledge*. London: Tavistock.

Foucault, M. (1982). *Madness and civilization: A history of insanity in the age of reason*. London: Tavistock.

Foucault, M. (1997). *Ethics: Essential works of Foucault 1954–1984, Volume 1* (ed. P. Rabinow). London: Penguin.

Garvey, B. & Stokes, P. (2022). *Coaching and mentoring: Theory and practice*, 4th edn. London: SAGE.

Garvey, B. & Stokes, P. (2023). 'Ethics and professional coaching bodies'. In W. Smith, J. Passmore, E. Turner, Y. Lai & D. Clutterbuck (eds.), *The ethical coaches' handbook: A guide to developing ethical maturity in practice*. Abingdon: Routledge.

Giraldez-Hayes, A. (2021). 'Different domains or grey areas? Setting boundaries between coaching and therapy: A thematic analysis'. *The Coaching Psychologist*, 17(2), 18–29.

Githens, R.P. (2015). 'Critical action research in human resources development'. *Human Resources Development Review,* 14(2), 185–204.

Grant, A.M. (2007). 'A languishing-flourishing model of goal striving and mental health for coaching populations'. *International Coaching Psychology Review* 2(3), 250–264.

Grant, A.M. (2017). 'Solution-focused cognitive-behavioural coaching for sustainable high performance and circumventing stress, fatigue and burnout'. *Consulting Psychology Journal: Practice and Research*, 69(2), 98–111.

Hart, V. & Leipsic, S. (2001). 'Coaching versus therapy: a perspective'. *Consulting Psychology Journal: Practice and Research*, 53(4), 229–237.

Hartog, M. (2018). 'Becoming a scholarly practitioner: as a teacher in higher education "how do I improve my practice?"' *Action Learning: Research and Practice*, 15(3), 224–234.

Haydon, G. (2006). *Respect for persons and for cultures as a basis for national and global citizenship*. London: Institute of Education, University of London.

Heikkinen, H.L.T., Huttunen, R., Syrjälä, L. & Pesonen, J. (2012). 'Action research and narrative enquiry: five principles for validation revisited'. *Educational Action Research,* 20(1), 5–21.

Heller, L. & Kammer, B. (2022). *The practice guide for healing developmental trauma. Using the neuroaffective relational model to address adverse childhood experiences and resolve complex trauma*. Berkeley, CA: North Atlantic Books.

Herman, J.L. (1992). 'Complex PTSD: A syndrome in survivors of prolonged and repeated trauma'. *Journal of Traumatic Stress*, 5(3), 377–391.

Heron, J. (1999). *The complete facilitator's handbook*. New York, NY: Kogan Page Limited.

Holmes, P. (2014). 'Researching Chinese students' intercultural communication experiences in higher education: researcher and participant reflexivity'. In J. Byrd-Clarke and F. Dervin (eds.), *Reflexivity and multimodality in language education: Rethinking multilingualism and interculturality in accelerating complex and transnational spaces*. New York, NY: Routledge.

Joplin, A. (2007). 'Part One: The "fuzzy space": Exploring the experience of space between psychotherapy and executive coaching'. Unpublished MSc dissertation, New School of Psychotherapy and Counselling, London. Available at www.scribd.com/document/17168 879/Research-Thesis-The-Fuzzy-Space-Between-Psychotherapy-and-Executive-Coach ing (Accessed: October 2018).

Joseph, S. (2006). 'Person-centred coaching psychology: A meta-theoretical perspective. *International Coaching Psychology Review*, 1(1), 118–134.

Josselson, R. (2011). 'Narrative research constructing, deconstructing, and reconstructing story'. In F.J. Wertz, K. Charmaz, L.M. McMullen, R. Josselson, R. Anderson & E. McSpadden (eds.), *Five ways of doing qualitative analysis: Phenomenological psychology, ground theory, discourse analysis, narrative research, and intuitive enquiry*. New York, NY: Guilford Press.

Jost, J. & Kruglanski, A.W. (2002). 'The estrangement of social constructionism and experimental social psychology: History of the rift and prospects for reconciliation'. *Personality and Social Psychology Review*, 6(3), 168–187.

Keyes, C.I.M. (2003). 'Complete mental health: An agenda for the 21st century'. In C.I.M. Keyes & J. Haidt (eds.), *Flourishing: Positive psychology and the life well-lived*. Washington, DC: American Psychological Association.

Mallon, R. (2007). 'A field guide to social construction'. *Philosophy Compass*, 2(1), 93–108.

Maté, G. (2022). *The myth of normal: Trauma, illness and healing in a toxic culture*. Toronto: Knopf Canada.

Maxwell, A. (2009). 'The co-created boundary: Negotiating the limits of coaching'. *International Journal of Evidence Based Coaching and Mentoring*, 4(1), 82–94.

McIlveen, P. (2008). 'Autoethnography as a method for reflexive research and practice in vocational psychology'. *Australian Journal of Career Development*, 17(2), 13–20.

McNiff, J. (2002). *Action research for professional development: Concise advice for new action researchers*, 3rd edn. Available at: http://www.jeanmcniff.com/ar-booklet.asp (Accessed: August 2018).

McNiff, J. & Whitehead, J. (2010). *You and your action research project*, 3rd edn. London: Routledge.

Nieto, S. (2003). *What keeps teachers going?* New York, NY: Teachers College Press.

Paper Tigers (2015). Directed by James Redford. KPJR Films.

Paterson, M., Higgs, J., Wilcox. S. & Villeneuve, M. (2002). 'Clinical reasoning and self-directed learning: key dimensions in professional education and professional socialisation'. *Focus on Health Professional Education*, 4(2), 6.

Popovic, N. & Jinks, D. (2014). *Personal consulting*, 1st edn. London: Routledge.

Price, J. (2009). 'The coaching/therapy boundary in organisational coaching'. *International Journal of Theory, Research and Practice*, 2(2), 135–148.

Reason, P. & Marshal, J. (1987). 'Research as personal process'. In D. Boud & V. Griffin (eds.), *Appreciating adult learning: From the learner's perspective*. London: Kogan Page.

Rose, N. (1999). *Governing the soul: The shaping of the private self*, 2nd ed. London: Free Association Books.

Rutkowski, N. (2014). 'Coaching and therapy: finding common ground in gestalt practice'. *Gestalt Review*, 18(2), 146–153.

Schön, D.A. (1983). *The reflective practitioner: How professionals think in action.* New York, NY: Basic Books.

Sime, C. & Jocob, Y. (2018). 'Crossing the line? A qualitative exploration of ICF master certified: coaches' perception of roles, borders and boundaries'. *International Coaching Psychology Review*, 13(2), 46–61.

Taylor, J. (2022). 'Views and perspectives. on being trauma informed'. Available at: Dr Jessica Taylor | About (Accessed: January 2022).

Teicher, M. & Samson, J. (2016). 'Annual research review: Enduring neurobiological effects of childhood abuse and neglect'. *Journal of Child Psychology and Psychiatry,* 57(3), 241–266.

Trede, F., Macklin, R. & Bridges, D. (2012). 'Professional identity development: a review of the higher education literature'. *Studies in Higher Education,* 37(3), 365–384.

van der Kolk, B. (2005). 'Developmental trauma disorder: Towards a rational diagnosis for children with complex trauma histories'. *Psychiatric Annals,* 35(5), 401–408.

Vaughan-Smith, J. (2019). *Coaching and trauma. From surviving to thriving.* London: Open University Press.

Wetherell, M., Taylor, S. & Yates, S.J. (2001). *Discourse as data: A guide for analysis.* London: Sage Publications Ltd.

Wilson, D. (2009). '"What price respect" – exploring the notion of respect in a 21st century global learning environment'. *Journal of College Teaching & Learning Clute Institute.* 6(2), 1544-0389.

Winters, R. (2003). 'Contextualizing the patchwork text: addressing problems of coursework assessment in higher education'. *Innovations in Education and Teaching International,* 40(2), 112–122.

Chapter 5

Navigating the grey space Part II

Surveying the grey space

Overview

This chapter presents the themes and sub-themes from Workshop 1 (Cycle 4). The extracts presented are representative of the collaborative enquiry group workshops and cross-boundary experts' one-to-one conversations. The enquiry groups comprised of three groups. These three groups consisted of: Group 1: coaches from various training and knowledge landscapes; Group 2: a coaching psychologist and psychologically informed coaches, who had formal/academic training in psychology/therapy; and Group 3: a mix of both, those from various training and knowledge landscapes, and those with formal/academic psychological/therapeutic studies. The composition of the groups remained the same throughout the research, all attending the workshops within a similar timeframe. Data from the cross-boundary experts' (see p.71) and trauma-informed coaches' one-to-one conversations were included in this round of discoveries. Various extracts for each theme and sub-theme are presented to demonstrate the relevant themes and sub-themes. One or more extracts are presented for each theme and sub-theme to illustrate the focus of the theme. A combination of co-enquirer, cross-boundary expert and trauma-informed coach extracts have been selected. Once the structure of the workshops had been established, I adopted the position of co-enquirer alongside an action research approach. My voice then became one of the co-enquirers, thereby contributing to the themes and sub-themes produced.

Due to the linear nature of writing and presenting information, the themes are presented as individual and separate. However, there are themes that interlink, and multiple themes may be employed or experienced at any one time, with all the themes corresponding with each other holistically.

Collaborative group enquiry – Workshop 1

Research question

How can I and other coaches improve the practice of dealing with ethics and managing boundaries in the grey space when working with clients experiencing health and well-being issues such as stress management, resilience and personal development?

DOI: 10.4324/9781003509776-6

The aim of the collaborative enquiry group cycles (Cycle 4) was to begin to explore how coaches experience navigating the grey space. Essentially, what they do, how they may become aware that they are entering this terrain, how they know when they are in the grey space and how they navigate their way through it. The objective was to get a better understanding of how we as coaches traverse this territory and to develop "actionable knowledge", which is produced from "reflection on reflection" (Argyris, 2003); a process of stepping back at every cycle to evaluate the process, the meanings and the experience, all of which then inform further planning for action. It is through this process that insider action research gains its quality and how the knowledge that emerges has the capacity to become actionable (Coghlan, 2006).

The workshop was a collaborative process to involve individuals in the creation of actionable knowledge regarding themselves, the actions taken and their work. In so doing, a dynamic space was created, allowing for a wealth of knowledge to emerge; thereby creating self-reflexivity as practitioners, and deepening our understanding of ourselves and our practices.

Action research is an iterative process, the aim of which is to reflect, review and implement gained actionable knowledge (Argyris, 2003).

The workshops consisted of three groups meeting at separate times. These four-hour discussions were held at a venue in London. My role was that of facilitator, I drew on Heron's (1999) co-operative mode within the workshop blended with a hierarchical mode with the development of the workshops and research questions asked.

Workshop agenda

- Boundaries
- Purpose action research/my role as facilitator
- Introductions and 500-word reflection pieces
  - Who you are?
  - What type of coaching do you do?
  - Why are you participating in this research?
  - Why were you drawn to coaching?
  - How might having more knowledge around the grey space help you as a coach?
- Questions to discuss as a group
  - In the type of coaching you do, how does the grey space show up?
  - What does the grey space mean to you?
  - How comfortable are you in the grey space?
  - What would you suggest to another coach about how to manage the grey space?
  - Any other reflections on the grey space?
  - Reflections on 500-word reflection pieces.

- Reflections and discussion
  - How do you feel/think about reflections? What are the similarities? What are the differences?
  - Is there anything you have heard that you think could benefit the way you practice? If so, what?
  - After hearing the discussions, is there anything that you want to do differently going forward?
  - Has anything been confirmed for you? If so, what?
  - What will stay the same in the way you manage the grey space?
  - Any other reflections?
- Facilitators share examples of grey space clients – story
- Current boundaries/guidelines – coaching
- Values exercise
- Agree on reflective exercise between workshops
- Facilitators' feedback from past clients
- Agree next meeting.

Four main themes (with sub-themes) were produced, as detailed in Table 5.1.

Table 5.1 CTA of action research from collaborative enquiry groups Cycle 1 and cross-boundary experts' conversations. How are coaches currently navigating the grey space?

Constructionist Thematic Analysis			
Theme 1 Holding Space	*Theme 2* Keeping A Watchful Eye	*Theme 3* Normalising	*Theme 4* Embodied Awareness
Sub-Themes			
Room to let it out	Deep listening	Mental health literacy	Sensing the grey
Bracketing	Helicopter view	Human emotions	Gut feel
Contracting and re-contracting: setting the scene		Seeing beyond the label	Dig deeper
Something is better than nothing		Appropriate humour	
The deeper you go			
Holding a mirror			
Glancing in the rear-view mirror			
Curiosity aids the coach			
All of you			
Holding space mentally			

Overview of themes

Theme 1: Holding space

This theme presents the position taken up by the coach when encountering the terrain of the grey space and how they may utilise this position to navigate this terrain.

Theme 2: Keeping a watchful eye

This theme considers how the coach may adopt a stance of awareness when coming into contact with the grey space, observing moment to moment how the coaching work is unfolding, in addition to what is happening, emerging and evolving for the client.

Theme 3: Normalising

This theme focuses on coaches aiming to 'normalise' the element of distress they may be experiencing, much in line with the "Distressed but Functional" quadrant (Grant, 2007, pp.26–27).

Theme 4: Embodied awareness

This theme demonstrates the manner in which coaches use their embodied self-awareness to navigate and know when they may be entering or experiencing the grey space.

Theme 1: Holding space

Theme 1 is the concept of 'holding space': an encompassing stance of presence. This theme presents the position taken up by the coach when encountering the terrain of the grey space. The coach may respond in this manner as they enter this space, which may subside, or it may be an ongoing stance throughout the coaching work as a tool to navigate the grey space. This can be seen much in line with Plett's (2020) concept of "bearing witness", which "is showing up without the answers. It is listening without needing to change the narrative or the situation" (p.38), to honour, see and pay attention to the coachee. Furthermore, Plett (2020) suggests that there are ten elements when it comes to the art of holding space: witnessing; containment; compassion; non-judgement; selective guidance; space for complexity; autonomy; flexibility; connection; and allyship. I propose that, as we move through the sub-themes, these elements are viewed.

Sub-theme: Room to let it out

In this sub-theme, the coach demonstrates holding space by providing a container within the coaching session for the coachee to 'let out' what is happening to them. Furthermore, there is a sense of clearing and dispelling of emotional or mental

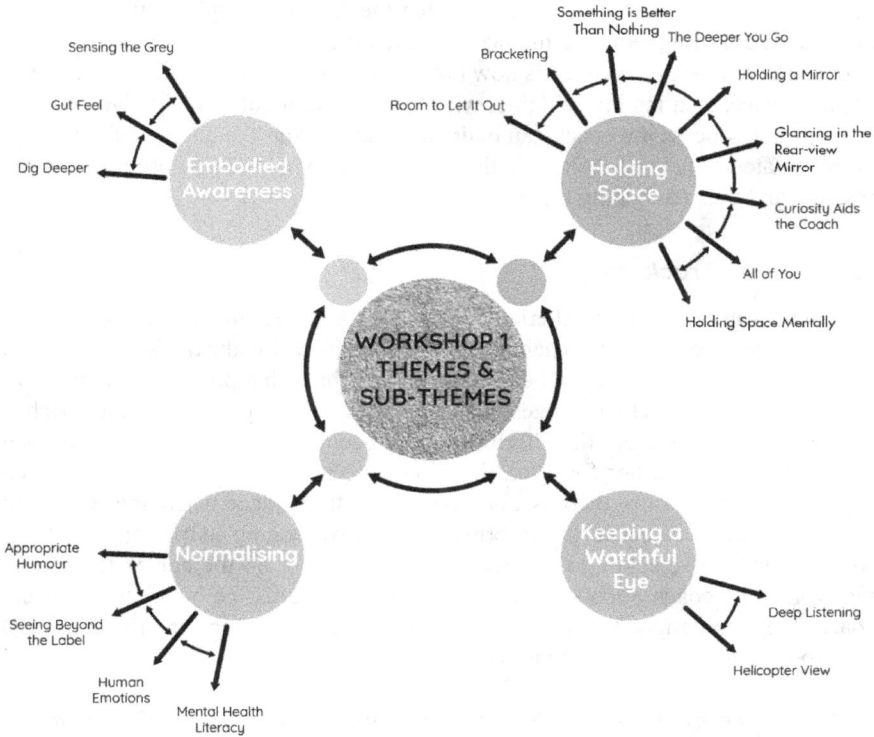

Sensing the Grey

Gut Feel

Dig Deeper

Embodied Awareness

Something is Better Than Nothing   The Deeper You Go

Bracketing

Room to Let It Out

Holding Space

Holding a Mirror

Glancing in the Rear-view Mirror

Curiosity Aids the Coach

All of You

Holding Space Mentally

WORKSHOP 1 THEMES & SUB-THEMES

Appropriate Humour

Normalising

Seeing Beyond the Label

Human Emotions

Mental Health Literacy

Keeping a Watchful Eye

Deep Listening

Helicopter View

Figure 5.1 The interlinked relationship between themes and sub-themes from action research collaborative enquiry groups Cycle 2

content that frees up space for the coaching work to progress, akin to 'unburdening'. Once again, a parallel can be drawn with Plett's (2020) element of "containment" surrounding the concept of holding space from Plett's viewpoint. Containment is the capacity to provide a space where an individual can move through their emotional process while not being concerned that the practitioner is unable to cope.

A2.3: *But they're full up. They're just full up with whatever has gone on … just needs to get some stuff out.*

In this extract, the coach describes how they create a container holding space for the client with 'room to let it out'. The client has a lot to get off their chest. Once this has been given the space to be heard, coaching work can begin.

A3.3: *'So, we just had to re-contract. I said, 'Right. We're going to talk about this. But you're outside my limit.' But, actually, what he wanted to do, I found very quickly, was download.*

In this extract, the coach acknowledges that the subject brought to the session is beyond the coaching remit. To maintain boundaries, the coach re-contracts with the client and the role of the coach is now taking the position of active listener; one of holding space, creating the container with 'room to let it out'. This is significant as through this process the coach can maintain being within the bounds of coaching, despite material that may belong in the therapeutic domains being brought into the session, and thus navigating the grey space.

Sub-theme: Bracketing

Within the sub-theme of 'bracketing', a coach is presented with information, which is grey space, or beyond the coaching context and sits within the therapeutic terrain, such as past abuse and mental health diagnoses. Through a process of transparent dialogue, the coach acknowledges this information and explores with the coachee how they wish to address this disclosure. If it becomes apparent that the coachee does not want to further focus on the disclosure information or seek additional support through therapy, there is a bracketing that takes place where the coach and coachee agree to 'bracket' the information, acknowledging its presence, yet not working with the disclosed material; rather, refocusing on the contracted coaching work. The coach adopts a stance of working towards the best interest of the coachee, either signposting towards additional support or honouring the coachee's decision to focus on the coaching work.

> **A3.3:** *You know, if they say, 'Oh, yes, I believe that I can bracket that', and they want to go ahead with that, my way of working with the coachee, it would be unless there is strong reason to know that that's not the case, I would work with that person. I would be coachee-led and I would listen to what they're saying, not think that my expert view on them is better than theirs.*

In this extract, the coach takes the position of bracketing to stay within the bounds of coaching because the client has disclosed a topic that sits within the bounds of therapy. The coach adopts a client-led approach. This is consistent with the Rogerian person-centred approach (Rogers, 1951). In this approach the client is trusted as they are viewed as the 'expert' on their own well-being, thus providing a sense of holding space for the client and all they may bring.

Sub-theme: Contracting and re-contracting, setting the scene

In this sub-theme, 'contracting' is an instrument to manage boundaries and navigate the terrain and the route that may be taken during the coaching. It grants permission to the coach to open certain dialogues within the coaching context. During initial contracting, the coach establishes the difference between coaching and therapy, setting the scene for the conduct of coaching. Contracting acts like a boundary where a coach outlines: this is where I go, this is where I do not go, this is how we work, this is how we do not work, this is my area, this is not my area; all the while checking in with the client so that a co-created contract is made. Thus, contracting draws on two elements to create a procedural contract: the nuts and bolts and the psychological contract "working alliance" (O'Broin & Palmer, 2006).

This allows coaches to open up a dialogue within the coaching work should there be a need, otherwise the coaching work would move beyond the grey and into therapeutic territory. Contracting can be viewed as a living thing, dynamic and constantly shifting and changing depending upon what clients bring to each coaching session. Through contracting and re-contracting, a space is provided and the framework in which to discuss elements that may emerge in the grey space is established.

Using contracting and re-contracting, coaches are "legitimately" (Harré & van Langenhove, 1999) able to open up difficult conversations should that be necessary, for example, conversations regarding signposting and additional support. In addition, a space is created which acts as a container for both coach and coachees, thereby holding space, creating psychological safety (Edmondson, 2019).

> **L3.2:** *You know, you can then also come back to the contracting. Because you've got a contract that is obviously stating that you are doing coaching rather than therapy; you can mention this point. You can also make the point that you know the reason you're bringing this up is because you've noticed this.*

In this extract, using initial contracting, permission is granted to the coach to open up a dialogue and to create a container of psychological safety – holding space – for the client at later points in their work should it appear that the work is moving into grey space.

> **B1.1:** *I liked what you said earlier about transparency and I think that's vital … I've got much more confident about being transparent in terms of, 'Let's think this through together. Is this an issue we can deal with here? Do we need to think about recruiting somebody else?'*

In this extract, transparency becomes part of the coach's initial contracting, acting as a resource to draw on and a way in which to create micro/in-the-moment contracting. Here we see the coach utilising transparency to open up conversations – a way of holding space regarding signposting; once again re-establishing the boundaries of coaching.

Sub-theme: Something is better than nothing

Coaches are faced with dilemmas within coaching at times. This theme highlights the way in which a dilemma is faced. During coaching work, it may become apparent that the scope of the clients' needs may be better supported through therapeutic support and so the coach signposts.

However, clients may be resistant to therapeutic support as there may be a perceived stigma (Grant, 2007). In this sub-theme, a position of 'something is better than nothing' is presented, where the coach adopts a position of support, still working in the role of a "skilled helper" (Egan, 1994) within their competencies and capacities of a coach, where the client navigates the coaching relationship. The coach is still utilising markers such as assessing how helpful the work is for the client (Cavanagh, 2005) and whether the client is engaged in the coaching work so that the work can continue (Grant, 2007). Context may come into play and be a deciding factor, as it may seem more favourable to have coaching rather than therapy (Grant, 2007) within certain working environments. Through transparent dialogue and supervision support, coaches navigate with the client whether coaching could be useful.

> **A3.3:** *'No, hang on, you've got to remember, in this organisation having a coach is a good thing. If you think I'm going to commit career suicide, think again.' And I was left with an ethical dilemma, which I took to my supervisor of actually, I could have said I'm not the right professional, but then you actually leave the individual with nothing, because they won't go to therapy.*

In this extract, the coach takes up an ethical stance; the coach is holding space for the client. This may not be the ideal support for the client, but the coach believes that something is better than nothing, thereby ensuring that the client is not left completely unsupported, once again demonstrating how a coach may approach moments of grey space. In addition, this may highlight that the organisation may need to do more to ensure a variety of support and well-being services are in place for employees to access, with a culture that normalises rather than stigmatises mental-health difficulties. Furthermore, this ensures that safeguarding policies are in place when coaches are commissioned, so that they are able to signpost clients correctly and have an appropriate source of support within the organisation.

Sub-theme: The deeper you go

As a coach, the deeper the psychological work you have done, the more able you are to contain, hold and feel comfortable with difficult emotions or challenges that may arise in the grey space. The 'you' in this theme refers to the coach. and the more self-development and/or therapeutic work a coach has gone through the easier it is on a personal psychological level for them to contain, hold and navigate challenges that may occur during the coaching work. Coaches highlight the importance of being able to stay emotionally and psychologically regulated and not be triggered. This is achieved by the coach being able to create a sense of safety within their own body, and be self-regulated, which in turn acts as a resource to the client (Porges, 2016; Schwartz, 2018).

H1.1:*[Y]our coachee will read you before you've even said anything. They pick up what they sense you're capable of holding. I talk about this concept of the 'container', just like a baby can feel whether the mother or the primary caregiver is strong enough and able to cope, manage or absorb, if you like, without damaging the strong emotions, the powerful emotions that the baby expresses. I think coachees tend not to go places if they don't feel – and this is all unconscious, in my view.*

In this extract, the level of self-work a coach has done – 'the deeper you go' – is a factor contributing to the level of psychological safety – holding space – a client will experience when working with a coach. This extract illustrates that coaches believe that doing the self-work is vital to creating a safe coaching container.

B1.1: *I would agree that we need to do work on ourselves. So, the fitter we are, either mentally, physically, whatever, coaching wise, the more able we will be to turn up for the person that's in front of us.*

This extract demonstrates that, by doing the self-work – the deeper you go – coaches are able to show up more fully for their clients – holding space – and are not clouded by their own internal process. Self-work helps to develop a coach's capacity, furthermore knowing one's limits and good supervision is pertinent to the deeper you go and consequently navigating the grey space.

Sub-theme: Holding a mirror

Within the grey space, the coach is not aiming to 'fix' the client; rather, by 'holding a mirror' for the client, the client may come to some new insight or understanding about themselves or the challenge(s) they are facing. Once again, the coach takes a position of holding space when encountering the grey space, and in so doing employs the tool of reflection. Coaches use the tool of reflecting back to the client what is being heard, observed and sensed in the coaching sessions.

A2.3: *We talked about whether or not it was appropriate in the context of coaching to go back into somebody's childhood or deeper history. But my experience is, we talk about holding a mirror up and it's all a bit – it sounds a bit trite, because coaches say it a lot, but I believe it to be true, a key part of the work is to hold a mirror up.*

In this extract, the coach takes the position of holding space for the client through the use of reflecting back to the client what is brought to coaching: holding a mirror. Then, the client can reflect on how this content may serve their coaching work. This may be seen as similar to techniques used in client-centred therapy, such as 'reflective listening', through "mirroring the client's attitudes in order to bring them more clearly into consciousness" (Rogers, 1942, p.361). However, in this context the holding a mirror or 'reflective listening' (Rogers, 1942, p.361) is utilised to bring to awareness the terrain the coach and client are entering. The client and coach can then discern where this material belongs, does it aid the coaching process or is it something to be signposted to therapy? Or do the coach and client negotiate bracketing this content and focus on the goal of coaching, in which case holding a mirror aids the coach to steer through the grey space.

Sub-theme: Glancing in the rear-view mirror

Again, this is a way for coaches to manage and navigate the grey space when information/knowledge/experiences are drawn on from the past, which may be viewed as therapeutic terrain (Giraldez-Hayes, 2021). Coaches manage this information by acknowledging it, and adopting a stance of 'glancing in the rear-view mirror', taking the information shared and working with the client to facilitate a way forward in light of this knowledge. Therefore, information/experiences that are situated in the past, which may be viewed as therapeutic terrain, are utilised in a coaching manner to inform the forward motion of the coaching process.

> **F1.1:** *Sometimes we need to take a step back to go two steps forward. I mentioned that client because she was a fully functioning individual and it was that one bit in her life that she needed to explore.*

In this extract, the coach is holding space for the client to reflect on an aspect from the past that may be blocking the forward momentum of their coaching work. In this situation, the coach does not step into therapeutic terrain; rather, the client glances at the past, 'glancing in the rear-view mirror' in order to move forward in the present and in line with their coaching goals. This is important, as looking back is often associated with therapy whereas coaching is seen as forward-facing. Such black-and-white messaging is unhelpful and can add to the dilemmas of working and managing the grey space and territory that coaches can find themselves in.

> **S1.3:** *Because coaching is looking forward to something and deals with change. But if you're driving, you have a look in the rear-view mirror every so often … have a quick look in the rear-view mirror to see where you've been and what's been going on.*

In this extract, the coach draws on the metaphor of driving and looking in the rear-view mirror, which acts as a navigational tool. As in the extract above, the coach is holding space for the client to reflect after glancing in the rear-view mirror in order to take stock.

Sub-theme: Curiosity aids the coach

At the time of encountering the grey space, coaches can hold space through eliciting curiosity, as a way to manage the terrain. Curiosity aids the coach to remain in a coaching space, as well as to further explore what may be occurring for the client. Curiosity opens dialogue and is also utilised to demonstrate the Rogerian core conditions (Rogers, 1951), and so, through the use of curiosity – a space of containment – holding space is created.

> **S1.3:** *It doesn't matter where it falls on the spectrum of therapy or – and they were going to say 'coaching'–which I think I said in my reply between therapy and coaching. Just be there, just be curious.*

In this extract, a sense of holding space is created through the use of curiosity. The coach is able to maintain the bounds of coaching and open up dialogue: 'curiosity aids the coach'. In this way, the client and coach can together explore how to navigate the subjects and terrain of the coaching work.

Sub-theme: All of you

Coaches see clients from a holistic perspective – 'all of you' mental, spiritual, emotional and physical beings – as a result holding space for all the client may be brought into the coaching session. Furthermore, from this perspective, coaches recognise that clients may be unable to 'silo' one life domain from another. As a result, the coach is open to receive the client as a whole, recognising various aspects in which work and life domains may intersect. Consequently, coaching may not be situated in just one life domain or aspect.

> **A3.3:** *Oh, you've got a personal life and it's there and you've got a professional life and we talk about this. But, actually, it didn't work like that. I'm a great believer that there is a whole human being in front of you.*

In this extract, the personal and professional spheres of a client's life are not seen as separate. The coach takes the position that every facet of the client is in the coaching room – all of you – thus enabling holding space for what the client may bring.

> **A3.3:** *'Can I talk to you about stuff outside of work?' I'm like, Yes. Last time I looked you're not different people. You're one person. Let's integrate the whole being.*

This extract demonstrates once again the position the coach takes, viewing the client as one person who is multifaceted – all of you – and therefore holding space for the client.

Sub-theme: Holding space mentally

The coach engages in an internal dialogue with themselves at times when in the grey space and navigating their way through it. Through this internal dialogue, and drawing on 'conceptual self-awareness' (Fogel, 2009), the coach constructs a narrative enabling them to create a sense of safety within their own body and be self-regulated, which, in turn, acts as a resource for the client (Porges, 2016; Schwartz, 2018). 'Holding space mentally' acts as a resourcing tool for the coach, so that they do not feel overwhelmed by the content the coachee may be disclosing.

Conceptual self-awareness is viewed as consisting of rational, logical, explanatory, abstract and cognitive aspects of the self thinking about itself, and is based on language and symbols.

> **A2.3:** *Calm down, it's okay, you're not going to do any harm here. All you're doing is listening. I wasn't writing anything down; I wasn't trying to be smart or anything. I was simply giving her the Carl Rogers unconditional positive regard.*

In this extract, the coach draws on internal dialogue to self-regulate when confronted by the grey space unexpectedly. This creates a sense of containment and psychological safety, a holding space for the coach, which is enacted through holding space mentally in this internal dialogue seen above.

> *[I]t's kind of a conscious effort … So, you're directing some of your mental efforts towards remaining calm. Then, also, desperately trying not to think of the next bright question, which is always, whatever your coachee wants to hear. So, what is the next question I'm going to …? Actually, no, not to think about asking a question, but just to, kind of, be there …*

Once again, this extract demonstrates the coach holding space for themselves, through holding space mentally by use of internal dialogue; at the same time acknowledging the mental effort required to enact holding space mentally.

I suggest holding space mentally is indicative of reflection in practice. Schön's (1983) concept of "reflection in action" suggests that to make decisions as a practitioner in the course of one's work, there is a continued interplay between thought and action. Through reflection, one gains the ability to move from being reactive to being proactive in practice. Consequently it helps the coach to develop competency in practice, whilst also helping them journey through the grey space.

Theme 2: Keeping a watchful eye

The coach adopts the standpoint of 'keeping a watchful eye' in moments when they begin to experience or find themselves navigating the grey space; maintaining an overview of what might be happening, emerging and evolving in the coaching work itself. The coach retains an awareness as to whether the client is still benefiting from coaching and is coachable (Cavanagh, 2005; Grant, 2007), or whether the client may need to be signposted to additional support.

Sub-theme: Deep listening

Coaches described drawing on 'deep listening' as a tool to traverse the grey space; one that allowed the coach a deeper insight into which terrain they may be entering. Senge et al. (2004) define presence as "deep listening" or "letting go and letting come"; letting go of any preconceptions and being open to what may emerge. From this viewpoint, presence may be seen as having the capacity to be fully in the moment, fully aware and directly experience what may be going on in mind, body and client, devoid of distraction. This requires one to have "embodied presence" (Blake, 2018) with oneself (see Theme 4) and simultaneously with another.

> **A3.3:** *[T]the real skill about what I would now call deep listening. When people say something and you go, 'Yes, that's very nice, but that's not what, actually, you're talking about'.*

In this extract, the coach takes up the position of keeping a watchful eye through the use of deep listening. In this way, the coach is able to sense more beyond the words being said; as a result they are able to explore with the client the terrain in which the coaching work is taking place, and whether it is moving beyond coaching bounds.

> **F1.1:** *... difficult space to just sit and listen and hear what is not being said more often than what is being said.*

Once again, in this extract, the coach utilises deep listening to acknowledge what is not being said but is being implied. This then shifts the coaching into keeping a watchful eye, ensuring that the coach keeps within the bounds of coaching should more issues emerge that are beyond the coaching territory.

Sub-theme: Helicopter view

When coaches begin to encounter the grey space, they adopt a macro position: a 'helicopter view' of what's happening in the moment with the coachee. They observe feedback from the client, this may come in the form of emotions, cognition or non-verbal cues.

The coach considers what is happening in the coaching work itself, drawing on their own professional experience and "professional identity" (Paterson et al., 2002; Trede, 2012), as well as drawing on "everyday taken-for granted" (Schön, 1983), the experience that is unfolding in the work with the client. The coach is able to keep a watchful eye from the vantage point of a helicopter view, considering what they may need to be aware of. Observing what unfolds, the coach can then discern whether or not they need to address concerns immediately (drawing on 'contracting', as seen in Theme 1) or at a later stage.

A conceptual self-awareness is taking place, which is viewed as the rational, logical, explanatory, abstract, cognitive aspects of the self thinking about itself, which is based on language and symbols. This self is experienced as narrative, story, facts, information, insights, self-assessment and interpretation (Fogel, 2009). I suggest that synergistic interaction between 'embodied self-awareness' (as seen in Theme 4) and a helicopter view takes place in order to keep a watchful eye. The key is effective conceptual evaluations; a helicopter view (conceptual self-awareness) of our senses (embodied self-awareness) (Blake, 2018). This synergy assists the coach when navigating these moments.

S0.1: *So, you know, at points along the way, I think we need to use that helicopter view of all our knowledge and experience and experience of this particular coachee and even sessions we're having with them, as to whether it's still appropriate to work with them. If, later on, we find that they're still struggling, I'm trying to track which direction the person is moving in. So, we might be in the grey space, but if it's less grey than it was.*

In this extract, the coach holds in mind all the knowledge and experience they have gained whilst working with this client: a helicopter view. This ensures that the coach is able to keep a watchful eye as sessions with the client unfold. It also enables the coach to discern when they are moving into the grey space, and beyond, which may inform how the coach navigates.

Theme 3: Normalising

Viewing coaching from the perspective of the "Distressed but Functional" quadrant (Grant, 2007) and navigating the grey space, in this theme coaches aim to normalise the element of distress experienced by the coachees, with to the objective of working towards the "Flourishing" quadrant. Einzig calls for coaches to be "brave" and to step into the space of emotions, particularly those that are challenging, so as not to fall into the "tyranny of the positive" (Einzig, 2011. However, this should be done within the ethical considerations of what it is to be a coach, recognising one's own limits and boundaries, while ensuring a basic awareness of psychological and personality disorder, with the ability to recognise disorders. Einzig goes on to further suggest that we as coaches should learn from indigenous cultures who "have a different view of illness or emotional distress, seeking to learn and integrate them" (Einzig, 2011). If we pose the question: "What if the answers we seek lay in the darkness?" rather than fearing this space, the question becomes one that helps clients to entertain a different perspective; one that assists in finding meaning, rather than fearing and avoiding emotional content with our clients (Einzig, 2011, p.41).

Sub-theme: Mental health literacy

This is the first theme relating to 'mental health literacy' (Jorm, 2012) and relates to how the coach interacts with the client at these times and how normalising happens. What came out of this theme is that normalising not only relates to the coach's mental health literacy but also helps the client gain and develop mental health literacy, so that they can normalise what's going on for them in the moment.

> **H1.3:** *We need to ... Mental health literacy is so poor in this country. We really need to just normalise it and understand it. The good mental health let alone just when it's gone wrong ... I think, coaching schools, really, should be educating people in this.*

In this extract, the coach calls for normalising mental health, viewing it as sitting on a continuum much like physical health. Here, the act of normalising is done through the use of mental health literacy, both for the coach and client. Furthermore, from this position, anyone in a helping or service profession can and should become mental health literate, not just those working in areas of psychology/therapy. I would suggest that this is particularly important post-pandemic because of the impacts that COVID has had on many individuals' mental health, as previously discussed (see p.31).

Sub-theme: Human emotions

Coaches, through reflection, support coachees in normalising the range of emotions they may be experiencing, in addition to developing the coachees' vocabulary around emotions in order to label emotions more effectively, creating emotional agility (David, 2016). This is one of the ways of navigating the grey space coaches found to help the client normalise some of the emotions that they were experiencing, and utilise emotional labelling.

> **H1.3:** *Most of the time I hear people say, 'It's normal'. Yes, it is normal, it's very normal. You just don't know. You believe it is just in your head and it's not, it's normal. So I think there is the key thing that I take away from it.*

In this extract, the coach reassures the client through the use of normalising and educating the client on the array of human emotions. As a result, the client no longer discredits or views themself as experiencing something wrong; rather, their emotional awareness develops.

Sub-theme: Seeing beyond the label

Coaches adopted a stance of 'seeing beyond the label' of mental health diagnosis, utilising Grant's (2007), "Distressed but Functional" quadrant. Coaches felt strongly that coaching should be made available, even if a coachee had had a prior mental health diagnosis, if the client was benefiting from the coaching work.

> **A3:** *... and actually we go, 'Okay, a person has mental health issues; it doesn't mean they can't succeed'. If we're helping people to succeed, then, actually, we're in a whole new space.*

H3:   *I love that. I think we need to get away from labels and we need to be func-*
tioning and dysfunctional …

A current challenge might be a mental health condition. But that doesn't
underlie that spirit of that person … if you can hold that for somebody, whilst
they're going through this distress, you're playing a very powerful role.
I think that's what we do as coaches. We point out those other facets to help
normalise it, really.

This extract demonstrates a conversation about the position the coach can take
when working with a client with current or previous mental health conditions.
Through engaging in the coaching work, alongside someone managing the client's
mental ill health, coaches act to normalise mental health being on a continuum.
Once again, the view is that coaching work can be engaged in appropriately and not
clients with mental health issues do not need to be excluded; thus seeing beyond
the label.

Sub-theme: Appropriate humour

The last sub-theme surrounding normalising the human experience is through the
coach's use of 'appropriate humour'. Here, humour may enable the client to change
state or gain a new perspective (Martin & Ford, 2018). This may be seen much in
the same light as the use of "adaptive humour" (Cann & Collette, 2014). From a
positive psychology perspective, humour is seen as a strength to draw on (Peterson
& Seligman, 2004).

A1.3: *I think, reflecting back, I have, depending on who the person is, used a bit of*
humour to try and break the state for everyone. Appropriate humour.
Z3:   *Because I thought, 'We just make everything so serious'. And I thought, 'Wit*
is not a word I would have used but fun would have been something I'd
put in'.
X2:   *And humour. I absolutely agree.*
Z3:   *Yes, absolutely.*
X2:   *… because sometimes there are moments in the coaching context where*
laughing at a situation actually dissipates it and helps to move forward.

In this extract, a dialogue is unfolding, which, through the use of appropriate
humour the coaches look to normalise, as well as to shift the client's perspective
when they are navigating challenges.

Theme 4: Embodied awareness

This theme demonstrates the way in which coaches use their embodied awareness to navigate and know when they may be entering or experiencing being in
the grey space. Coaches utilise their embodied awareness to sense that something

has shifted within the dynamic; again, monitoring moment-by-moment changes. Coaches describe a physical embodied knowing or physical embodied sense of something happening, leading them to want to enquire with the client further; to dig deeper.

Blake (2018) defines 'embodied awareness' as present-moment, non-judgemental attention to sensation, movement and emotion. From this perspective, the body is viewed as a social and emotional sense organ – whole body awareness – with our bodies acting as antennae, always picking up sensory information from the emotional and social atmosphere we live in. There are three embodied perceptions: 1) exteroception, responsible for the five senses, which are sight, sound, smell, taste and touch; 2) interoception, or internal visceral sensitisation, involving the heart, lungs, gut, skin and fascia; and 3) proprioception, the position of the body in space, which includes the inner ear, specialised muscle cells and fascia.

Embodied self-awareness is viewed as a whole-body phenomenon, the self experiencing itself, based on sensing, feeling and acting in the present moment. This may be experienced as physical sensation, temperature, pressure, movement, shape, breath, mood and energy levels with interoceptive and proprioceptive neural networks involved. This is unlike conceptual self-awareness, which is viewed as the rational, logical, explanatory, abstract and cognitive aspects of the self thinking about itself based on language and symbols. This self is experienced as narrative, story, facts, information, insights, self-assessment and interpretation, and the "conceptual self-awareness informed by embodied self-awareness is the best source of making decisions beneficial to both self and others" (Fogel, 2009, p.61). "Bridging our embodied perception and our conceptual perceptions of life, the world ourselves are our emotions, which are effectively evaluations of our sensations. They're conceptual evaluations of sensations" (Blake, 2018, p.10).

Sub-theme: Sensing the grey

As the coach enters the grey space, or, as the dynamics within the coaching work shift, when the coach is using their bodied awareness, they sense that something has shifted within the dynamic.

> **B1.2:** *How do I know if I'm in the grey space? There is something that happens within me; my body tells me whether or not I'm in a space that is …*

In this extract, the coach speaks of a knowing embodied awareness that something in the coaching work with their client has changed and that they are moving into complex territory – 'sensing the grey'.

> **J1.2:** *I think there's something about a felt sense you get when you've been around for a bit. And even if you can't, you know sometimes I think actually, it's how you feel at the end of your time with that person, and if you're feeling either unusually tired or maybe quite agitated. You know, it's something about how do*

you respond, how do you resonate with that person, and what you are left with at the end can sometimes be a clue as well, I think.

Once again, this extract demonstrates a felt sense of embodied awareness from the coach. At such times, the coach will reflect on what is happening for them within their bodies, as the body acts as a data source and indicates what may be taking place moment by moment in the session.

Sub-theme: Gut feel

Coaches described having a 'gut feel' that they may be entering the grey space or that something is or has shifted that the coach may need to pay attention to. Initially, the coaches may experience interception, the internal visceral sensitisation of body perception (Blake, 2018), which is utilised to help the coach navigate this terrain. Furthermore, coaches have learnt from experience developed as a result of years of practice to trust this experience or "professional identity" (Paterson et al., 2002; Trede et al., 2012), viewing this information as practically assisting the navigation of the grey space.

S0.1: *I don't know. For want of a better word, that gut feel that something is just off, or something not sitting right, that you get.*

In this extract, the coach speaks of a visual gut feel that a shift within the coaching work has occurred. The coach utilises this embodied awareness to advance the session further.

S0.1: *So, I think there is something about gut instinct and I think that means gut instinct gets a bad press. And I think you're right, when you've been practising for a while, there is a lot of procedure, rules, that you develop – if A, then B. You know, you're building up. So I don't think gut instinct actually is always gut instinct, I think actually there is a lot of thinking that sits behind that, so I trust that.*

In this extract, the coach indicates that embodied awareness such as gut feelings are developed over time through practice and experience, resulting in trust for these visceral experiences.

Sub-theme: Dig deeper

This embodied self-awareness and felt sense – interoception (Blake, 2018) – signal the coach to explore further with the client what may be emerging in the session; exploring whether they are still working within the coaching territory or whether there has been a move towards the therapeutic space. A counterpoint to this is pace, and the theme of 'slowly does it' (see p.97).

S0.1: *Where I might be tempted to … Or it might raise questions for me, if there are any signals in any one of those four areas that would lead me to dig a little deeper. I would be confident to just dig a little deeper if I felt that there was information that could help me make a better decision with the client about what was needed.*

In this extract, because of the trust the coach has developed in felt sense or embodied awareness, Blake (2018, see p.118 for definition), they will explore what they are sensing with their clients. The coach looks to 'dig deeper' through dialogue; thereby confirming or denying the information they have detected. In so doing, the coach can navigate the grey space by drawing on earlier themes such as re-contracting. By picking up information from felt sense, the coach utilises this information to dig deeper with the client, which acts as a technique and resource when entering the grey space.

Summary

This chapter outlined Workshop 1, the first of two collaborative group enquiries. The workshop aimed to explore how and when coaches experience the grey space, in a collaborative process. After outlining the workshop agenda, action research presented four main themes. Through the exploration of these themes, and multiple sub-themes, the grey space was surveyed in detail. The next chapter focuses on the second collaborative group enquiry, Workshop 2, in which more themes are explored.

Discussion points

1. What themes, sub-themes and codes do you recognise in your own practice?
2. What is your awareness/experience of the grey space?

Recommended reading

Aquilina, E. (2016). *Embodying authenticity. A somatic path to transforming self, team & organisation.* London: Live It Publishing.

Blake, A. (2018). *Your body is your brain: Leverage your somatic intelligence to find purpose, build resilience, deepen relationships and lead more powerfully.* Truckee, CA: Trokay Press.

Campone, F. (2014). 'At the border: coaching a client with dissociative identity disorder'. *International Journal of Evidence Based Coaching and Mentoring*, 12(1), 49–62.

Day, A. (2012). 'Working with unconscious relational process in coaching'. In E. de Hann & C. Sills (eds.), *Coaching relationships: The relational coaching field book.* Faringdon: Libri Publishing.

Edmondson, A. C. (2019). *The fearless organization: Creating psychological safety in the workplace for learning, innovation, and growth*. Hoboken, NJ: Wiley.

Fook, J. (2010). 'Beyond reflective practice: Reworking the "critical" in critical reflection'. In H. Bradbury, N. Frost, S. Kilminster & M. Zukas (eds.), *Beyond reflective practice: New approaches to professional lifelong learning*. London: Routledge.

Garvey, B. & Stokes, P. (2022) *Coaching and mentoring: Theory and practice*, 4th edn. London: SAGE.

O'Broin, A.O. & Palmer, S. (2006). 'The coach-client relationship and contributions made by the coach in improving coaching outcomes'. *The Coaching Psychologist*, 2(2), 16–20.

O'Broin, A. & Palmer, S. (2010). 'Building on interpersonal perspective on the coaching relationship'. In S. Palmer & A. McDowall (eds.), *The coaching relationship: Putting people first*. Abingdon: Routledge.

Porges, S. (2016). 'Co-regulation'. Relational impact. Available at: Porges-2016-09 (relationalimplicit.com (Accessed: December 2021).

Schön, D.A. (1983). *The reflective practitioner: How professionals think in a*ction. New York, NY: Basic Books.

Schwartz, A. (2018). 'Connection and co-regulation in psychotherapy'. Available at: Connection and Co-Regulation in Psychotherapy | Dr. Arielle Schwartz (drarielleschwartz.com) (Accessed: December 2021).

Strozzi-Heckler, R. (2014). *The art of somatic coaching: Embodying skillful action, wisdom and compassion*. Berkeley, CA: North Atlantic Books.

Whittington, J. (2016). *Systemic coaching & constellations: The principles, practices and applications for individuals, teams and groups*, 2nd edn. London: Kogan Page.

References

Argyris, C. (2003). 'Actionable knowledge'. In T. Tsoukas & C. Knudsen (eds.), *The Oxford handbook of organizational theory*. Oxford: Oxford University Press.

Cann, A. & Collette, C. (2014). 'Sense of humor, stable affect, and psychological well-being'. *Europe's Journal of Psychology*, 10(3), 464–479.

Cavanagh, M. (2005). 'Mental-health issues and challenging clients in executive coaching'. In M. Cavanagh, A.M. Grant & T. Kemp (eds.), *Evidence-based coaching, Volume 1: Theory, research and practice from behavioural science*. Bowen Hill, Australia: Australian Academic Press.

Coghlan, D. (2006). 'Insider action research doctorates: Generating actionable knowledge'. *Higher Education*, 54(3), 293–306.

David, S. (2016). *Emotional agility. Get unstuck, embrace change and thrive in work and life*. London: Penguin Random House.

Egan, G. (1994). *The skilled helper*, 5th edn. Pacific Grove, CA: Brooks.

Einzig, H. (2011). 'The beast within'. *Coaching at Work*, 6(3), 40–43.

Fogel, A. (2009). *The psychophysiology of self-awareness: Rediscovering the lost art of body sense*. Portland, OR: Ringgold Inc.

Giraldez-Hayes, A. (2021). 'Different domains or grey areas? Setting boundaries between coaching and therapy: A thematic analysis'. *The Coaching Psychologist*, 17(2), 18–29.

Grant, A.M. (2007). 'A languishing-flourishing model of goal striving and mental health for coaching populations'. *International Coaching Psychology Review*, 2(3), 252–264.

Harré, R. & van Langenhove, L. (1999). *Positioning theory*. Oxford: Blackwell Publishers Ltd.

Heron, J. (1999). *The complete facilitator's handbook*. New York, NY: Kogan Page Limited.

Jorm, A.F. (2012). 'Mental health literacy: Empowering the community to take action for better mental health'. *The American Psychologist*, 67(3), 231–243.

Martin, R. & Ford, T. (2018). *The psychology of humor: An integrative approach*. Cambridge, MA: Academic Press.

O'Broin, A.O. & Palmer, S. (2006). 'The coach-client relationship and contributions made by the coach in improving coaching outcomes'. *The Coaching Psychologist*, 2(2), 16–20.

Paterson, M., Higgs, J., Wilcox. S. & Villeneuve, M. (2002). 'Clinical reasoning and self-directed learning: key dimensions in professional education and professional socialisation'. *Focus on Health Professional Education*, 4(2), 6.

Peterson, C. & Seligman, M. (2004). *Character strengths and virtues: A handbook and classification*. Washington, DC: American Psychological Association.

Plett, H. (2020). *The art of holding space: A practice of love, liberation and leadership*. Winnipeg, Canada: Page Two Books.

Porges, S. (2016). 'Co-regulation'. Relational Impact. Available at: Porges-2016-09 (relationalimplicit.com (Accessed: December 2021).

Rogers, C. (1951). *Client-centered therapy: Its current practice, implications and theory*. London: Constable.

Rogers, C.R. (1942). *Counseling and psychotherapy: Newer concepts in practice*. Boston, MA: Houghton Mifflin.

Rogers, C.R. & Farson, R. (1957). 'Active listening'. Available at: activelistening.pdf (Accessed: 7 January 2021) (an excerpted version).

Schwartz, A. (2018). 'Connection and co-regulation in psychotherapy'. Available at: Connection and Co-Regulation in Psychotherapy | Dr. Arielle Schwartz (drarielleschwartz.com) (Accessed: December 2021).

Senge, P., Scharmer, C.O., Jaworski, J. & Flowers, B.S. (2004). *Presence: Human purpose and the field of the future*. Cambridge, MA: The Society for Organizational Learning.

Trede, F., Macklin, R. & Bridges, D. (2012). 'Professional identity development: A review of the higher education literature'. *Studies in Higher Education*, 37(3), 365–384.

Chapter 6

Navigating the grey space Part III

Further surveying, and charting what emerges

Collaborative group enquiry – Workshop 2

Research question

How can I and other coaches improve the practice of dealing with ethics and managing boundaries in the grey space when working with clients experiencing health and well-being issues such as stress management, resilience and personal development?

The aim of Workshop 2 was to reflect and consider how co-enquirers may have developed, altered or adapted their own practice, including reflections, possible insights, implementation of any actionable knowledge and alternative ways of thinking regarding the grey space, during the six months between Workshop1/ Cycle 3 and Workshop 2/Cycle 4.

Once again, the extracts presented are representative of the collaborative enquiry group workshops. The enquiry groups consisted of three groups: Group 1: coaches from various training and knowledge landscapes; Group 2: a coaching psychologist and psychologically informed coaches, who had formal/academic training in psychology/therapy; and Group 3: a mix of coaches from various training, knowledge landscapes and those who had received formal/academic psychological/therapeutic training. The groups remained the same for the duration of the research, all attending the workshop within a similar timeframe. Extracts that are deemed to be representative of each theme and sub-theme have been included in the text from all three groups of co-enquirers. As with Workshop 1, once the structure of the workshops had been established, I adopted the position of co-enquirer and took an action research approach. My voice became one of the co-enquirers; thereby contributing to the themes and sub-themes produced.

The objective was to discover the benefits gained from participating in Workshop 1/Cycle 3 hearing co-enquirers' critical conversations and sharing learning and to explore any changes in in-between workshop reflective practices. In line with the iterative process of action research, the aim of each cycle was to reflect, review and implement gained actionable knowledge (Argyris, 2003).

DOI: 10.4324/9781003509776-7

The workshops consisted of a four-hour enquiry via Zoom, due to COVID-19 restrictions. My role was that of facilitator, drawing on Heron's (1999) co-operative mode within the workshop, gradually blending the hierarchical mode as the workshops developed, and seeing what emerged, based on the research questions provided in the agenda. These questions provided areas for exploration and a focus for enquiry.

Workshop agenda

- Open general group reflections regarding practice, insights and reflections since Workshop 1
- Reflection on any living contradiction in values identified by a practitioner as a result of participating in the research
- Group discussion based on semi-structured questions:
  - Have you identified any elements of your practice in the grey space that you would like to develop?
  - Why would you like to develop these elements?
  - Are there any modifications you have made or would like to make to your coaching work as a result of reflections, discussion and participation in this research?
  - Going forward, how do you intend to further develop your practice in the grey space?
  - Have there been any changes in how you refer since taking part in this research (how, frequency, etc.)?
  - What are your views on coaches dealing with challenging emotions?
  - What positive impact can coaches have on stress-related mental health issues.

Three main themes were created, which gave an overarching sense of what developments had come about for the coaches as a result of them having participated in the research, as well as what changes had been made or were planned for the future because they had participated in the reflection on the grey space.

Overview of themes

What has been the development of practice within navigating the grey space?

Theme 1: Permission to show up

This theme presents the position adopted by coaches as they grapple with the notion of permission to inhabit the grey space, highlighting how coaches enable, engage and navigate its complexities.

Theme 2: Position

This theme explores how coaches actively situate themselves within the grey space. Coaches reflect on their position within the grey space, navigating role fluidity, identity and the tensions around how they show up. There is a conscious

Table 6.1 CTA of action research collaborative enquiry groups in Workshop 2

Constructionist Thematic Analysis

Theme 1 *Permission to Show Up*	Theme 2 *Position*	Theme 3 *Voice*
Sub-Themes		
Presence: holding space	Tensions at play	Disillusionment
Proficiency	Radical inclusion	Normalising
Reflexivity: a living compass	Deeper purpose	Presence of trauma
Context	Coaching towards	Referral: coaching's
	therapy	'ugly step-sister'
Utilise professional practice		Research gives voice
and communities		
Arc of transformation		
Values		

positioning of self within this space, where roles are fluid and shaped by personal and professional stories. Coaches resist rigid role definitions, embracing complexity in service of deeper, more integrated practice.

Theme 3: Voice

Coaches give voice on behalf of their clients, the tensions within the profession and disillusionment with the system. There is a resistance to the discourse surrounding the term 'referral'.

Theme 1: Permission to show up

The main theme of 'permission to show up' demonstrates how coaches grapple with permission to be in the grey space, in addition to navigating the space itself. I present the following sub-themes that coaches drew on to give them permission to show up as a way of navigating this space. In addition, I suggest that coaches obtained permission through the coach-coachee dynamic, as well as drawing on the wider professional communities and practice. This would indicate that permission to show up is warranted through utilising three elements: 1) the inner landscape of the coach; 2) collaboration with the client; and 3) the wider coaching professions and practices. All these are an active way of positioning themselves in this space, such as is present in 'reflexive positioning': "reflexive positioning is a process by which one intentionally or unintentionally positions oneself in unfolding personal stories told to oneself" (Harré & van Langenhove, 1999, p.75). Additionally, because coaches critically reflected on how they manage the boundaries between therapy and coaching, practitioners created a process for gaining awareness through the exploration of "everyday taken-for-granted" (Schön, 1983). This resulted in a new awareness being obtained. Coaches could confirm or reconstruct their identities as practitioners (Fook, 2010), which granted them permission to show up.

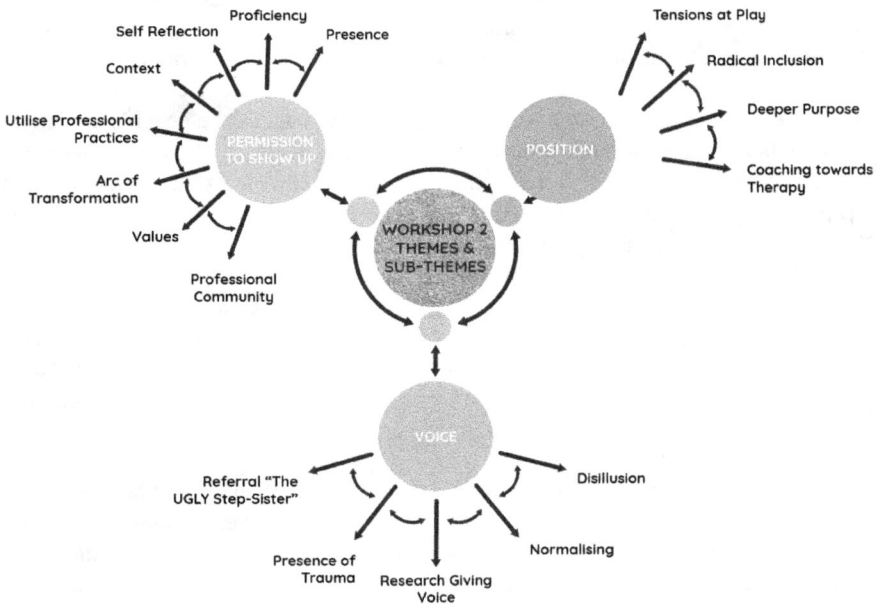

Proficiency
Self Reflection
Presence
Context
Utilise Professional Practices
Arc of Transformation
Values
Professional Community

PERMISSION TO SHOW UP

Tensions at Play
Radical Inclusion
Deeper Purpose
Coaching towards Therapy

POSITION

WORKSHOP 2 THEMES & SUB-THEMES

VOICE

Referral "The UGLY Step-Sister"
Disillusion
Presence of Trauma
Normalising
Research Giving Voice

Figure 6.1 Theoretical framework for navigating boundaries in coaching practice

Sub-theme: Presence: holding space

This sub-theme considered how coaches grant themselves permission to show up in the grey space through the application of 'holding space': an encompassing stance of presence. This is much the same as seen in the first cycle of CTA (see p.51). The concept of holding space, an encompassing stance of presence, presented a position taken up by the coach when encountering the terrain of the grey space. Furthermore, by holding space, permission was warranted for the coaches to show up. Plett (2020) suggests that there are ten elements involved in the art of holding space: witnessing; containment; compassion; non-judgement; selective guidance; space for complexity; autonomy; flexibility; connection; and allyship. I propose that these elements can be viewed in several ways, including witnessing, embodied presence, relational presence (which encompasses being attuned to the client/client-led), pace and spirituality.

Code: Holding space

Plett's (2020) concept relates to "bearing witness", which "is showing up without the answers. It is listening without needing to change the narrative or the situation" (p.38), to honour, see and pay attention to the coachee, which can be seen in this aspect of holding space. Furthermore, coaches utilised elements of unconditional positive regard (Rogers, 1956) and active listening (Rogers & Farson, 1957) to be fully present with the client. The importance of the quality of presence was high-lighted. It was agreed the coach's role is not to 'fix' the client; rather, to be with the client, thereby providing safety through presence for both client and coach. Therefore, granting permission to show up not only reduces the coach's anxieties, it also acts as a navigational tool in the grey space. Extract M1.1 and the poem below demonstrate that, when a coach is 'doing', in the role of fixing, a tension is created. Therefore, moving into a state of 'being' away to hold space allows greater clarity, awareness and safety within this space.

A3.3: *I think I'm making modifications as we go. I think there are certain areas where I used to be quite proactive, that I'm now looking to do less, so less questioning and more just being, to hold the space that I'm hearing from feedback, that the people I work with, the coaching clients, are saying that they appreciate and value.*

In this extract, through the act of doing less, by holding space and being present with the client – 'presence: holding space' – the coach is granted permission to be in the grey space with the client. Furthermore, clients reported appreciation and value for the space created by the coach.

T2.1: *No, it is holding a space for them … It is not therapeutic and so I actu-ally think, in some ways, it is safer because you are potentially minimising the chance of re-traumatisation, because it is just holding a space.*

Here, again, the coach takes up a position of doing no harm in the grey space through presence: holding space granting permission to show up in this terrain.

M1.1: *I just first wrote something that I kind of knew, but I felt, 'It would be so useful for me to have on my own wall', which was, 'Being is doing and doing is being', as an acknowledgement. But then I wrote it in a different way. I put, 'I'm doing and not being', because the productivity can be, very often, 'I'm doing'. My focus is just doing and not being. 'I'm being and not doing', 'I'm doing and I'm being'. And then, 'I'm being and I see the doing in that'.*

The poem was presented like this:

Being

I am doing and I am not being.
I am being and I am not doing.
I am doing and being.
I am being and seeing the doing in my being.

This extract and poem 'Being' by one of the participants, Magdalena Bak-Maier, reiterate that presence: holding space is not about an active doing. The lines from Bak-Maier, "I am doing and I am not being./I am being and I am not doing" are particularly relevant as they apply to the state the coach is holding – the being, the presence the coach adopts and in so doing, feeling confident to be in the grey space with a client's permission to show up.

Code: Embodied/somatic presence

In addition to holding space, presence is created with the client through the coach being in a present and calm embodied state. Aquilina states that the person that we are "is the most potent and versatile tool we have" (Aquilina, 2016, p.98). Coaches reported developing a greater somatic awareness when encountering the moment of grey space, meaning that the coach is aware of their own somatic experiences as well as those of the client. By using this somatic awareness, we can "learn to access deeper wisdom that resides within each of us" (Aquilina, 2016, p.98). It is suggested that emotional co-regulation is created through the coach's embodied presence. Co-regulation is a complex automatic stimulation process that occurs due to mirroring between individuals through relationship. As a result, the autonomic nervous system can either be in regulation or dysregulation (Porges, 2016). From a somatic perspective, emotional co-regulation is accomplished through the process of body awareness, which develops a greater capacity to notice moment-to-moment sensory experience changes. Through the practitioner's calm attention and by creating a sense of safety within their own body, being self-regulated, this presence acts as a resource for the client (Porges, 2016; Schwartz, 2018). This is a proactive response, with practitioners being present and holding a present-moment awareness, including that which may be unspoken yet present (Aquilina, 2016). In these circumstances, embodied awareness acts as a guidance system for the coach; a safety permission to show up.

M1.1: *We're having a conversation about what keeps us safe. I was thinking, 'This is about the quality. The more present we are with ourselves – i.e. the more aware of our own internal territory in our own felt sense and our own presence – being able to really work that for ourselves, in turn, is what makes sure that we keep our clients safe'. Those two things go together.*

S1.1: *It's about holding that emotion and being okay – this container. 'How much space have I got in me to hold this right now?'*

B2.1: *So that, I think, is what we'd call embodiment, isn't it? There's an embodied sense of self and who you are and what you're bringing, and all of that is good and "'s enough, and you've got what you need.*

In this extract, the coaches are having a dialogue regarding the importance of one's quality of presence as a coach: presence: holding space. This quality of presence can be impacted by the level of embodied presence the coach has. Furthermore, this presence can be enhanced through the development of one's felt sense and ability to negate one's internal terrain. Through greater 'embodied presence', the coach has a greater capacity to be present and hold space for the client and therefore permission to show up in the terrain the coach and client are navigating.

Code: Relational presence

Through reflective/reflexive practices (Schön, 1983), coaches viewed relational presence as a fundamental quality for any good work to occur because, through the coaching relationship, a container is created where the collaborative coaching work can take place (O'Broin & Palmer, 2010). Furthermore, Critchley (2012) proposes that coaching is a profoundly relational process, with effective coaching being dependent on the ability of the coach to work skilfully with this relational dimension.

Through the relational presence, coaches gain permission to show up in the grey space. Not maintaining the relational presence is seen as unethical; one that could reinforce 'attachment or relational wounds' (Bowlby, 1988); therefore causing the client greater harm.

Owing to the relational aspect of coaching, coaches concentrate on the quality of the relationship itself. Day (2012) states: "coaching values the perspective of the client as much as that of the coach" (p.45).

Coaches hold that maintaining the quality and bond, the "affective bond" (Martin et al., 2000), involves liking, trust and respect, 'attachment or relational need' (Bowlby, 1988), being 'there for them [the client]', and being in relational presence with the client is an ethical position to take within the grey space.

Consequently, when navigating their way through the grey space, the coach anchors to the quality of the relationship. Coaches value the relational aspect and view it as essential and to be honoured. Critchley (2012) suggests that by far the greatest factor in effective coaching outcomes is the relationship itself rather than any specific process or method.

K2.2:   *Again, it is building the working alliance, isn't it? Once that working alliance is strong, when the client feels that the space is safe to express emotions, then they will come out and say something, which can be really significant in terms of the coaching ... So, for me it is really about developing my own and being comfortable in myself to open that space up for the client for when they are ready to explore those emotions, whether it is in coaching or in therapy.*

S1.1:   *... It's the implication of working in the grey space from a relational perspective, not just from a kind of ethical perspective by way of practice and intervention, but actually, a very ethical dimension, because of the relationship and the quality of the relational space.*

B1.1:   *It's always relationship, yes.*

S1.1:   *It's always relational, yes.*

B1.1:   *Yes, and yet, we don't talk about it in … Well, we do talk about it in those ways.*

Once again, this extract demonstrates permission to show up with a client in the grey space should the client want to bring emotional content into sessions. Through the use of presence: holding space, the nuance here is the quality of the relational presence the coach can provide. The greater the relational presence, the greater the container the coach provides presence: holding space while navigating the complexities of the grey space. The coaches viewed the importance of creating this relational presence as being of great ethical importance.

Code: 'Slowly does it'

Another application of holding space is through pace. Coaches described that, through applying more conscious awareness when navigating the grey space, their need to slow down to be present with the client increased. In these instances, the coaches paced themselves, so they could be fully present, aware, holding space, with the client. Pacing became an instrument for coaches, enabling them to 'show up' when navigating this terrain.

Brems (2001) suggests that speed is essential, with the client's pace being accommodated. However, it is not only the client, the coach too seems to have a pace at which they feel able and competent to navigate the grey space; one which is more measured or uses a slower approach, as highlighted below.

S1.1:   *I think that taking a really paced approach.*

B1.1:   *I can say, I have a client who is in such a great deal of mental stress that even on our initial contracting session, the person said to me, after about ten minutes, 'My brain has now switched off. I can't really do anymore.' Basically, I went, 'Well, how are we going to have a lengthy session?' Because actually, this person's physiology doesn't support, at the moment, as a proper being – I don't know – twenty minutes or thirty minutes. Part of the reconditioning work is, 'Can we do ten minutes safely? What can we do in that?' There's even a kind of dosage of time, as well, to that.*

These two extracts highlight that coaches actively adjust their pace, with their client and themselves in mind. Through actively pacing, the coaches demonstrate their presence and containment with the client presence: holding space; in so doing granting themselves permission to show up in the grey space.

Code: Spiritual presence

The other way of holding space as permission to show up is spiritual presence. Through the process of reflecting on how coaches navigate the grey space, several concluded that when navigating this space there was a spiritual quality. Plett (2020) suggests that "holding space is a spiritual act" (p.70), inferring that, as a 'space-holder', one is open to something far larger than oneself. From a systemic constellation perspective, this may be seen as the 'field of information', where, tuning into this aspect, amid the parts and people of the system, "is a source of the hidden resources and solutions held within systems" (p.32).

After reflecting on how coaches may adapt or improve their practice in the grey space, the groups resolved to develop and utilise spiritual presence more. This was to be done both in the moment with the client, as well as in their own spiritual practices, which act as a resource; a way of centring/coming back to oneself and allowing the coaching to take on meaning.

Desmond (2012) proposes that there are various ways of knowing that arise within a coaching relationship; spirituality being one. Furthermore, he suggests that "spirituality is intrinsic to being human and is an embodied experience" (p.68). Meaning-making plays a vital part in our quality of life as human beings. Frankl (1992, 1978) suggests that spirituality and meaning are closely linked, enabling individuals to construct a sense of their lives.

M1.1: *I have, for quite some time, come to a belief that I work in a field, and the field is boundaryless. What keeps you safe is actually presence … it does mean that it's not so much about what you do, but how you are with people. There's something that you were saying, Beverly, about purity of intention. That's a very metaphysical concept and a spiritual concept, but it really is an energetic quality as well. Children bring it. Animals bring it. It's why they are so healing to people. Nature brings it. There's a purity to things that I would say … I would say it's helping me develop my spirituality more. That's probably what I'd say.*

B1.1: *So what that brings up for me is, I was thinking, as you were talking M1.1 about this quality of presence … 'We're having a conversation about what keeps us safe'. I was thinking, 'This is about the quality'. The more present we are with ourselves – i.e. the more aware of our own internal territory in our own felt sense and our own presence – being able to really work that for ourselves, in turn, is what makes sure that we keep our clients safe. Those two things go together.*

Then I'm wondering whether there is absolutely something in here about the spiritual presence. It's about our felt-sense presence, but also felt sense in the sense of our spiritual presence as well. We can talk about presence as just how this felt body is being present, and how grounded and present is this felt body and my connection to my own felt sense? But how is this felt-sense body also connected with all of this – the spiritual world around me, and how I bring that into this space as well?

This extract highlights that coaches enact presences not only through embodied presence, pacing or adopting the core Rogerian principles. When a stance of spiritual presence is taken up, the coach steps into a sense of something greater; a connection with all. Through bringing this quality into themselves and therefore their coaching work, coaches felt that they had a greater sense of presence for their client and therefore permission to show up.

Sub-theme: Proficiency

The coaches described having a sense of increased 'proficiency' to manoeuvre through the grey space permission to show up since Workshop 1/Cycle 3; speaking of various dimensions that supported this development of competence and skill – for example, 'doing the work'. This talks to the importance of coaches undertaking their own psychological development, their 'dynamic edge'. Through confronting the boundaries of their capacity, an expiation took place and the coaches conveyed a sense of growth in competence, CPD, training and integration of knowledge, as well as adopting a "life-long learning" (Wise, 2010) stance. Through the act of working with clients, practical knowledge is acquired, 'depth through practice'. In addition to being an 'art form' a co-creating takes place between coach and client, with each situation being different from the next.

Code: Doing the self-work

This was seen in Workshop 1/Cycle 3, the sub-theme being 'the deeper you go' (see p.76). The importance of doing deep psychological work as a coach is seen as vital, not only to hold space (as seen in Workshop 1) but also as a way to gain proficiency in manoeuvring one's way through the grey space. 'Doing the self-work' is about dealing with one's psychological element. In so doing, one is able to be more present, to gain competency in manoeuvring, thus keeping the relational space cleaner. Self-care is involved in this too. Consequently, the coach can 'show up' for the client more proficiently.

Furthermore, as discussed in Workshop 1, doing the self-work was vital in order to stay emotionally and psychologically regulated and not be triggered. The coach creates a sense of embodied safety through self-regulation, which in turn acts as a resource for the client (Porges, 2016; Schwartz, 2018).

Moreover, within the sub-theme of 'proficiency', I suggest this code of doing the self-work can be viewed as a further development of the sub-theme 'deeper you go' from Workshop 1. So doing the self-work encompasses the sub-theme 'deeper you go' (Workshop 1) – and more. It is through doing the self-work that the coach develops greater proficiency in their own inner landscape; a greater sense of personal resource and psychological understanding, which acts to grant permission to show up.

K2.1:   *Although the coaching Master's introduced all of that relational coaching, without doing that work on yourself I do not think you can actually work relationally.*

L2.1:   *I completely agree. You have to have done the work on yourself, or continued to. There is no way anyone can do this without taking a hard look at themselves.*

A3.1:   *Well that's a wonderful thing to say, and thank you for saying that, that's very encouraging. I guess it's on me now, to make sure that I do the right things, to learn from … when actually what I could be doing is incorporating that into the work that I do. Because, as you say, we are the tool, aren't we? We are the vessel, the vehicle, for the coaching. It's about integrating, isn't it?*

Facilitator: *I am hearing what you are saying and this is my reflection back on it, and I am adding my own opinion in here too … For us, as practitioners, those who find the space something that we feel passionate about and like to work in, knowing our own triggers and doing that work on ourselves is extremely important to know what our capacity is to then be able to hold that complexity.*

L2.1:   *A hundred per cent, I really agree with that. I think, for me, that is why my own therapy has been absolutely essential. Actually, I do not think I would have understood myself as much as I do without that therapeutic … I have been with my therapist now since 2012, so a really long time. I have grown and learnt so much.*

In this extract, coaches discussed that theoretical study is not enough; in order to attain greater levels of proficiency, one must explore one's own psychological world through therapy, doing the self-work. Furthermore, coaches viewed themselves as active tools within the coach-client relationship, and therefore gaining greater proficiency through doing the self-work grants coaches permission to show up with clients in complex terrains.

Code: Dynamic edge: coach's boundary and proficiency

As previously suggested, Maxwell (2009) proposes that the boundary distinctions between therapy and coaching do not lie within the fields of coaching or therapy but rather within the practitioner; with the "willingness and ability of both coach and client to work with personal/psychological material" (p.82).

The coaches described a sense of a dynamic edge to their boundaries where, at times, they may get a feeling that they have come to the limit of their boundaries and capabilities within the grey space. Yet, at the same time, because of experiencing this edge, an expansion takes place in their competence within this space; extending the coach's sense of proficiency further, thus giving them permission to show up. Coaches reported a greater 'self-efficacy', which is defined as one's belief concerning task performance and capability to succeed (Bandura, 1977).

Furthermore, I suggest that this dynamic edge can be likened to the 'Learning/ Growth Zone'. Luckner and Nadler (1997) suggest that, by engaging with experiences beyond one's 'comfort zone', one can move into the 'growth zone'. However, this only takes place once the discomfort of moving from the comfort zone has been navigated.

L2.1: *... it was around your edge, where is your edge for anxiety. We have all got one but where do you actually locate it and are you aware of it? So, I suppose it is just these borders that just constantly change.*

Facilitator: *That makes sense as well because, again, what we are talking about here is a boundary. Where is your edge? Where is your boundary? Where is it therapy and where is it coaching? So, the analogy or the metaphor works wonderfully.*

T2.1: *Reminds me of a poem ... it is called 'Ridge Walking'. From what I remember of it, it really speaks to this ... It is called 'Ridge Walking', by Char March, and I am happy to share it.*

This is my life out here,
on this edge.
Windy here – a narrow ridge.
Often I am scared,
have to squeeze my eyes shut,
hug myself to the rock,
crawl along on all fours
mumbling mantras.
But sometimes
I dance the thin line,
whirling in the sun,
shouting in an arms-up,
head-back laugh.
This is my life out here.
A slim chance
with steep drops on either side,
but the views
are bloody marvellous.

[laughter].
There is something exciting about being on that edge, isn't there? It is that fine line between fear and joy or fear and excitement. L2, what you said there just reminded me of that poem.

Facilitator: *That poem really describes what it is like as a practitioner entering the grey space, right?*

T2.1: *Yes, I had not thought about it in the grey space context but, yes, I think absolutely.*

Facilitator: *You have clients who are like ... And there is all that fear. Then there are clients where you are on the edge and you are dancing on the edge, and it is a spectacular view because you can see the transformation, and*

you are aware of the potential transformation that can happen. Thank
you so much for sharing the poem. Personally, I see it as very apt for
the grey space. Is the poem your metaphor or would you like to...?

In this extract, coaches discuss a 'dynamic edge: coaches' boundary and proficiency'. Coaches also experienced the navigation and territory of the grey space
being dynamic. Being at the edge of what is comfortable for the coach when working with the client can be a source of anxiety. However, once the coach has navigated this territory successfully the next time they are confronted with a similar
scenario to navigate they find the sense of anxiety has reduced or is not there. As a
result, the coach's confidence proficiency grows when mapping and navigating the
complexities of the grey space, giving the coach permission to show up.

Code: CPD

In the course of the research, several coaches committed to various training courses
to enhance their practice. Some had received training previously, whereas others
became aware of gaps in their knowledge due to reflection and discussion in the collaborative enquiry groups. Furthermore, coaches reported that professional development was an essential part of their practice. When this learning is integrated into
practice, it enhances skills and competence, enabling coaches to tackle the complexity of the grey space more proficiently, giving them permission to show up.

T2.1: *There is something about learning [and growth] for me. For example,*
I am doing this listening space coaching course at the moment ... It is allowing
myself to have the courage to grow and learn and develop within this space.

In this extract, through continual training, the coach speaks of growth in self,
which then transfers to their practice through deeper proficiency; resulting in permission to show up with clients.

P2.1: *So, it is grounded in a lot of training, workshops, learning. So, I have not*
just made it up. I have not just plucked something out of the air. It draws on a
lot of great wisdom. Both from coaching and psychotherapy. I think it is about
transparency with the client, in the sense that I am continually refining explain-
ing how I work.

This extract highlights the way in which coaches draw from their training,
grounding their practices in proficiency; thereby granting permission to show up.

Code: Gaining depth through practice

Gaining depth of proficiency through applied practice is the act of working with
clients. The crucial aspect here is being able to approach one's practice with a

conscious awareness, which results in practical knowledge being acquired and a depth of managing the coaching boundaries being gained.

> **M1.1:** *I am learning at a depth that is a depth of a different depth So there is no such thing as showing up to it and always doing it the same. You are a different person, and it's different, and there is new awareness. That gives you a degree of master in something, because mastery is simply more differentiations; just more abilities to differentiate something.*

This extract demonstrates that, through the act of consciously engaging in the practice of being a coach, a new level of depth to one's skills is developed through the act of practising; thereby gaining greater proficiency and permission to show up.

Code: Navigating the grey space: an art form

The coaches described working well with a client in the grey space as not just a result of skill or modality but, rather, that there is an 'art form' or co-created 'magic' that takes place in this space between client and coach that cannot be quantified or defined. And when there is a push to define these boundaries in the grey space – to provide an overly scientific or deductive understanding of what may be taking place – something may get lost or it may do more harm than good.

> **M1.1:** *Yes. I think there's an art to it, and I think it's hard to teach and hard to model. I don't believe you can watch it, because the magic happens not because of a skill. Some skill, for sure, but I really do think it's like an inspired channel of something that gets co-created between you and your client when you are just really purely there, with a good intention, and stuff happens. It's like a field working through people. It's very spiritual, I think. It's very hard to capture.*

In this extract, the coach demonstrates proficiency by taking up the position of co-creation with their client 'navigating the grey space: an art form'. In doing so, permission to show up is granted.

Sub-theme: Reflexivity: a living compass

The grey space is not experienced as linear or with definite boundaries. Therefore 'reflexivity: a living compass' assists the coach to evaluate moment by moment where they might be when circumnavigating this territory, according permission to show up. The forming of this 'living compass' consists of constant questioning; 'safety in questioning' develops great awareness, which by its nature is always advancing.

Coaches said that when they felt that they may be encountering the grey space, they asked themselves such questions as: Am I in the grey space? Am I not in the grey space? Can I be here? Can I not be here? How am I managing this at the moment? This questioning was seen as a reflective practice with coaches drawing on the questions as a navigational tool, reflecting on those questions and feeling the 'yes' or 'no', drawing on their embodied awareness. Therefore, safety in questioning gave practitioners permission to show up when it felt appropriate.

Coaches also discussed greater self-reflection when they thought they might encounter the grey space. They spoke of having a greater sense of awareness, which is an aspect of reflexivity: a living compass. This means to sense an embodied knowledge of stepping into the grey space and a sense of the grey space itself. Consequently, coaches had a greater sense of confidence within this space, as they felt better equipped to know where to tread. There was also a cyclical aspect this reflexivity because, through reflection on how they navigated the grey space, a higher sense of self-awareness occurred which created further self-reflection, generating greater awareness. Subsequently, coaches felt a greater sense of competency to know when they were stepping into the grey space and how they might manage this terrain.

Code: Safety in questioning

As mentioned above, the grey space is not experienced as linear or as having definite boundaries. Therefore, continually asking themselves questions assists the coach to evaluate moment by moment the grey space territory. Utilising questions as a navigational tool grounds the coach, as they are being bolstered in the moment when negotiating their way through the grey space – a living compass in this terrain – safety is provided through questioning.

> **P2.1:** *So, one of the questions I am holding. Not actively, but it is there. So, sometimes a client will mention something from their past and I am wondering in that moment, 'Do we go to that? Or do we stay in the here and now, and the future?' So, very much the classic, stereotypical coaching [narrative]. Almost always, that is what I choose to do and that feels ethically right, based on what I have contracted for.*

In this extract, the coach draws on internal questions – 'safety in questioning' – which act to determine the direction the coaching takes. Is it moving more into therapeutic terrain or not? In this context, the coach is steered by what has been contracted with the client and what the coach believes to be in the best interest of the client – reflexivity: a living compass – thereby maintaining the coaching work's 'permission to show up.

Code: Greater self-awareness

Coaches reported a greater sense of self-awareness regarding their response within – and to – the grey space itself, acknowledging and recognising the complexity of this terrain. In addition, they described a greater sense of self-awareness regarding the client within this space.

Through actively participating in the research, hearing from other co-enquirers and engaging in the reflective exercises, "reflection in action" (Schön, 1983) brought "everyday taken-for granted" (Schön, 1983), such as practices and decisions, more into conscious awareness when entering the grey space. In addition, coaches acknowledged a heightened ability to recognise what they had the competency and capacity to manage – and what may be beyond their scope. Through this greater awareness, coaches reported a greater capacity and proficiency in navigating this terrain with clients.

Furthermore, as seen in Workshop 1/Theme 4 (see p.84), coaches drew on 'embodied self-awareness' (Blake, 2018). In addition to acting as a source of information to draw on and reflect back to the client, coaches had a greater embodied self-awareness (Blake, 2018) of when it was not appropriate to enter a coaching dynamic with a potential client. Consequently, knowing when to show up and when not to.

> **S3.1:** *I think for me it's about – Well, one, to kind of be more present, I guess, so that I'm open to the grey space. Or to create a better level of awareness about when we're kind of there, or not there. Some of it is very kind of tutorial, isn't it? How are we going to do this? How are we going to solve a problem? But then, in other times, you're going to get this kind of space. So I think for me, in terms of areas of development, it's, one, am I recognising that it's there? And I would have to say, in January, if someone said it to me and they waved it in my face, I probably wouldn't have recognised it. So I think, in the last six months, in the process of recording and reflecting, I think I am more aware of what I think the grey space is with the clients that I have.*

In this extract, the coach reflects that, prior to this research, they were not actively aware of the grey space. Through participating in this research, the coach reports a 'greater self-awareness' due to engaging in reflexive and reflective practice, which results in developing reflexivity: a living compass of the grey space and therefore a deeper awareness of when not to show up and when there is permission to show up within client work.

Sub-theme: Context

Permission to show up is context dependent. This sub-theme explores the wider context, such as whether the client has a stakeholder or is self-referred, amongst other things. This may impact whether the coach engages in the coaching work or looks to signpost any given coaching client and session. The level and depth of work, and therefore stepping into the grey space, is also seen as context specific.

> **T2.1:** *I think, for me, it is the context around those emotions and the stories associated to them which tells me whether I can work with it or not. For example,*

with that person that contacted me about grief, I just know that, yes, I can work with that person. I can hold a space and I can allow space for those emotions to come forward, but I have no expertise in bereavement counselling, grief therapy or coaching around grief. So that tells me that, yes, I can hold emotions but I am not going to be the right person to support this person through this part of their journey ... about contracting and about the goals of the session. If these are emotions that are emerging which we need to explore in order for us to move forward towards the coaching goals then that is something that I think I am able to do. If it then starts to emerge that, actually, there are other goals that are coming up or other needs that are arising, which falls outside of my area of knowledge, expertise or capacity, then I think that is the point when I know.

This extract shows how the coach determines permission to show up. Here, the coach demonstrates that 'context' plays a large role. Should there be an established coaching relationship and the client bring emotions to the coaching work beyond the coach's remit, the coach may draw on a mixture of themes seen in permission to show up with the client. However, should it be a potential client – therefore a different 'context' – the coach would not grant themselves permission to show up.

S1.1: *... depending on how you construct stress, if, actually, your source of stress is lack of attachment, then you're having a stress response to whatever it is that's happening in your life. So yes, primarily, absolutely, there's a lot of signposting that goes on. However, if I was to back out and have a look at the contract and the content of pretty much any coaching conversation, it is to do with stimulus and response to that stimulus. At that moment, if your brain is foggy because it's got too much sugar being fed to it, then signposting to a dietary recommendation might be beneficial in that moment, depending on the person and the context. So if you peel all the layers back, then you could say there's a through line all the way to stress for pretty much anything. Trauma is stressful.*

This extract demonstrates the 'context' in which stress is defined. Based on this, the coach will either engage in coaching work with the client – permission to show up – or signpost the client on.

Sub-theme: Utilise professional practice and communities

By using professional practice and communities, such as contracting, supervision, peer support or creating a network of helping professionals, coaches refined aspects of their practice. This resulted in coaches reporting greater clarity and a sense of being resourced, resulting in permission to show up.

Much like the first workshop, contracting (see p.74) was a fundamental tool coaches used to navigate the intersection between therapy and coaching. However, several coaches spoke of an iterative development of their contracting – which provided a greater sense of clarity – and of the territory becoming clearer. They were therefore more able to navigate the grey space.

In addition, because they were reflecting on the grey space, coaches engaged more in reviewing, refining and being more explicit with clients with regard to contracting.

Supervision was another professional practice that coaches made increasing use of after Workshop 1/Cycle 3. Several coaches reported taking up different types of supervision or starting supervision where they had not had supervision before and/or increasing supervision. Coaches sought out supervisors they felt were more able to handle the complexities of their work, such as those supervisors who either had psychological backgrounds or supervisors who were working within the grey space. This resulted in coaches being able to draw on this resource of professional practice.

In addition to changes in professional practice, coaches reported utilising professional communities more, such as peer support and developing networks of individuals from other helping professions, should signposting be required. A sense of community in this space was highlighted as important and was created in various ways, for example, the opportunity to speak with individuals, experiencing similarities and differences, such as they had during this process, enabled a sense of community. Furthermore, coaches identified supervisors who understood this space and built a network of trusted helping professionals, for signposting. As a side note, this may have reduced the feelings of isolation coaches reported in Workshop 1.

Code: Contracting

One of the modifications to practice owing to reflecting on the grey space related to contracting, with coaches actively reviewing, refining and being more explicit with clients with regard to contracting. Several coaches spoke of an iterative development of their contracting, which provided a greater sense of clarity, and territory becoming clearer, which, in turn made them more able to navigate the grey space.

> **P2.1:** ... *what I share upfront with the clients in chemistry sessions, in the contracting, but then checking in with them as we go. 'Is this exercise ...? This is what we could do now. How does that feel to you?'*

In this extract, the coach demonstrates permission to show up using contracting 'utilising professional practice'. The use of initial contracting, in addition to ongoing moment-to-moment contracting with the client, enables permission to show up and opens up the possibility of doing various exercises with the client.

> **P2.1:** *I have put more into my contracting recently ... The document I send people. What we talk about in the first sessions, about feelings, bodily sensations, emotions in the body. So, it is becoming more explicitly already, but this is a reminder really [in terms of] the huge power of that.*

This extract demonstrates the coach refining their contracting utilising professional practice, through transparency of their modality of coaching; thereby granting permission to show up and having discernment regarding the type of coaching they are engaging in.

Code: Supervision

Coaches reported increasing supervision when navigating the grey space as a way of utilising professional practices and communities. As previously highlighted, several coaches described initiating supervision for the first time, shifting the type of supervision they engaged in, or increasing its frequency. They actively sought out supervisors they perceived as better equipped to engage with the complexities of their practice – often those with psychological training or those experienced in working within the grey space. Supporting the work of models such as Proctor's Model of Clinical Supervision (2008) speaks to the resourcing aspect – the "resourcing function" – of supervision (Hawkins, 2019) and the resourcing aspect of the supervisory relationship (Henderson & O'Riordan, 2020).

> **P2.1:** *I think supervision is a big part of that. I have started working with a new supervisor, who is a psychotherapist coach and a supervisor. It feels important to me to have someone who can cover that whole landscape. So, I really feel my sense of her is she can hold in a very large space. That is important, so I can explore all of what I want to bring. But also in terms of role-modelling. So, she is, to me, exhibiting something that I would aspire to over time. So, it is having people as mentors, role models, people who can show the way really.*

In this extract, the coach is utilising professional practice by using supervision; the key element being engaging with a supervisor with a great breadth and depth of knowledge of a range of modalities and of experience. This enables the coach to feel that they have permission to show up in the grey space.

Code: Peers and community

A sense of community in the grey space was highlighted as important; coaches were actively creating this in various ways. Having peers and a sense of professional community provided a source of support, to brainstorm similarities and differences other practitioners may face when navigating this terrain.

> **P2.1:** *Because people sometimes say, "Oh, coaching can be quite lonely, quite isolating." Fortunately, I do not feel that. Because I have a community of coaches that I am in touch with quite a lot through my training. But I think if that generally can be true, I think it can be even more isolating for coaches interested in this space. Because people tend to avoid it often. So, just knowing*

*there are other people travelling ... It may not be on my train, it may not be
exactly taking my journey, but they are fellow travellers in the broader sense.
That is a reassuring, good, positive feeling.*

In this extract, coaches managed isolation and created a sense of camaraderie
through engaging and forming networks of 'peers and communities', 'utilising professional practice and communities'; thereby enabling the coach to feel reassured
in the grey space with permission to show up.

M1.1: *I have also, probably ever since we met* [ref to being a research co-
enquirer], *reached out to more people and become more conscious to find people
who work in unusual ways, to help me stay grounded. That's been quite good...
I can go to people. I can soundcheck things. I can ask for advice. I can make
sure that I can hold it, and that I don't wake up at night in cold sweats, thinking,
'What the hell?' and that it's safe for my client.*

In this extract, the coach speaks of hearing how other coaches work to develop support with peers and communities, which acts to help them stay grounded in their
own way of working utilising professional practice. Furthermore, these communities work as sounding boards and spaces in which to make to make sense of the
situation in order to ensure the safety of the coach's client, enabling permission to
show up in complex territory.

Code: Network of helping professionals to signpost to

Coaches had developed, or were developing, a network of helping professionals to
signpost clients to. This network included a range of individuals, not just within the
therapeutic space, who acted as a resource and enabled the coach to have permission to show up, knowing that they had other helping professionals on hand should
they need additional assistance.

A3.1: *Actually there would be other people to help this person move further
forward, and they clearly want to need to move further forward, so now is the
time for me to plug into my network and help them to find the right person for
them to work with next.*

In this extract, the coach feels able to work with the client in the grey space because,
should the client need expertise beyond the coach's scope, they have a network of
other professionals – 'peers and communities' – to signpost the client to utilising
professional practice and communities. This helps coaches to navigate the grey
space, as knowing they have a network within the helping professions holds multiple benefits, it reduces feelings of isolation, and enables shared learning and a
sense of resourcing.

Sub-theme: Arc of transformation

Through engaging in a level of critical reflection on how they are as practitioners and how they might navigate the grey space, their "professional identity" and how they go about "practice", coaches are able to gain new awareness so that they can confirm or reconstruct their identities as practitioners (Fook, 2010).

However, Fook (2010) proposes that the first stage of developing critical awareness of practice is to expose "(unsettling or 'shaking up') of fundamental (dominant) assumptions and their sources; the second stage develops this awareness into possible practice strategies" (p.41). In this sub-theme, the 'arc of transformation' presents how the coaches experiencing this exposure talked about it, describing being unsettled, shaken up, with a sense of deconstruction taking place, as a result of critically assessing themselves as practitioners in the grey space. Coaches depicted a groundlessness occurring, much like being in a "liminal space" (Turner, 1974), as they transitioned between what had been and what was to come. Furthermore, coaches conveyed that they felt that they were not sure where they stood in relation to how they should navigate the grey space, questioning what they had once felt comfortable with and how and who they were as practitioners. Strozzi-Heckler (2014) describes this as the "arc of somatic transformation", where one experiences an "unbounded state" when transitioning between ending and beginning.

However, through this shaking up phase, as Fook (2010) suggests, one gathers awareness, which can then be developed into improved or new practice strategies. This change is described as being "initiated by the possibility of a new beginning, or by the ending of something" (Strozzi-Heckler, 2014, p.144). Therefore a "new shape" forms (Strozzi-Heckler, 2014) and, by obtaining this new awareness, the coaches were able to confirm and reconstruct aspects of their identities as practitioners (Fook, 2010), coming full circle with new conviction as to how they show up in this space, and where they felt they had permission to be. In doing so, we negotiate "the unbound state, which is the ground between what has been and what has yet to form" (Strozzi-Heckler, 2014, p.144).

B1.1: *Then there's what we call the arc of transformation. There's a journey through, which is described, for the [concept] of language as linear, but it's not linear. We do this, and we move backwards and forwards, and so on. But in that transformation and in that journey, there's what they call the unbounded shape. I think the Americans describe it as between a quart and a pint cup, or something, or I might describe it as no-man's land. It's like I don't quite know who I am anymore. Then there's the risk that the old shape rears its head and tries to pull you back as you're trying to move forward to achieve a new shape.*

So, what it seems, to me, we're talking about is the unbounded territory, here, of what we're exploring … And when we get to new shape, quite often, we find that new shape becomes old shape, and there's another new shape.

Facilitator: *Absolutely. That takes us beautifully back to the action research. That's that whole cycle process, right?*

In this extract, a dialogue is created between coaches discussing a move from old to new awareness in their practice and navigating the grey space – permission to show up. This, however, is not a straightforward change – an arc of transformation. Rather, there is this sense of backward and forward between what they were doing in their practice and new ways of engaging in practice. Furthermore, as this is an ongoing experience that is cyclical in nature, the unknown becomes known and the search for new awareness continues through reflective and reflexive practice.

B1.1: *I feel like I've permanently been in that question for the last six months. I've had moments of a sense of ground shifting beneath me, almost not really knowing where my ground was. I've come to a point of being able to observe, 'Here's where I'm coaching, and here's where ''m stepping into something that feels more therapeutic, even though I'm not a therapist'. So then these whole stories come out of, 'Should I even be in here? Should I even be having this conversation? What am I up to? Is this what we contracted?' I've got all these internal narratives that go on … and I was thinking, 'Oh, is that what I'm really up to?' In some ways, it's not that this process has undermined what I'm doing, but it's shifted the ground underneath me, and that's had me feel less solid around what I'm doing. Then, as I've just said that, I've gone, 'What's at the back of that?' What's at the back of that is making sure that I get it right, which is part of my story. So, is what I'm doing here right? That's what's making the ground shift.*

In this extract, the coach describes a sense of the ground shifting due to the reflective and reflexive practice resulting in a constant state of questioning – arc of transformation – having to hold a sense of uncertainty, which directly impacts the sense of surety the coach once had. However, as seen in the sub-theme 'reflexivity: a living compass', through this groundlessness of questioning, the coach is ensuring that they are working in the best interest of the client; thereby granting permission to show up.

Sub-theme: Values

This sub-theme offers insights into how coaches arrange the themselves as practitioners and as ethical coaches in relation to negotiating the grey space.

Through the values they hold, coaches shape how they show up in the grey space when coaching. It is important to note McNiff's point, that "there are no overarching structures of values" (McNiff, 2002) to act as a stabilising factor, which coaches come back to when facing tension, ambiguity and the sense of the ground shifting, as a result of being in the grey space, in addition to the sense of everything being unbounded that critical reflection can bring (see sub-theme 'Arc of transformation'). However, at times, coaches find themselves grappling with conflicting values – 'living contradictions' (Whitehead, 1988) – because they may find dissonance between personal values and those of practice.

Foucault (1978) argues that our cultural values and social expectations both influence and shape us. Where one is unable to escape, or move beyond the cultural values and social expectations, one can learn instead which to accept and which resist; this being the art of existence (Foucault, 1978) and in so doing re-author the self (Foucault, 1997). Furthermore, action research is believed to have the capacity to assist us in making sense of our lives because it moves beyond the surface structure of method (while still regarding it as important) to look deeply at the underlying configuration of our values and intentions of our lived experience (McNiff, 2002).

> **B1.1:** *Well, I suppose that takes you right back to the values… but I think there's an observation in me about … There's the authenticity, for me, about how I show up and how I am in this space. Absolutely, there's something about being in service of taking care of the client and the relationship. That's really, really important. I think that's vital. Then, more personally, there's something about the authenticity of how I show up … but also, what comes up is how I hold this ambiguity, if you like. I found myself on a path, learning to work this way. I didn't choose a different coaching methodology. This is the one that I chose. So then I go, 'So this is okay. This is what it brings', and I lean into that.*

In this extract, the coach draws on their personal value of authenticity to navigate how they enter the coaching dynamic; ultimately granting permission to show up.

> **T2.1:** *I do not know if I am making sense. But that is what came up for me as you reflected that question back, really about how do we give ourselves permission to show up as who we are, and how do we give our clients that permission as well?*

This extract demonstrates that, through the value of authenticity, which is encouraged in both self and client, permission to show up for client and coach is made possible.

Code: Values and living contradictions

One of the core elements of action research is to reflect on our values and how we bring our values to our practice, and where we may be experiencing 'living contradictions' (Whitehead, 1988), because through these contradictions we are able to reflect on our practice and ways we may improve it.

At times we can see coaches finding themselves grappling with conflicting values as they find dissonance between personal values and values of practice.

Ultimately, how coaches reconcile their values shapes how they give themselves permission to show up, when encountering the grey space.

> **A3.3:** *Two values that really stick out for me, that have always been at the fore-front of my mind, and have caused me all sorts of dilemmas, and cognitive dissonance, to be fair, A3.2, as well, is collaboration and commitment. And I bring that into my coaching practice. And it causes me certain bother now and again, which is this thing to do with referring people on, or not.*
>
> *And you may remember, in fact I think it was in one of the first emails I sent to you, Lauretta, ''m not a member of any of the accrediting bodies. Because there is something for me around not being told what to do. I reject that, I want to carve out my own code of conduct, not adopt someone else's … And they bring that to my coaching, and I've got a values conflict around, 'I've made a commitment to you, I can't quit, but there is something here about bullying I can't handle'. And without the supervision space with my colleague, I wouldn't have been able to make sense of that. So I've had some real insights from this process around values, how they play out in the coaching.*

This extract demonstrates the conflicting values that professional bodies and coaches may have. Here, the coach holds the value of commitment as being important to practice, yet the body's code of conduct conflicts with it. Through supervision, the coach can navigate this living contradiction and gain permission to show up with their client.

> **T2.1:** *Yes, that comes along with bias and it comes along with subjectivity, and it comes along with all the things that are trained out of us as psychologists, and there is real value in that as well. I think an added layer to that is for those of us who are learning in a predominately Western context, but who have very different cultural groundings, backgrounds and ethics, there is even more that we need to do in order to practise in a way that is deemed acceptable.*

In this extract, the coach grapples with values that feel conflicting. On the one hand, the coach values traditional formal training – psychology – but on the other hand they feel that this conflicts with their personal values of freedom and authenticity; somehow feeling that the formal training restricts these values of freedom and authenticity as having been 'trained out of us'. The coach has to manage these inconsistencies in order to gain permission to show up. I suggest that coaches' personal core values form the foundations of their ethics in practices, assisting them as a means of manoeuvring the complexities of competing values. Additionally, these values inform the way coaches navigate the grey space and so grant permission to show up are similar to 'ethical thinking' where a coach "has the capacity to weigh up benefit versus harm on a case-by-case basis" (Garvey & Stokes, 2022, p.282). Ethical thinking is discussed on page 00.

Theme 2: Position

The second main theme relates to how coaches situate themselves within the grey space. This theme views how coaches take up a 'position' within the grey space. Harré & van Langenhove (1999) state that "the act of positioning thus refers to the assignment of fluid 'parts' or 'roles' to speakers in the discursive construction of personal stories that make a person's actions intelligible and relatively determinate as social acts" (p.17).

Four sub-themes were presented, including 'tensions at play', exploring how coaches face a range of dilemmas regarding how to position themselves within this space, however, through the position taken, coaches grant themselves permission to show up; an interlink can be seen between the main theme, permission to show up, and the position a coach takes.

Rather than excluding aspects from the coaching dynamic, 'radical inclusion' is a position taken up by the coach, acknowledging the wholeness of the client and themselves as practitioners; all their knowledge and experience across all domains being intrinsically linked to who they are as professionals informing their "professional identity" (Trede et al., 2012).

Coaches viewed working in the grey space as retaining a 'deep purpose' within their work. What's more, coaches described having actively worked in this space; hence engaging in the research itself. Coaches position their coaching work within this space. Ultimately, when coaches found that they were working with a particular grey space, they adopted a position of coaching towards therapy.

Sub-theme: Tensions at play

'Tensions at play' explores the position taken by the coach within the grey space. When faced with various dilemmas, such as 'politics at play', coaches conveyed tension between the different coaching bodies, codes of conduct and ethics held. Also, coaches felt that there was tension over what was described as political elements that they felt that these bodies had, and wondered whether the commercial money-making capitalistic machine was running underneath everything.

The second element of tension relates to how coaches positioned themselves in relation to the tensions they perceived between therapy and coaching within the helping discipline. Coaches felt that coaching can be therapeutic, whilst not being therapy, moreover they suggested that there was a territorial tension between the therapeutic profession and coaches. However, coaches wanted to engage in open dialogue, "relating to coaching as an ethical practice, rather than thwarting the therapeutic/counselling communities, or impeding the appropriate support for those individuals who suffer with mental illness" (Cundy, 2019, p.66).

Lastly, tension affected the psychologically informed coaches. They actually felt constrained by their knowledge and formal psychological training, because they thought they were unable to be as innovative and flexible as non-psychologically informed coaches, but, at the same time, they valued an evidence-based approach.

Code: Coaching professional boards/bodies

In the following extracts, we can see how coaches saw tension between the different coaching bodies, codes of conduct and ethics held. They also thought there was tension over what was described as political elements that they felt these bodies had, and wondered whether this was related to the capitalistic money-making machine that ran underneath everything. The tensions they felt were: whether to be part of a professional body – and if so which one; grappling with what comes with being a member: taking into consideration how these positions impacted their wider practice and how they should navigate the grey space.

A3.1: *I think that I tread lightly across values. So I read the list of ICF. I'm a member of the ICF, and I read the ICF values and their ethical framework. And I kind of don't disagree with anything, so I mentally give it a tick. But I wouldn't necessarily say that I buy in to all of the values that they espouse to the same degree ... So I'm kind of a bit laissez-faire about values. I think well yes, these organisations you've got, I don't know how many different coaching bodies there are, and I personally, like you A3.3, strongly believe that they are generally self-serving organisations and they want to make money. The purpose is to monetise rather than support, I think that's the front foot, maybe rather cynically ... So I'm very sceptical and cynical about professional bodies generally and what their purpose is.*

In this extract, the coach does not buy into the values presented by the professional body they are part of, viewing the body as being self-serving. On the one hand, the coach knows, from a career perspective, that they need to be associated with a professional body – the position taken. On the other hand, this is done out of an obligation – a box-ticking exercise – owing to conflicting values held by the coach: tensions at play.

A3.2: *I think A3.3 that's my problem ... It's the lack of commonality. So the ICF will say one thing, the ILM will say something else, the EMC say something else. And actually, if I was now coming into the coaching industry, I would feel very confused about what I should be doing.*

The tensions at play in this extract are to the result of a lack of commonality in ethics and codes of conduct across various associations and professional bodies; resulting in the position taken by the coach being one of confusion and resistance to any take-up of membership to the professional associations and bodies.

Professional boards and bodies can take lessons from these discoveries, such as greater dialogue, community engagement, joint conferences, publications and dissemination of research such as this. There should be active engagement within the profession to keep informed about issues and develop knowledge of practice. Knowledge does not stand still, therefore the wider coaching profession should be seen as a community of practice where knowledge and practice are ever evolving for the better in the service of the clients and practitioners.

Code: Therapeutic profession versus coaching profession

In these extracts, we can see tensions and how coaches positioned themselves in relation to the tensions they perceived between therapy and coaching within the helping discipline. Coaches felt that coaching can be therapeutic, whilst not being therapy, in addition they suggested that there was a territorial tension between the therapeutic profession and coaches. However, coaches want to engage in open dialogue.

> **P2.1:** *So, I think particularly that, what you were talking about with challenging the orthodoxy, there is also real value in the reflective conversations. Continuing discussions around, 'Okay, well, what are the challenges? What is the way of having a debate and where would you most usefully have those discussions?'*

The tensions at play in this extract relate to the conventional 'helping' tradition associated with the world of psychology and therapy. Here, coaching may be viewed as non-traditional, bringing with it tensions. However, coaches position themselves as wanting open dialogue with these more traditional professions.

> **A3.1:** *Just following on from that, A3.2, I wonder where the walls come from. I certainly have worked with counsellors and I've worked with coaches, and some people are really very keen on making sure that I understand the difference between the two professions, as the new kid on the block, as I say.*

This extract highlights tensions at play regarding professional territories. Coaches experience barriers to open dialogue with other helping professions, experiencing instead a warning not to step into territory that is not coaching. Coaches try to adopt a cooperative approach position, which is not met by other helping professions.

> **A3.1:** *And I've found that some counsellors can be hugely protective of the space – 'It's taken me three, five years to feel qualified to be a counsellor – you guys come along after whatever back of a fag packet course you've just finished and charge three times as much as I do, and you have nowhere near the depth of skill and quality of listening to offer as I do as a therapist.' They don't actually say it as brutally as that obviously, but that's kind of the gist, the thrust of it. What I pick up is behind some of those conversations. And I do wonder, and I've read obviously about the boundaries in the various books that we all read, and you can see it in the professional bodies and how the BACP and how the ICF and the other coaching bodies. They're very clear, aren't they, to make sure …?*

Now you've got to be really clear what the differences are between mentoring and consulting and coaching and counselling. And it's really important that you understand these dividing lines, and that you don't start encroaching into these other professions.

And I wonder whether that is skill-based or whether it is just an artificial construct that's put together by professional bodies, that want to protect their profession, that they've probably built up with a great deal of skill and care, and they want to protect what they've grown and their own interests. I don't know. Maybe it's as simple as that. Maybe I'm being just really cynical again. [laughter]. *I don't know.*

In this extract, the coach questions the origins of the tensions at play between the helping professions, resulting in the coach taking the position of cynicism towards the divide across the professions. I suggest that, owing to these tensions between the therapeutic and coaching professions regarding "territory", open transparent dialogue and therefore learning is hindered between professions. This hampers collaborative working and exploration of manoeuvring in the grey space, which would be of benefit to the client.

Code: Tension psychologically informed coaches grapple with

Psychologically informed coaches grappled with tension. They actually felt constrained by their knowledge and formal psychological training, sensing that they were unable to be as innovative and flexible as non-psychologically informed coaches. However, at the same time, they valued an evidence-based approach.

Psychologically informed coaches described being constrained by their 'rigid' traditional psychological training, with one individual likening it to having innovation and flexibility 'trained out of us as psychologists'. This suggests that a psychologically informed position is one that is evidence-based and methodical in of its approach to doing things; it prevents an individual from being able to be more intuitively informed or more innovative in a way that the non-psychologically informed coaches were in practice.

T2.1: *I might be wrong, but one thing … I have got a lot of close friends who are Indian like me – I know I am a very pale skinned Indian, but I am Indian – who work in this space, either as coaches, psychologists or therapists. We often notice how these rules, boundaries, constraints and practices do not fit with our culture. So, again, this tension around, 'How do we bring ourselves and who we are, and create space in the coaching practice for who our clients are, if they come from diverse backgrounds, but still follow all these things that we are meant to follow?'*

It is something that I always feel scared about raising, actually, because whenever I talk about D&I, particularly about race, it always feels threatening. I do not how this relates to grey space, but for some reason it does. I think it comes back to the sense of, what you were saying about, 'Can we be more authentic in terms of the way that we work?' These non-psychology coaches, somehow, seem to have the freedom to do that. Yes, that comes along with bias and it comes along with subjectivity, and it comes along with all the things that are trained out of us as psychologists, and there is real value in that as well. I think an added layer to that is for those of us who are learning in a predominately Western context, but who have very different cultural groundings, backgrounds and ethics, there is even more that we need to do in order to practise in a way that is deemed acceptable. (Viewpoint from psychologist/psychology-informed coach.)

Similar to the theme 'values', we see 'tension at play' resulting from conflicting values, which are professional, cultural and personal. This extract in particular highlights the tensions a psychologist/psychology-informed coach has to grapple with.

L2.1: *It is funny how we have just said about psychologists, I have got it here as well and I thought, 'Oh my God, it is actually really constrained',* [laughter] *as I am reading it.* (Viewpoint from psychologist/psychology- informed coach.)

In this extract, the psychologist/psychology-informed coach reflects and experiences the constitution of psychology as being constrained and rigid – tensions at play – which conflicts with the broader meaning that the word 'coaching' holds for them.

M1.1: *Academics and researchers are always a step behind … The world will move on, which is why whenever I read management literature, I'm never impressed, because I always feel like, 'Are you kidding me? I've experienced this phenomenon. I've got many colleagues who have done something useful with it, and you're telling us, now, this is true?' It's very difficult. So this is a really good space.* (Viewpoint from non-coaching psychologist.)

In this extract, academics and researchers, as well as psychologists (including coaching psychologists) are seen as being a step behind. Here, the tensions at play come as the non-psychologists/psychology-informed coaches experience their proficiencies not being validated. Only once the research has 'proved' it does, does it become 'true', which is long after the lived experience non-psychologists/ psychology-informed coaches are having in practice. I suggest that in order to manage these tensions at play the coaches adopt a position of valuing experience more than 'proven' research when approaching and navigating the grey space.

Sub-theme: Radical inclusion

I suggest that there was an evolution from Workshop 1 'bracketing' (see p.74) to 'radical inclusion' where information is disclosed, which is grey space, or rather it is beyond the coaching context and sits within the therapeutic terrain, for example, past abuse and mental health diagnoses. This evolution is a subtle shift: from reactively holding space through bracketing to a response stance in which the position of radical inclusion is taken, brought about by a duty of care, a sense of moral obligation to allow the person to bring the whole of themselves to the practice. This forms part of the coach's "embodied understanding of, and in practice" (Dall'Alba & Sandberg, 2006; Heidegger, 1962).

Furthermore, radical inclusion is a position adopted by the coach, acknowledging the wholeness of the client and themselves; all their knowledge and experience across all domains being intrinsically linked to who they are as professionals which informs their "professional identity" (Trede et al., 2012). This is demonstrated in the codes 'All of you' and 'All of me'. This response stance of radical inclusion does not mean that coaches work beyond their scope and boundaries; it is one of acknowledgement. Systemic coaching and constellation work suggest that when something is excluded from or denied by the system the whole system is sent into disarray, as the system tries to "re-member" (Whittington, 2016). Through acknowledging that "everything is given a place, ... then the system can settle and move on" (Whittington, 2016, p.14).

Code: All of you

Here we can see a similarity to Workshop 1, Theme 1, Sub-theme 'All of you' (see p.79).

Coaches see clients from a holistic perspective – all of you – mental, spiritual, emotional and physical beings, and as a result they hold space for everything the clients may bring into the coaching session. Furthermore, coaches recognise that clients may be unable to silo one life domain from another one. As a result, the coach is welcoming and open to the client as a whole, recognising that various aspects and work and life domains may intersect. Therefore, coaching may not be situated in just one life domain or aspect. However, the difference is that coaches come from a position of radical inclusion. Systemic thinking proposes that when an element is excluded or denied within a system, it can disrupt the system's balance, prompting a process through which the system attempts to 're-member' or reintegrate what was lost (Whittington, 2016).

> **S3.2:** *I think for me, the answer would be that it's okay to be in the grey space. One thing I've learnt out of this whole process actually, and through real reflection, perhaps everybody is in the grey space. It's just how close to the door, as S3.1 so nicely put it, that we actually are. Because I can't find a human being that doesn't sit there.*

In this extract, the coach, through this research process, has become aware that every person brings complexity – all of you – and so each client at various times may enter the grey space as a position of radical inclusion for whatever may emerge in session.

Code: Coaching as 'all of me'

Coaches are compelled by a duty of care and a sense of moral obligation to bring the whole of themselves to the coaching session; forming part of the coaches' "embodied understanding of, and in practice" (Dall'Alba & Sandberg, 2006; Heidegger, 1962). This position was adopted, as it was considered to be service to the client. Here, it is important that coaches are fully aware of their situation, as they bring to "plenary existence the situation on the one hand and human reality on the other. This presupposes a patient study of what the situation requires, and then a way of throwing oneself into it" (Sartre, 1999, p.54). Coaches may 'change hats' within the coaching work, with the client's consent and transparency, using the lessons learned by being authentic and determining themselves to "be-for" the situation. (Sartre, 1999).

> **A3.2:** *Isn't it incumbent upon me to bring every possible skill that I've ever gone to, to the coaching room, in the service of the client, to help them make change, solve an issue, do whatever? Rather than be in this very kind of closed box, which says, 'What do you want to focus on? How would you know when you've got it? Where are you? Let's recap, let's reflect. What action should we take? Goodbye, we'll see you next time.'*
>
> *So, I think whatever training we've had, whatever influences we've had, from whatever teachers, lecturers, workshop managers, whatever, whatever CPD we've done, and whether it comes from a completely discipline, then I think my belief is it's incumbent on me to present myself with all of that baggage. And we can have a rummage through a bag from time to time and see if there is something of use for somebody. But so long as you're offering it …*

In this extract, the coach takes the position of radical inclusion of all they have to offer a client to support their goal attainment. Again, an interlinking in themes/sub-themes can be seen because the coach is driven by 'values' and therefore permission to show up and taking the position of radical inclusion: 'all of me'.

Sub-theme: Deeper purpose

'Deeper purpose' is a position coaches take regarding the space in which they work, their reason for doing the work they do and how they wish to work. Through this exploratory process, coaches concluded that previously they were 'drawn to the work', viewing it as holding a deeper purpose; rather than discovering the grey space through the research process – and that through reflecting on their practice a confirmation occurred, they wanted to work with the complexity the grey space brings, viewing it as valuable. Coaches shared how they have become more comfortable in the complexity of the grey space and with transformational work in general. Several coaches experienced an ontological shift around becoming more content to work within complexity, resulting in a deepening of the sense of their work. "Ontology is the study of being. It is concerned with 'what is' with the nature of existence, with the structure of reality" (Crotty, 1998, p.10).

Code: Drawn to the work

Coaches conveyed that previously they had been on the path 'drawn to the work', viewing it as holding deeper purpose, rather than discovering the grey space through the research process. Furthermore, several coaches shared experiencing an ontological shift around becoming more drawn to do deeper work.

> **A3.3:** *I think I'm making modifications as we go ... And then actually being more comfortable and willing to explore and navigate these grey areas, should they wish ... So, there is more confidence and more comfort and more willingness to go on that collaborative journey of exploration with them, should they wish but making sure they're aware of it, if that makes sense. I think that's a shift away from ... To give it some labels, a slight shift away from a cognitive behavioural approach, which is probably where I was at, to a more existential approach, which is where I think I'm travelling to, which is the acceptance piece which is coming in. That's me.*

The coach in this extract describes a shift in their approach to working with clients: a greater willingness and confidence to explore greater depth with clients – taking up a new position. Here, the coach recognises this is who they are – "that's me" – being 'drawn to the work' navigating the grey space; a sense of a deeper purpose.

> **S1.1:** *... is what engages me. You have touched on this before, this very superficial kind of Grow Model, "I need to do A, B, and C and it will give me the right results." That really does not interest me at all.*
>
> *I think just being mindful of I want it to be a lot deeper, I want to encourage people ... Not to force them but obviously for them to lead it, but for them to actually challenge their own thinking and to not be constrained by it at the same time ... I want to actually sit in that space around coaching. It does seem very much around significant change.*

In this extract, the coach is very clear about the position they take within their coaching work. They view coaching as a possibility for significant change and doing deep work – deeper purpose – in which they are drawn to the work.

Code: Comfortable with complexity

Through reflecting on what and how the grey space may appear in practice for coaches, coaches began to recognise the levels of complexity faced in their day-to-day practice. They shared how they have become more comfortable in the complexity of the grey space, and with transformational work in general.

T2.1: *I think what I am really talking about is being able to manage complexity. I think that is the same with this. It is resonating, I think, with what L2.1 and K2.1 and saying as well, that that is where I enjoy working ... to move into the areas that I am really passionate about, which is the diversity and inclusion space.*

In this extract, the coach indicates that they are 'comfortable with complexity' in the grey space; positioning this work in the grey space as having a deeper purpose and passion for them.

Sub-theme: Coaching towards therapy

There are times within coaching work when coaches recognise that material beyond the scope of the coaching context is present. However, clients are not ready or do not want to be signposted to therapeutic support. To navigate this terrain, coaches adopt the position of 'coaching towards therapy', which may mean that the client they are working with may eventually be signposted to therapy, whilst coaching acts to destigmatise the notions of therapy/helping professions. In this situation, coaches work to destigmatise the helping professions, as well as normalise such support. Furthermore, coaches work to empower clients through the coaching work to investigate and understand what type of support may suit their current needs best. On occasion, coaches work with the client as a way of preparing, resourcing, and encouraging awareness and insight development, until the client chooses to engage in therapeutic work.

This sub-theme suggests that coaches are working with the therapeutic profession (this may not be at a personal level), leading the client towards therapy, at times when coaches recognise work beyond their scope. However, within this position, coaches are still honouring the client, the clients' choice and being client-led. In this situation, a position of coaching towards therapy can be seen as one of working in an ethical way, rather than thwarting the therapeutic profession.

The greatest concern for the coaches was to ensure that clients were not left without support. Therefore, they viewed their role as acting as a bridge, stepping into 'helper role' to facilitate finding the support the client needs: *T1.2: "I think the risk comes if the client is left hanging."* Once again the question arises of how coaches signpost and the processes behind their signposting. One of the key learnings and take-aways for co-enquirers was related to this topic, which links back to the discussion and resistance to the term 'referral' (see 'Referral: coaching's ugly step-sister' on p.00)

Code: Coaching as resourcing, transition/preparation for therapy

T2.1: *Another thing that I have experienced is sometimes somebody is not ready to dig deeper. Actually, the coaching space offers them enough to build up resource, almost. What I have experienced in my own coaching work is that*

I can see, because I have the background and the understanding, that there is a deeper issue at play that the client may need to address, but the client does not want to go there. They are not ready and resourced for it. Actually, the work that we are doing in our coaching work is to help them to become more resourced in their day-to-day life here and now, knowing and also very transparently discussing the fact that this may be a blockage for them, and they will need to dig deeper.

Here, the coach adopts the position of 'coaching as resourcing, transition/preparation for therapy'. In this extract, there are issues beyond the coaching that is taking place, but the client is not ready to move towards therapy. Therefore, the coaching work is focused on ways of resourcing the client. Again, an interlinking between multiple themes and sub-themes can be seen, such as 'contracting', 'holding space' and 'normalising', to name but a few.

Code: Coaching to develop awareness and insights

T2.1: *If they are not ready to do that work on themselves then we would stay in that coaching space, but maybe developing their insights and awareness of how aspects of their experience might be impacting on them achieving what they want to achieve in the workplace. So, bringing that into awareness, and in that situation, I am not doing the work that is required but perhaps recommending that they might want to explore it, at a deeper level, through psychotherapy.*

Through encouraging the client to 'develop awareness and insights', the coach acts to bring to light aspects that may be explored in therapy and therefore takes up the position of coaching towards therapy. Therefore, by the coach skilfully working in the grey space, the client gains awareness of material that would be better suited to therapy. What has come to light through the coaching work offers the client an opportunity to develop 'willingness' (Hayes et al., 2004) (see p.144) which may later result in the client choosing to engage in therapy coaching towards therapy.

Code: Signposting to therapy

H3.1: *So just knowing that that is at your disposal sometimes is enough, and then help clients through the process of interviewing therapists or choosing one that is in an … That they're feeling some kind of … They have a rapport with. Because I don't think people choose therapists the same way they choose coaches. I've often been told to try three coaches and see which one resonates the most with you. But a therapist, you tend to be so desperate for help that you just say, 'I need to talk', and you grab whoever will give you an ear.*

Coaches take a coaching approach 'position' when 'signposting' clients 'towards therapy'. In this extract, the coach actively encourages the client to find a therapist who resonates with them, much in the same way one would be encouraged to do when choosing a coach, rather than choosing the first option.

> **A3.3:** *And then that conversation, between L3.1 and H3.1 in particular, around referring on, the advice you gave. I had in my head this personal construct that referring on was abandoning someone. It's not, is it? And actually, the thought about coaching someone through the process and potentially still staying with one is a major re-think for me, and very useful, so thank you.*

This extract highlights that, through participating in the workshop conversation, this coach shifted their view of referring on to one of signposting the client towards therapy. Here, the coach's perspective and position shifted from viewing this action as abandoning the client to one of a coaching process, researching the client towards appropriate support.

Code: Coaching in parallel to therapy

> **S1.1:** *I've not referred people on. I seem to be working with a handful of people who are also working with therapists at the moment, and being quite open about ... I always check in with someone, when we're contracting, as to are they working with anyone else, and how would we honour those boundaries, so I either don't collude with them or their therapist on a topic? ... I noticed that differentiation. Increasingly, I'm of a view that there's a space for coaching and a space for therapy that can be quite comfortably sitting alongside each other.*

In this extract, the position adopted by the coach is one of working in 'parallel to therapy' with clients. Here the coach and client experience adequate differentiation between the two helping roles, viewing coaching and therapy as sitting comfortably alongside each other. From this position the coach navigates the grey space with greater confidence. Moreover, this position taken by the coaches aligns with Campone's (2014) study.

Code: Destigmatising therapy

> **A3.1:** *Yes. And there's also something, I think, about humility as well, and recognising our own imperfections and saying, 'Yes, I go to therapy too from time to time, and that's enormously helpful to me in this way – X and Y.' And it somehow makes it more accessible for other people.*

Even if they'd had therapy in the past – and there seem to be a lot of people out there who have had a bad experience of therapy – and of course they're not always because it was a terrible therapist, it could be any combination of reasons why they didn't have a good experience with somebody at that time in their lives, and that doesn't mean the same is going to happen again. Yes, it's an interesting area, referral.

This extract demonstrates that coaches actively take up the position of talking about attending their own therapy. Therefore, by normalising and 'destigmatising therapy' in this way, coaches are coaching towards therapy, should a client decide therapy is of interest to them.

> **H3.1:** *When I'm doing my training, I quite often share at certain points, 'I saw a therapist just recently, in order to deal with my dad and grief and blah, blah, blah'. And you have people saying, 'Really?' And they start asking questions about it – 'That's really brave of you to tell me that'. And I think, 'Well how can I be here, asking you guys to do this, if I'm not doing it myself?' It just seems like a no-brainer to me.*

As this extract demonstrated, through actively sharing about engaging in personal therapy, the coach's destigmatising therapy engages in coaching towards therapy. Furthermore, themes and sub-themes can be seen, such as 'values', 'proficiency' and 'holding space' through the 'position' taken: "Well how can I be here, asking you guys to do this, if I'm not doing it myself? It just seems like a no-brainer to me. "

Theme 3: Voice

Gergen (1989) puts forward the concept of 'warranting voice', proposing that, during social interactions, an individual attempts to gain 'voice' through warranting their conduct as socially acceptable, within any given context.

Through this theme, coaches can be seen to engage in warranting voice on behalf of their clients and themselves with regard to the disillusionment with social systems and structures; bringing to light tensions observed within the profession and warranting how coaches step into and navigate the grey space.

Coaches also look to resist the term 'referral', which is seen to be inherited from psychological tradition because it is considered to hold a 'power-knowledge' (Foucault, 1979) differential.

Five sub-themes were created within this main theme. 'Disillusionment' gives voice to the level of disillusionment with the mental health profession and the way in which traditional psychology and psychiatry operate. 'Normalising' is called for regarding mental health and emotions, acknowledging the 'presence of trauma' and calling for practitioners to be trauma-informed or sensitive. 'Referral: coaching's "ugly step-sister"' calls for signposting rather than 'referring' and all that this term implies because it is viewed as a term which is inherently 'loaded'. Finally, it is acknowledged that coaches have had the opportunity to gain voice through the vehicle of this research: 'research facilitating voice'.

Within this theme of taking up voice, coaches may be seen to be engaging in the art of existence, whereby they 'cultivate' themselves by challenging and resisting power structure (Foucault, 1997) in how they work and navigate the intersections between therapy and coaching, in addition to enabling voice for discourses that may otherwise go unacknowledged.

Sub-theme: Disillusionment

This sub-theme relates to the 'disillusionment' regarding therapy in the wider traditional mental health profession. There were several individuals affected by this in all three groups, who spoke about either themselves having had negative experiences with therapy or having clients who reported negative experiences with therapy. What was interesting was that 90 per cent of the coaching psychologists had had a negative experience with therapy. Foucault (1982) suggests that, from our cultural perspective, madness is "owned" or resides within the disciplines of psychology/psychoanalysis and psychiatry, which assume the position of expert, retaining power through assessing and determining another's behaviour, with significant consequences.

Code: Disillusion with traditional psychological professions

Coaches spoke to give voice to personal experience and client experience as well as critically reflecting on professional knowledge, regarding the system and structure of the traditional mental health profession. Coaches called out the power imbalances that they and their clients had experienced. This affects the way coaches signpost, which is illustrated further in the main theme. This position does not, however, prevent coaches from signposting 'coaching towards therapy' (see p.122). Rather, this theme calls for more from the wider professions.

Taylor (2022) considers "the mental health movements to be misguided, often with good intentions – but ultimately lead to people believing that they have something wrong with them which needs treating or managing".

> **L2.1:** *It is by Judith Herman, and it is called* Trauma and Recovery. *She is an associate professor at Harvard, but she goes into a lot of this, about the early development of that diagnostic manual, run by groups of men and women who were subject to battery in the home, victims of domestic abuse, and how they were categorised as… I cannot remember what the term is she uses now, but it is basically about having a masochistic personality disorder. It was the women who had the masochistic personality disorder and made themselves into victims. It is a fascinating look at how the whole process evolved and how psychiatrists interpreted different disorders and how they victimised the victims, really.* (Viewpoint from psychologist/psychologically informed coach.)

In this extract, the coach gives voice to the mistrust they have of psychiatry and broader therapeutic professions because of the way in which the *Diagnostic*

Statistical Manual was developed, which is used to determine pathology. As a result, this highlights the wider systemic issues and the disillusionment.

> **L2.2:** *I think with psychotherapy, even though I hear what you are saying, K2.1, for me, and this is only my experience from a psychodynamic counselling course where we were told the same thing, but there is absolutely a power imbalance. When that power imbalance goes wrong it can be incredibly dangerous.*

In this extract, the coach is recounting their own experience of being in and studying a type of therapy; in addition to sharing stories from the client, they give voice to the imbalance of power within a psychotherapeutic relationship and the dangers thereof. This points to their disillusionment about psychotherapy.

> **L2.2:** *I hear you in terms of, when we are in the room with a client it is absolutely that co-creation, and that is what we were taught in the programme. But if you then look at the institutionalisation and the systemic nature they are absolute significant power imbalances. Then you add in ethnic minorities and all of these other things to it and it's just a complete minefield really.* (Viewpoint from psychologist/psychologically informed coach.)

Once again, this extract demonstrates the wider systemic issues within the traditional mental health professions and gives voice to the disillusionment across different cultures. It is in these situations that coaches view their work in the grey space as offering an alternative narrative of co-creation and one which has a greater balance of power between coach and client.

Code: Call for an integrative holistic approach

Coaches give voice to a sense of compartmentalisation that takes place within the traditional helping professions, calling for a more holistic approach, seeing the human as a whole system and working across specialisms. For example, psychology has only recently recognised the importance of the gut microbiome, gut-brain axis and the impacts this can have on mental health (Cryan, 2019). Furthermore, this position informs how coaches navigate the grey space, particularly when it comes to signposting, and how signposting is done.

> **L2.1:** *I hated the fact that even at university there was no crossover. You would suggest to, 'Well, why do you not link up there, because I am sure that something else is going on?' It was almost like, 'Get out of my room, f-off'.*

This extract demonstrates the lack of shared knowledge across various domains this coach experienced when studying. Therefore, issues are not dealt with in a systemic way. Here, the coach voices their disillusionment and calls for a more 'integrative holistic approach' to health and mental health.

S1.2: *So, yes, primarily, absolutely, there's a lot of signposting that goes on. However, if I was to back out and have a look at the contract and the content of pretty much any coaching conversation, it is to do with stimulus and response to that stimulus. At that moment, if your brain is foggy because it's got too much sugar being fed to it, then signposting to a dietary recommendation might be beneficial in that moment, depending on the person and the context.*

In this extract, the coach is demonstrating taking up an integrative holistic approach – i.e. their position – due to the disillusionment of an individual's symptoms being viewed in isolation. Here, the coach takes into account the broader context of what may be happening in the client's life, as a result they signpost in a more holistic way.

Sub-theme: Normalising

Coaches give voice to 'normalising' mental health. In addition, coaches look to 'normalise emotion', facilitating voice to the holistic nature of the human experience. A crossover with the sub-theme 'Radical inclusion' (see p.118) can be seen. Furthermore, through normalising, a destigmatising effect can occur for clients. With the result that, if additional therapeutic support was required, clients felt more open to being signposted.

Code: Normalising stigma: mental health

Once again, the theme of normalising was presented, as in Workshop 1's sub-theme 'Mental health literacy' (Jorm, 2012) (see p.82).

Coaches felt that the current rhetoric surrounding mental health was damaging. Therefore, there was a need to encourage mental health awareness, as well as view mental health on a continuum. This meant viewing coaching as providing a space for normalisation and voicing the message of 'there's nothing wrong with you', and challenging the rhetoric of being 'broken' or 'needing to be fixed'. Through coaching activities such as strengths and values, coaches feel that they are encouraging the client to have greater self-efficacy, thus enabling the client to begin to feel empowered to make choices. Within the grey space, coaches looked beyond the label of a mental health diagnosis, yet still worked within the parameters of coaching. Once again, we can consider Grant's (2007) 'Distressed but Functional' quadrant.

T2.1: *… or me, the current rhetoric around mental health is incredibly, incredibly problematic for so many different reasons.*

This extract represents calling for giving voice for greater normalising of the narrative around mental health.

A3.3: *One piece of common feedback I've had from three different individuals, all of which I would say, when I started, were grey space clients. A very common theme across them is they've said the process normalised what they're experiencing, and helped them to realise that actually there wasn't something wrong with them.*

In this extract, the coach gives voice to the coaching process acting as a way of normalising the emotional experience the client had, resulting in a new narrative take-up by clients: "there wasn't something wrong with them."

Code: Emotions

Coaches actively resist the rhetoric of pathologising emotions; viewing them as part of being human, thereby creating a space within the coaching work for emotions. Furthermore, coaches act as a voice in that normalises moments when clients experience emotions. A parallel can be seen with Workshop 1 (see p.56) with coaches supporting clients to normalise emotions. However, in comparison to Workshop 1, coaches were more active in voicing their views against the wider societal stigmatisation of emotions. I suggest that coaches, through 'voicing', are being 'brave' and are stepping into the space of emotions, particularly those that are challenging, so as not to collude with the "tyranny of the positive" (Einzig, 2011); however, this is still done within the ethical considerations of what it is to be a coach, recognising one's own limits and boundaries.

L2.1: *That also feeds back into what we were saying before about normalising and reducing the stigma. The emotions are just there. There is nothing wrong with whatever they are. They are trying to say something, more often than not, so it is another example really. It is just part of being a human being.*

In this extract, the coach actively reduces stigma for the client by voicing that there is nothing wrong with emotions; thereby normalising the client's experience.

H3.1: *There is an emerging field in psychology now, about emotion. You went from behaviouralism to cognition and now it's emerging around emotion. And I think we stigmatise emotion, we make it pathologised, we make it … You're talking about the uncontrollable. But actually, it's perfectly normal.*

And there is something about, if we could embrace that as part of coach training, then there wouldn't be such a false dichotomy between this is therapy, this is coaching. Because we work with emotions all the time. Why are we not just helping people look at the shades of it, to go back to your grey colour? It's about human beings, isn't it, and what's …?

This extract highlights the disillusionment felt through the stigmatisation and pathologising of emotions. Here, emotions are seen as a part of the human experience – normalising. Furthermore, giving voice that there is a false dichotomy to viewing the coaching space as one that should remain free of difficult emotions. Once again coaches view their work in the grey space as offering an alternative narrative surrounding the stigmatisation and pathologising of emotions.

Sub-theme: Presence of trauma

Voice was given in recognition of the 'presence of trauma' within the grey space and coaching as a whole. Acknowledging that, in coaching, trauma can be present coaches and the wider profession need to consider tis. Elements of the sub-theme 'Radical inclusion' can be seen as a form of acknowledgement that trauma is present, even though this is not an area the coach will actively work with. Coaches also recognised the need for training regarding a 'trauma-informed' approach, to ensure that they had the capacity to hold whatever a client may bring. "Trauma-informed coaching is the practice of understanding the presence of trauma in a coach-client relationship and how to use it as a guide for resilience and solution-forward resolution" (Canadian Company, n.d.).

Taylor (2022) considers "the mental health movements to be misguided, often with good intentions – but ultimately lead to people believing that they have something wrong with them which needs treating or managing". A trauma-informed position talks instead about 'trauma responses', which can be both physiological and psychological rather than 'symptoms' and 'coping mechanisms' or 'disorders' or 'psychosis', as seen in the medical model. This suggests that helping professionals are encouraged to see clients from a trauma-informed position rather than a position of pathologising, medication and psychiatric diagnosis; further suggesting that individuals are experiencing trauma responses and coping mechanisms because they "have been subjected to trauma, harm, abuse and distress of any kind" (Taylor, 2022).

> **B1.1:** *Because clearly, I have an interest in more complex client work. Clients show up. There is always trauma present of some description. Always. It's there. There's always a break in the attachment somewhere, and that was showing up in the space.*

The coach in this extract gives voice to the presence of trauma, particularly when undertaking more complex client work in the grey space.

> **K2.1:** *You can if you are coming at it from a psychotherapeutic or psychological background, but a lot of coaches out there do not have that background and they are not qualified to go into things that might trigger earlier traumas and stuff. Knowing how to deal with that and also the pace …*

Once again, this extract gives voice to the presence of trauma. However, here the coach calls for coaches to ensure that they are skilled and equipped to navigate coaching work. I suggest that it is likely that trauma will be present when entering the grey space is entered, and so to ensure that coaches are equipped to travel this space well it is essential that coaches working in the grey space are trauma informed (see p.130 for definition).

Sub-theme: Referral: coaching's 'ugly step-sister'

When creating codes and gathering themes, the codes and themes that were considered may not have been demonstrated across all groups. Furthermore, important issues raised by one group or individual were also considered because these might have been relevant to all groups (Braun & Clarke, 2013). This was the case within one group with regard to this particular sub-theme.

In this sub-theme, the term 'referral' is seen to be in direct conflict with the position of the coach and the coaching profession. The coaches are not challenging the notion of signposting, or facilitating the client towards therapy, as seen in sub-theme 'Coaching towards therapy'. Rather, the implicit historical and discursive implications that the term 'referral' holds are what they give voice to.

Foucault (1982) suggests that from our cultural perspective, madness is 'owned' or resides within the disciplines of psychology/psychoanalysis and psychiatry, which assume the position of expert, retaining power through assessing and determining another's behaviour, with significant consequences. This is comparable to Rose's (1996) notion of the "power of psychology".

Coaches believed that the term 'referral' has several underlying meanings, relating to a medical model from a psychiatric/psychology standpoint. The implications coaches felt this held up related to the notions of diagnosis and pathologising, which are in direct conflict with the position a coach takes up. The word 'referral' is inherently in conflict with the position that a coach takes up because the word itself implies that the coach needs to engage in some form of analysis in order to refer a client. Therefore, this shifts the coach into an imbalanced position of power: power-knowledge (Foucault, 1978).

> **M1.1:** *And again, that is my construct of how I hear, 'referring on' – is loaded in my mind, as in 'referring on', to me, has a quality to it of a parcel being moved. I think there is that kind of somatic feel for me about that language … I know, for a while, I've explored, with my supervisor, this idea of power in a relationship, be you a guide, a priest, a coach, a therapist, or somatic experiencer, or anything. Clients come and there is a dynamic. But when you bring in another expert of some kind, it has this colluding-like element of there being yet another power that is being given, which can disempower someone, in some way, and at the same time, break the relationship they already have with you, where they are being empowered.*

In this extract, the coach gives voice to the way in which the term 'referring a client on' is a loaded term for them – one of breaking a relationship, while conjuring up images of the client being passed on like a parcel to other 'experts'. Here, the term holds a power dynamic; one that is viewed as disempowering to the client.

> **L3.1:** *It's interesting, because, for me, again, clarity and thinking happening there, if I reflect about the way that I language things with my clients, I would never say to them, 'I'm referring you on'. However, if we look at any of the texts, normally, around coaching and coaching boundaries, the language in those texts is all around referring on. Those are the words that are used.*

This extract demonstrates the use of the term 'referral' being used in all texts in the field of coaching.

> **L3.1:** *Then it's like if you've got to the edge of your boundary, that's where you refer on. We're being encouraged, as coaches, to almost step into this model that, actually, might not feel comfortable for us, as coaches, possibly, depending on our context and framework. Again, as you say, is there a disempowering element in that, maybe, in those terms?*

In this extract, the coach gives voice to the inherently opposing position the term 'referral' places the coach in; one that is not in alignment with what coaching values stand for.

Sub-theme: Research facilitating voice

The coaches felt that the research itself acted as a spotlight on the grey space and 'gave voice' to what they had been experiencing: the grey space. In addition, the research enabled them to voice and bring to light experiences that, at times, felt isolating. Many coaches spoke of having started this journey of working in this space before the research, which may have been one of the incentives for participating. Several coaches felt that the research provided a container, a space or a spotlight to reflect and grow; crystallising the journey that they had begun and bringing ways of practising that are "taken for granted" (Schön, 1983) to light; much like a greenhouse, creating the right conditions for rapid growth to occur.

> **B1.2:** *I think just the process itself of us meeting and us discussing is also quite helpful … But again, it's nice just to almost be in the space of sharing that and being part of it, and feeling less lonely. Do you know what I mean? Just even seeing the breadth and diversity of it and a different stage of it, it's not better or worse; it's just simply different. Because there are clients who need all of it, and they need it in certain permutations. So yes, 'spotlight' is a nice way to … When you said that question and I wrote it down, I just wrote, 'spotlight'. I hope that helps.*

B1.1: *But yes, so that has all just presented itself. Would it have done without this?* [referring to participating in the research]. *I don't know what my response would have been without this. But that has been present recently, in that I was able to go, 'There's something not right. I'm really going to reflect upon this'. I had a focusing practice. Body said, 'Absolutely not', and then after came the rationalisation of, 'And here is why not'.*

In this extract, a dialogue between coaches highlights the journey the coaches were on within the grey space prior to the research. However, through the research, coaches 'facilitated voice' of the experience of being in the grey space – this being experienced as a spotlight.

Limitations and further research areas

This study framed the experience of the grey space from a majority demographic of the white middle class. The study was not culturally diverse; there was only one coach who represented the black, Asian and minority ethnic (BAME) population. She and I had discussions regarding this, inquiring as to whether the lack of minority individuals is a broader reflection of the coaching industry and field, or if the grey space is experienced differently by those from different ethnic backgrounds. This calls for further research.

Additionally, the experience of and navigating the grey space is viewed purely from the practitioner's perspective. To offer a balanced insight, future research may look to understand how this space is experienced by the client/coachee and why coaching is selected over other support.

What emerged

Coaches felt strongly about normalising mental ill health and the need for more mental health education; giving voice to normalising mental health within the ethical considerations, limits and boundaries as a coach. Coaches also held a conviction that emotions are part of the human experience and that they are open to 'seeing this person as a whole' and normalising experiences with their clients.

They also viewed coaching as having an ameliorative effect on stress-related mental health illness; adding to the development of psychological flexibility. Thus providing a stepping stone towards therapy through destigmatising, normalising helping professions (various therapies, etc.) and coaching the client 'towards therapy', with the various roles a coach can play to facilitate support.

Coaches indicated that the grey space is a dynamic and complex space, with questions arising as to whether the signposting process needs further development when considering clients who may be in this space. In these situations, coaches position themselves in relation to signposting so as to support/facilitate the client through coaching towards creating a 'wellness team', with the client at the centre of this team; encouraging the client to draw support from the most appropriate resource at the time, be that therapy/counselling, coaching, their GP, functional practitioners, etc.

However, a juxtaposition regarding therapy, traditional psychology and systemic issues surfaced. The coaches' stance was that of facilitating, giving voice on behalf of their client and themselves to the tensions within the wider helping and mental health professions and the system as a whole. This brought to light the disillusionment felt by the clients and the coaches themselves – both professionally and, at times, personally – and they voiced the difficulties and negative experiences their clients reported regarding therapy both in the past and currently. Interestingly, within the coaching psychologists/psychologically informed coaches group, a discussion arose regarding the potential risks and harm that can be done in coaching, and ended with a conversation about the potential risks and harm that can be done in therapy. All except one of the coaching psychologists/psychologically informed coaches shared that they had had a negative experience within their own personal therapy, resulting in a question emerging as to whether this is why we became coaching psychologists rather than therapists. Taylor (2022) argues that the traditional current medical model treatment and perspective regarding mental health is ill-advised, "the mental health movements to be misguided, often with good intentions – but ultimately leading to people believing that they have something wrong with them which needs treating or managing" (Pope, 1709, line 625).

The coaching psychologists/psychologically informed coaches spoke of conflicting views being held and tensions arising: on one hand, viewing non-psychologically informed coaches as 'fools rush in, where angels fear to tread' and, on the other, viewing them as unencumbered and therefore able to be innovative, creative and advancing coaching. In some respects, they envied coaches who did not have the psychological underpinning because they felt that they owned a sense of freedom – an ability to be creative within the coaching space – drawing on practical knowledge and unencumbered by academic knowledge. This suggests that, through schooling, innovative thinking is trained out of you. Therefore, the psychologists felt that they were more rigid. Western (2012), defines coaching as "a vital and dynamic space that enables creativity to emerge, whereas other 'helping relationships' are often saddled with more restrictive cultures" (p.10).

That said, they also believed that the speed and depths non-psychologically informed coaches may work at with a client may differ from psychologically informed coaches. This suggests that the non-psychologically informed coaches may enter the grey space and find that questions such as, "Should I be here?" and "Is this therapeutic terrain?" do not emerge as quickly as with the psychologically informed coaches, This indicates that non-psychologically informed coaches may feeling competent and comfortable working with what emerges in session. However, psychologically-informed coaches may have more moments of experiencing 'analysis paralysis' due to the information that they hold, with psychologically-informed coaches needing to define the territory they are working in, unlike coaches who do not have an academic psychological education (this may be because of the way in which education takes place, creating certain constructs of territories). Therefore, non-psychologically informed coaches may experience more fluidity and, along with psychologically informed coaches, seek a greater need for definition of territory, which is seen as both a hindrance and an advantage. This raises the question of awareness and training and whether having the territory mapped may hinder freedom, albeit, when it comes to navigating the grey space, having psychological education in coaching creates greater safety. This again echoes the 'cross-boundary expertise' which calls for foundational training in mental health.

Coaches within this research acknowledged that they were drawn to the work in this complex grey space, with the co-enquirers reflecting that they felt that they were already on a journey of exploration. Hence, their interest in participating in this research.

Furthermore, coaches recognised and held the belief that they had the competency and capacity to hold and manage the complexities, tensions and ambiguities that come with navigating this terrain. There is a sense of a 'calling' – a deeper purpose to this space. In addition, they reported that the grey space is not experienced as linear or with definite boundaries. Consequently, to navigate this terrain, coaches maintained a state of questioning regarding ethics, care, competency and capacity to assist; evaluating moment by moment the territory of this space. I too can relate to this, as this state of questioning is what brought me to this research. As previously discussed, this state of questioning, rather than requiring a definitive answer, becomes a navigational tool – a living compass within this terrain.

Moreover, there is a conviction that, to traverse the complexities of the grey space, one must be actively engaged in 'work on the self' – whether this is through therapy, coaching or training – which results in becoming a better coach and holding that relational space required for this work. Additionally, through participating in the research, modifications to practice were made, with "reflection in action" bringing "everyday taken-for granted" (Schön, 1983) more into conscious awareness, such as practices and decisions, when entering the grey space; particularly regarding contracting, with coaches saying that they actively reviewed and refined their practice and were more explicit with clients. Coaches also reported a greater sense of self-awareness regarding their response within – and of – the grey space itself, acknowledging and recognising the complexity within this terrain and conveying having obtained further embodied self-awareness (Blake, 2018) relating to when and when not to enter a coaching dynamic with a potential client.

Several coaches spoke of an iterative development of their contracting, which provided a greater sense of clarity, as well as making the territory become clearer; consequently they became more able to navigate the grey space with further adjustment surrounding supervision. What's more, several coaches reported taking up different types of supervision, starting supervision where they had not had it before and/or increasing it. Coaches sought out supervisors who they felt were more able to handle the complexities of their work, such as those who either had psychological backgrounds or were working within the grey space. Thus, coaches are more 'resourced' (Henderson & O'Riordan, 2020) and equipped to manage whatever emerged during coaching sessions.

What became apparent is that the coaches' approach to this space is much like that of a 'personal consultant' (Povick & Jinks, 2014), drawing on an array of training and skills, with a continuing desire through CPD to develop their knowledge and skill set base in order to better support clients with whatever may arise during sessions.

All three groups, but in particular Group 1, had a lively discussion regarding the term 'referral'; they proposed that the term is inherently in conflict with the position that a coach takes up. The act of signposting was not the issue because all the coaches felt comfortable signposting clients towards other professionals. It was rather the term 'referral' itself, everything that the term suggests, the power dynamic and the position that that word contains within it. It was therefore suggested that the term 'referral' does not belong in the coaching lexicon.

Having reviewed the data, I suggest that grey space was experienced by all three groups, with co-enquirers expressing that talking about this space was particularly beneficial and supportive.

As discussed, each group faced different tensions as a result of the type of training they had received, their professional standing and their ontological positions. Throughout this process, the group I viewed as gaining the most value for themselves and developing as practitioners was Group 3, which consisted of the blended group of psychologically-informed coaches and non-psychologically informed coaches. This was probably because of the group's exposure to different reference points and perspectives, in addition to the group dynamic being that of taking an open, receptive, respectful position with a willingness to learn from each other. This was experienced particularly by one of the non-psychologically informed coaches, who did not view – and was unaware of – mental health coming into coaching. As the discussion unfolded, with various experiences being voiced in the room, the fact that everyone has mental health that sits on a continuum was understood, resulting in the coach in question recognising a need for training and subsequently enrolling for mental health first aid training. Furthermore, Group 3 has subsequently formed a peer-to-peer supervision group (which I am involved in) that meets every six weeks.

Even though this stance was also adopted by the other two groups, they may have acted as 'echo chambers' because they comprised of non-psychologically informed coaches or psychologically-informed/coaching psychologists. Therefore, it could be argued that this would result in them holding similar views, knowledge and reference points.

Finally, in addition to the complexity of the grey space within the coach-client context, it was suggested that there are multiple levels of complexity and grey areas through which coaches must steer within the field of coaching in terms of definition, codes of conduct, ethics and the industry as a whole. There were levels of frustration, cynicism and confusion across all three groups relating to the different guidelines and ethical considerations, depending on which body, society or association the individual was affiliated to.

A recommendations section has deliberately not been included because, in the final chapter, I have analysed what has emerged and incorporated it into a framework (see p.159).

Summary

As previously discussed in Chapter 3, action research takes place within cycles of enquiry, with data generated in the moment, which identified core themes for knowledge and practice. Through the use of action research enquiry, there was a facilitation of voice and of bringing to the fore and illuminating hidden experiences and understanding of our practice, and how coaches work in the grey space.

This chapter has focused further on the importance of discussions between coaches and coachees to help better understand clients, the grey space and the challenges faced by professionals. It also considered the limitations connected with the grey space and contemplated how this could be addressed – and improved – in the future.

Discussion points

1. What themes, sub-themes and codes from Workshop 2 do you recognise in your own practice?
2. Having reflected on the themes and cycles of enquiry presented, are there any revisions you will be making to your practice?

Recommended reading

Aquilina, E. (2016). *Embodying authenticity. A somatic path to transforming self, team & organisation.* London: Live It Publishing.

Blake, A. (2018). *Your body is your brain: Leverage your somatic intelligence to find purpose, build resilience, deepen relationships and lead more powerfully.* Truckee, CA: Trokay Press.

Bradbury, N. Frost, S. Kilminster & M. Zukas (eds.), *Beyond reflective practice: New approaches to professional lifelong learning.* London: Routledge.

Campone, F. (2014). 'At the border: coaching a client with dissociative identity disorder'. *International Journal of Evidence Based Coaching and Mentoring,* 12(1), 1–13.

Dall'Alba, G. & Sandberg, J. (2006). 'Unveiling professional development: A critical review of stage models'. *Review of Education Research,* 76(3), 383–412.

Day, A. (2012). 'Working with unconscious relational process in coaching'. In E. de Hann & C. Sills (eds.), *Coaching relationships: The relational coaching field book.* Faringdon: Libri Publishing.

Fook, J. (2010). 'Beyond reflective practice: reworking the "critical" in critical reflection'. In H.
Garvey, B. & Stokes, P. (2022). *Coaching and mentoring: Theory and practice*, 4th edn. London: SAGE.
O'Broin, A.O. & Palmer, S. (2006). The coach-client relationship and contributions made by the coach in improving coaching outcomes. *The Coaching Psychologist*, 2(2), 16–20.
O'Broin, A. & Palmer, S. (2010). 'Building on interpersonal perspective on the coaching relationship'. In S. Palmer & A. McDowall (eds.), *The coaching relationship: Putting people first*. Abingdon: Routledge.
Porges, S. (2016). 'Co-regulation'. Relational Impact. Available at: https://proactivemindfulness.com/zug/transcripts/Porges-2016-09.pdf (Accessed: December 2021).
Schwartz, A. (2018). 'Connection and co-regulation in psychotherapy'. Available at: https://drarielleschwartz.com/connection-co-regulation-psychotherapy-dr-arielle-schwartz (Accessed: December 2021).
Schön, D.A. (1983). *The reflective practitioner: How professionals think in action*. New York, NY: Basic Books.
Strozzi-Heckler, R. (2014). *The art of somatic coaching: Embodying skillful action, wisdom and compassion*. Berkeley, CA: North Atlantic Books.
Whittington, J. (2016). *Systemic coaching & constellations: The principles, practices and applications for individuals, teams and groups*, 2nd edn. London: Kogan Page.

References

Aquilina, E. (2016). *Embodying authenticity. A somatic path to transforming self, team & organisation.* London: Live It Publishing.
Argyris, C. (2003). 'Actionable knowledge'. In T. Tsoukas & C. Knudsen (eds.), *The Oxford handbook of organizational theory.* Oxford: Oxford University Press.
Bandura, A. (1977). 'Self-efficacy: Toward a unifying theory of behavioral change'. *Psychological Review*, 84(2), 191–215.
Bettelheim, B. (1976). *The uses of enchantment: The meaning and importance of fairy tales.* London: Penguin.
Blake, A. (2018). *Your body is your brain: Leverage your somatic intelligence to find purpose, build resilience, deepen relationships and lead more powerfully.* Truckee, CA: Trokay Press.
Bowlby, J. (1988). *A secure base: Clinical applications of attachment theory.* London: Routledge.
Braun, V. & Clarke, V. (2013). *Successful qualitative research: A practical guide for beginners.* London: Sage Publications.
Brems, C. (2001). *Basic skills in psychotherapy and counselling.* Belmont, CA: Wadsworth/Thomson Learning.
Campone, F. (2014). 'At the border: coaching a client with dissociative identity disorder'. *International Journal of Evidence Based Coaching and Mentoring*, 12(1), 1–13.
Canadian Company. (n.d.). 'Moving the human spirit'. Available at: https://www.movingthehumanspirit.com/trauma-informed-coaching (Accessed: October 2019).
Cann, A. & Collette, C. (2014). 'Sense of humor, stable affect, and psychological well-being'. *Europe's Journal of Psychology*, 10(3), 464–479.
Cavanagh, M. (2005). 'Mental-health issues and challenging clients in executive coaching'. In M. Cavanagh, A.M. Grant & T. Kemp (eds.), *Evidence-based coaching,*

Volume 1: Theory, research and practice from behavioural science. . Bowen Hill, Australia: Australian Academic Press.

Coghlan, D. (2006). 'Insider action research doctorates: generating actionable knowledge'. *Higher Education,* 54(2), 293–306.

Critchley, B. (2012). 'Relational coaching: Dancing on the edge'. In E. de Hann & C. Sills (eds.), *Coaching relationships: The relational coaching field book.* Faringdon: Libri Publishing.

Crotty, M. (1998). *The foundations of social research.* London: Sage Publications Ltd.

Cryan, J.F. (2019). 'More than a gut feeling'. *The Psychologist,* 32(1), 30–35.

Cundy, L. (2019). 'The role of coaching psychology and coaching in "the Grey Space"'. *Coaching Psychology International,* 12(1), 59–68.

David, S. (2016). *Emotional agility. Get unstuck, embrace change and thrive in work and life.* London: Penguin Random House.

Day, A. (2012). 'Working with unconscious relational process in coaching'. In E. de Hann & C. Sills (eds.), *Coaching relationships: The relational coaching field book.* Faringdon: Libri Publishing.

Desmond, B. (2012). 'Spirituality in the coaching relationship'. In E. de Hann & C. Sills (eds.), *Coaching relationships: The relational coaching field book.* Faringdon: Libri Publishing.

Einzig, H. (2011). 'The beast within'. *Coaching at Work,* 6(3), 41–45.

Egan, G. (1994). *The skilled helper,* 5th edn. Pacific Grove, CA: Brooks.

Fogel, A. (2009). *The psychophysiology of self-awareness: Rediscovering the lost art of body sense.* Portland, OR: Ringgold Inc.

Fook, J. (2010). 'Beyond reflective practice: reworking the "critical" in critical reflection'. In H. Bradbury, N. Frost, S. Kilminster & M. Zukas (eds.), *Beyond reflective practice: New approaches to professional lifelong learning.* London: Routledge.

Foucault, M. (1978). *The history of sexuality, Volume 1: An introduction.* New York, NY: Vintage.

Foucault, M. (1982). *Madness and civilization: A history of insanity in the age of reason.* London: Tavistock.

Foucault, M. (1997). *Ethics: Essential works of Foucault 1954–1984, Volume 1* (ed. P. Rabinow). London: Penguin.

Frankl, V.E. (1978). *The unheard cry for meaning: Psychotherapy and humanism.* Oxford: Simon & Schuster.

Frankl, V.E. (1992). *Man's search for meaning,* 4th edn. Originally published in 1959 under the title *From death-camp to existentialism.* London: Random House Group.

Garvey, B. & Stokes, P. (2022). *Coaching and mentoring: Theory and practice,* 4th edn. London: SAGE.

Gergen, K.J. (1989). 'Warranting voice and the elaboration of the self'. In J. Shotter & K.J. Gergen (eds.), *Text of identity.* London: Sage.

Giraldez-Hayes, A. (2021). 'Different domains or grey areas? Setting boundaries between coaching and therapy: A thematic analysis'. *The Coaching Psychologist,* 17(2), 18–29.

Grant, A.M. (2007). 'A languishing-flourishing model of goal striving and mental health for coaching populations'. *International Coaching Psychology Review* 2(3), 252–264..

Harré, R. & van Langenhove, L. (1999). *Positioning theory.* Oxford: Blackwell Publishers Ltd.

Hawkins, P. (2019). *Leadership team coaching: Developing collective transformational leadership,* 3rd edn. London: Kogan Page.

Hayes, C. & Fulton, J.A. (2015). 'Autoethnography as a method of facilitating critical reflectivity for professional doctorate students'. *Journal of Learning Development in Higher Education*, 8(8), 252–264.

Hayes, S. C, Follette, V. M., & Linehan, M. M. (eds.). (2004). *Mindfulness and acceptance: Expanding the cognitive behavioral tradition.* New York: Guilford Press.

Heidegger, M. (1962). *Being and time.* London: SCM Press.

Henderson, A. & O'Riordan, S. (2020). 'Resourcing the supervisory relationship during the COVID-19 pandemic'. *International Coaching Psychology Review*, 9(1), 51–66.

Heron, J. (1999). *The complete facilitator's handbook.* New York, NY: Kogan Page Limited.

Jorm, A.F. (2012). 'Mental health literacy: Empowering the community to take action for better mental health'. *The American Psychologist*, 67(3), 231–243.

Luckner, J.L. & Nadler, R.S. (1997). *Processing the experience: Strategies to enhance and generalize learning,* 2nd edn. Dubuque, IA: Kendall Hunt.

Martin, R. & Ford, T. (2018). *The Psychology of humor: An integrative approach.* Cambridge, MA: Academic Press.

Martin, D.J., Garske, J.P. & Davis, M.K. (2000). 'Relation of the therapeutic alliance with outcome and other variables: A meta-analytic review'. *Journal of Consulting and Clinical Psychology*, 68(3), 438–450.

Maxwell, A. (2009). 'The co-created boundary: negotiating the limits of coaching'. *International Journal of Evidence Based Coaching and Mentoring*, 4(1), 82–94.

McNiff, J. (2002). *Action research for professional development: Concise advice for new action researchers*, 3rd edn. Abingdon: Routledge.

O'Broin, A.O. & Palmer, S. (2006). The coach-client relationship and contributions made by the coach in improving coaching outcomes. *The Coaching Psychologist*, 2(2), 16–20.

O'Broin, A. & Palmer, S. (2010). 'Building on interpersonal perspective on the coaching relationship'. In S. Palmer & A. McDowall (eds.), *The coaching relationship: Putting people First.* Abingdon: Routledge.

Paterson, M., Higgs, J., Wilcox. S. & Villeneuve, M. (2002). 'Clinical reasoning and self-directed learning: key dimensions in professional education and professional socialisation'. *Focus on Health Professional Education*, 4(2), 6.

Peterson, C. & Seligman, M. (2004). *Character strengths and virtues: A handbook and classification.* Washington, DC: American Psychological Association.

Plett, H. (2020). *The art of holding space; A practice of love, liberation and leadership.* Vancouver: Page Two Books.

Pope, A. (1709). 'An essay on criticism'. Available at: https://www.poetryfoundation.org/poems/44893/an-essay-on-criticism (Accessed: December 2021).

Popovic, N. & Jinks, D. (2014). *Personal consulting,* 1st edn. London: Routledge.

Porges, S. (2016). 'Co-regulation'. Relational Impact. Available at: https://www.relational-%C2%ADimpact.com/co-regulation

Porges, S. (2016). 'Co-regulation'. Relational Impact. Available at: https://www.relational-%C2%ADimpact.com/co-regulation (Accessed: December 2021).

Proctor, B. (2008). *Group supervision: A guide to creative practice.* London: Sage.

Rogers, C.R. (1942). *Counseling and psychotherapy: Newer concepts in practice.* Boston, MA: Houghton Mifflin.

Rogers, C.R. (1951). *Client-centered therapy: Its current practice, implications and theory.* London: Constable.

Rogers, C.R. & Farson, R. (1957). 'Active listening'. Available at: https://wholebeinginstitute. com/wp-content/uploads/Rogers_Farson_Active-Listening.pdf (Accessed: 7 January 2021).

Rose, N. (1996). 'Power and subjectivity: critical history and psychology'. In C. Graumann & K.J. Gergen (eds.), *Historical dimensions of discourse*. Cambridge: Cambridge University Press.

Sanderson, C. (2015). *Counselling skills for working with shame*. London: Jessica Kingsley Publishers.

Sartre, J-P. (1999). *War diaries: Notebooks from a phoney war, 1939–1940* (trans. Q. Hoare). London: Verso.

Schön, D.A. (1983). *The reflective practitioner: How professionals think in action*. New York, NY: Basic Books.

Schwartz, A. (2018). 'Connection and co-regulation in psychotherapy'. Available at: https:// drarielleschwartz.com/connection-co-regulation-psychotherapy-dr-arielle-schwartz (Accessed: December 2021).

Senge, P., Scharmer, C.O., Jaworski, J. & Flowers, B.S. (2004). *Presence: Human purpose and the field of the future*. Cambridge, MA: The Society for Organizational Learning.

Sigel, D.J. (1999). *The developing mind*. New York: Guilford Press

Strozzi-Heckler, R. (2014). *The art of somatic coaching: Embodying skillful action, wisdom and compassion*. Berkeley, CA: North Atlantic Books.

Turner, V. (1974). 'Liminal to limioid, in play, flow and ritual: An essay in comparative symbology'. *Rice University Studies*, 60(3), 53–92 .

Taylor, J. (2022). 'Views and perspectives. On being trauma informed'. Available at: https:// www.drjessicataylor.com/contact (Accessed: January 2022).

Trede, F., Macklin, R. & Bridges, D. (2012). 'Professional identity development: a review of the higher education literature'. *Studies in Higher Education,* 37(3), 365–384.

Western, S. (2012). *Coaching and mentoring: A critical text*. London: Sage.

Whitehead, J. (1988). 'Creating a living educational theory from questions of the kind, "How do I improve my practice?"' *Cambridge Journal of Education,* 19(1), 41–52.

Whittington, J. (2016). *Systemic coaching & constellations: The principles, practices and applications for individuals, teams and groups,* 2nd edn. London: Kogan Page.

Wise, E. (2010). 'Maintaining and enhancing competence in professional psychology: Obsolescence, life-long learning, and continuing education'. *Professional Psychology: Research and Practice*, 41(3), 289–292.

Chapter 7

Viewing beyond trauma

Within my personal, professional and research arenas I experienced – directly and indirectly – trauma, in varying degrees. This chapter seeks to describe real-world examples of trauma in order for coaches to better understand their clients as a result of considering the presence of trauma and the management of boundaries.

"As we draw to the end of this chemistry session, I would like to check in. Do you have any questions, reflections or comments?" I say to my potential client.

"Yes, actually I do. I felt a bit anxious when you were saying you can't work with my trauma. I felt as though you might reject me," she responds.

Here, the word 'trauma' is utilised to refer to the incident shared by the client, as this is not my story to share. In our actual discussion, I employed her language when discussing her experience.

My heart drops to my stomach as I hear this reflection. I thought that I had made it clear that I was able to work with her on her goals but was not qualified to work with her to make sense of her traumatic experience.

"Thank you for sharing that with me. I really appreciate you being so honest. I want to reassure you that, as I mentioned, your well-being is my top priority. And part of that is to be clear where I have the skills to work and where I don't. I can, am able and am happy to work with you on the goals we spoke about such as work-life balance, stress management, work-life boundaries, well-being and enhancing resilience. However, if you wanted to explore and work through the trauma you shared with me, this would not be my area of expertise. But what I could do is support you in finding the right person to do this work with you."

I hope to convey that I am not rejecting her; rather, I am highlighting my competencies and capabilities.

"No, no. I don't want to go there. I just want to move forward from that. I want to focus on my business and being there for my kids," she says vehemently.

"I am very happy to work with you towards these goals. I think it's important that we have very open lines of communication. Could we make an agreement to be very transparent with each other? So, if at any point you feel your focus shifts, or that the trauma you shared is coming up, and you would like to focus on this aspect, we can find the best support for you."

DOI: 10.4324/9781003509776-8

My intention is to demonstrate the boundaries of our work, and how we may navigate this terrain should she become aware that her trauma is coming to the fore, whilst also maintaining my value of seeing the whole person. I also aim to demonstrate to her that she has choice and control over this situation, establishing the 'container' of our potential working relationship, contracting our boundaries and setting the stage for empowerment. I am also very aware and honoured that the client has entrusted me because I am one of a handful of people to whom she has disclosed her trauma.

As it happens, boundaries become a theme of our work, which is no surprise when one experiences trauma resulting from boundary violation. There are moments in our work when we discuss blocks to goals, and she can identify that they root back to the trauma. However, she is adamant that she does not want to go to therapy. Once again, I find that we 'bump up' against this fear of abandonment and rejection, as she shares openly her fear of not performing in the coaching. Sanderson (2015) suggests that a client can become increasingly anxious that they will be judged with the "flawed self-risks being exposed" including the risk of being rejected by others (p.176). And so, again, I honour my client and where she is, re-contracting on my remit, as described above, moving at her pace and working towards manageable action steps. Some steps might be as simple as packing the folded washing away, but she is in charge, and I believe that this is empowering.

I have had several experiences in my coaching practice of disclosure of sexual trauma. At times, I am the first person the client has disclosed to; having made it very clear that they do not want to go to therapy and that they would prefer to engage in coaching. In Bailey and Taylor's (2022) report, a resistance in women and girls to report or disclose abuse or sexual assault to mental health professionals was noted. The reasons given included embarrassment, lack of trust in professionals and concerns regarding available treatment. They were also afraid of being diagnosed with a mental health condition, which would remain on their medical records and might have repercussions in the future (Taylor, 2022).

I am aware of the impact the experience of trauma has had and is having on lives as it becomes apparent in our coaching work whether this is confidence, lack of assertive skills or poor boundary management across different life domains. As discussed in Chapter 1, I draw from a range of both personal and professional learning and experiences that have shaped my professional practice (Trede et al., 2012) and "professional identity" (Paterson et al., 2002), such as having been a psychology and counselling undergraduate. Furthermore, as previously discussed, the specialism of an influential lecturer, Christiane Sanderson, during this time was sexual trauma and childhood sexual abuse. She would use case studies to bring to life the concepts we were learning. Through this process, my own lived experience and learning through theory and experience and participating in my own therapy (for more on my professional identity please see Chapter 1), I have gained an "embodied understanding of and in practice" (Dall'Alba & Sandberg, 2006, pp.389–390). Therefore, I bring this lens into my coaching practice; not to work as a therapist but to assist me in navigating this terrain – the grey space, sensitively.

There is something to be said for readiness – I personally know only too well the position of not being ready to step into the work of unpacking one's trauma. To do so requires a level of resource, as a single mother, being the sole provider and trying to keep life running. The last thing I had was the capacity to 'root around' in my trauma. That would require me to have a level of stability and the resilience to begin to unpack the abuse I had experienced. Coming away from each therapy session, I was raw; I had little to offer in terms of energy to anyone. And so I relate to my client when she says, "No, I don't want to go there. I just want to feel less tired, less overwhelmed, more balanced in my life."

Yes, one could argue that addressing the trauma would free up these aspects. However, perhaps one needs a level of resources to tackle such things and to hold a business and a family together. This is the role I see that a coach can offer: the building of resources, identifying strengths, providing psychoeducation on the nervous system and building towards resilience. What's more, coaching offers a focus away from the trauma, such as discovering values, strengths and "visions I may have for the future". Utilising positive psychology coaching exercises, such as "Best Possible Future Self' (King, 2001), supports the development of optimism and motivation and also draws on strengths when considering how one might work towards this. It assists in developing "willingness", which in this context can be seen as openness to experience discomfort, uncertainty or challenging emotions, thoughts or behaviour without engaging in experiential avoidance (Hayes et al., 2004). I truly believe that it is necessary to spend time integrating and deriving meaning from our traumas through therapy. However, it is just as important to focus on what is working well and how we can opti-mise and use these aspects to gain resilience. And, yes, there are many ther-apies that do this. However, coaching holds a different dynamic. Vaughan-Smith (2019) suggests that individuals often turn to habitual survival defences in a bid to resource themselves, which are well-founded neuropathways. The role of the coach is to "explore the resources not caught up in trauma response and lay down new pathways" (p.16).

I see a parallel in the coaching approach, viewing it as inherently aligned with the trauma-informed approach (as seen on p.00). Stepping back and reflecting on these approaches, once again I understand more deeply why I was drawn to coaching.

The Crime Survey for England and Wales (CSEW) year ending March 2020 estimated that 2.9 per cent of women aged 16 to 74 experienced sexual assault. The National Society for the Prevention of Cruelty to Children (NSPCC) esti-mate that one in twenty children in the UK have been sexually abused. However, it is difficult to determine the full extent of sexual assault in the population as prevalence statistics are likely to be underestimated.

(cited in Bailey & Taylor, 2022, p.7)

Sanderson (2022) suggests the figure to be one in four: "evidence shows as many as one in four adults have experienced some form of sexual abuse before the age of

18. Only one in eight children come to the attention of the authorities" (p.7). I high-light these figures, and most of the disclosures I have experienced in my coaching practice have been by women, regarding sexual violence. However, it is not only women who experience this type of trauma. Moreover, with statistics like these, it is highly probable that many coaches have faced similar experiences to the ones I have highlighted.

Therefore, as coaches, we need to be informed and agile enough to 'dance' with our clients in such situations. I would argue that this is particularly the case for coaches working in the sphere of resilience, well-being and stress manage-ment because these are all areas that will be impacted and affected by trauma. Furthermore, I suggest that trauma is inherent to the grey space, in which there is a greater likelihood of trauma being present, therefore is vital that coaches be trauma informed.

Moving from the 'ugly step-sister' to 'beloved bonus sister'

In addition to gaining skills in navigating disclosure with our clients, it is important to consider how coaches support their clients in seeking additional support, par-ticularly when relational trauma (see p.39 for definitions) is involved, so as not to naïvely cause more harm.

We are all too familiar with the classic tale of Cinderella and her bullish, mean 'ugly stepsisters', who derive pleasure from making Cinderella's life hellish. Fairy tales are seen to convey significant messages to the conscious, preconscious and unconscious mind, focusing on concerns surrounding universal human difficulties (Bettelheim, 1976).

As the story goes, Cinderella's ugly stepsisters interfere, trying to hold her back from attending the ball. I would like to draw a parallel between this tale and the term 'referral' in terms of the impact it has within coaching. I suggest that the term 'referral' is very much like the ugly stepsisters interfering, holding us back from the ball: the values we hold within the coaching profession. We inherited the term from the medical model, which is rooted in analysis, diagnosis and instruc-tion. "A medical discourse typically contains positions of those who offer treat-ment through their medical knowledge ... and less knowledgeable patients who receive their care" (Burr, 2003, p.112). I propose that this is in direct conflict with the stance of coaching, or 'Cinderella getting to the ball'. From a social construc-tionist perspective, the language and terms we use are discourses. These discourses assign specific "meanings, metaphors, representations, images, stories, statements and so on that in some way produces a particular version of events" (Burr, 2003. p.64), thus shaping how we make meaning and interact in the world. You see, dis-courses define "our knowledge of the world, our common understanding of things and events", and inform our shared understanding and social practices. And so, "it becomes clear that there is an intimate relationship between discourse, knowledge and power" (Burr, 2003, p.67).

Therefore, I would argue that when we use the term 'referral' in any context related to coaching, a shift in the power dynamic immediately occurs; one that is in direct conflict with the position coaching takes.

As coaches, we pride ourselves on being "client-led" (Palmer & McDowall, 2010) in creating a collaborative and facilitative relationship (Grant, 2003), whilst supporting the ideas of ownership and responsibility for one's own life (Wilson, 2007). The International Coaching Federation (ICF) believes "that every client is creative, resourceful, and whole" (ICF, n.d.). However, beneath this belief in 'resourcefulness' are the principles of choice and self-responsibility (Rogers, 2008). Nevertheless, being subject to any form of oppression brings with it "the internalisation of oppressive beliefs (Shoukry, 2016, p.17). Shoukry (2016) suggests that such a "journey has a strong emotional demand that often acts as barriers to meaning-making. Coaching can facilitate 'emotional fitness', supporting the client to move away from feelings of fear, self-blame and victimisation, and towards self-efficacy, agency and clarity" (p.23).

My interpretation of this statement is that we are to hold the mirror of creativity, resourcefulness and wholeness up for our clients, through the coaching applications of power questions, encouragement, challenge and accountability because our clients, particularly those who have been impacted by trauma, may not be in a creative, resourceful and whole state when entering the work with us. Here, the coach is in the role of facilitator, with the coachee as "expert in the relationship" (O'Broin & Palmer, 2010). This may be viewed as an emancipatory journey.

And so we experience a dilemma: one of trying to hold the position of coaching being client-led, whilst making a decision on behalf of our client, because of the connotations the term 'referral' holds – which I have bumped up against many times in my practice and through this study; particularly through the discussions in the collaborative enquiry groups in the second meeting, Cycle 5 (see p. 60) in relation to the use of the term 'referral' in our coaching practices. So, I propose a shift – a subtle one, but one that could have huge ripple effects. Furthermore, it is much like the tale and narrative of Cinderella and her ugly stepsisters which have become outdated in these modern times, and been replaced by happier, more cohesive, blended families.

So, I propose a move from the term 'referral' or 'ugly stepsisters' to that of 'signposting' or 'beloved bonus sister'. From this position, we are no longer in conflict with our core values as coaches. We can retain the stance of being client-led, encouraging the client to be empowered in their choice. Signposting brings with it the connotations of many options and directions; at the same time the client has a guide supporting them so that they can make a discerned choice based on what is right for them in the moment. It moves away from the power imbalance that the term 'referral' holds.

Yes, I hear you say, what is the big deal? It's only a word. One that I would never use with my client anyway. One that only gets used in textbooks and professional writing. What is in a word? Sometimes everything! As argued by Burr, words do not belong to any "particular discourse" (Burr, 2003). Rather, what we say depends upon the "discursive contexts" in which our words lie (Burr, 2003).

The view of words only being a means of communication, rather than them having a set meaning (Shotter, 1993) may be even more relevant when it comes to individuals who have experienced trauma. As the 'hook-up' between words and circumstances are created, (Shotter, 1993) the client's power to decide can be taken away from them through trauma. And so, enabling the client to make the decision of how and when to move from coaching to therapy has the potential to either empower or re-traumatise the client. If it is done ineptly, it reinforces messages of the client not being able to trust themself and stories about them being broken. Therefore, through the term 'signposting', we facilitate the client to make their own decision. This is the subtle difference; one that may engender a vastly different experience.

Diary extract: 3 August 2020

I came face to face with the experience of needing to examine myself and practice up close. I felt my values, practice and epistemological position were called into question. Bassot (2016) proposes that, by using "the metaphorical mirror", we can reflect on and make sense of practice, to make change and avoid future mistakes. Using the metaphor of "the magnifying mirror", "this is indispensable in situations where we need to look at our faces closely … The close examination of an incident can mean that we avoid mistakes in the future" (Bassot, 2016, p.6). I have come to evaluate, make sense of and adjust my practice, as a result of discussions that took place in the second meeting of Group 1 in Cycle 5 of the collaborative enquiry groups, regarding the topic of referral as a coach and in particular the use of this term in general and all the connotations it holds.

I will be removing the word 'referral' from my vocabulary as a coaching psychologist as I have come to recognise that this word has a significant impact on the way that I conduct practice. You see, I would never use this word directly with my clients. However, I have used this term with my supervisors and my peer coaches when discussing my clients, it has been used in coaching literature. What I have come to discover is, using the word 'referral' in these ways, I as a practitioner subconsciously take up a position of power and decision making when it comes to my client, and this happens on such a subtle level. This happens through discussion as to whether I should still be working with a client or whether they may need therapeutic support during supervision. What I am suggesting is not that we as coaches do not signpost our clients to receive the most appropriate support. What I am suggesting, however, is that words hold power, and this may lead us as coaches to take up a position that goes against all that we stand for. We do not diagnose; we are client-led; we reflect to the client that they are whole and capable.

Diary extract: 10 October 2020

The difference is subtle. I no longer use the term 'referral', and therefore I find that my approach to my client is more in line with the ethos of coaching – 'client-led'. I may bring to light my observations, as well as highlight my expertise, indicating what I can work with and where my remit ends. Engaging in a coaching conversation, inviting the client to share if they agree with my observations as well as how they may want to proceed. I will then offer up a range of information regarding all the possibilities of what may be available. Drawing on a solution-focused style, I will invite the client to engage in a coaching process where the client finds the best support they require at the time. I will also trust the client to determine if they are coachable, as this is not my role and is in direct conflict with the position of coaching. My role is to investigate with the client if coaching is working for them. However, there are exceptions, and this may be if a client discloses suicidal ideation, current ongoing abuse or harm to self and or others. My practice has changed immensely when it comes to the term 'referral'.

How I and my practice have changed as a result of this research

Owing to exposure to a range of coaches and discussions with my critical friends, I have bumped up against new avenues to explore, such as somatic/embodied coaching and trauma-informed practice. This experience has had both a personal and a professional impact and has created change. As previously mentioned, as 'the scientist', I view myself as the laboratory. So, I threw myself into somatic, bioenergetic psychotherapy to understand the roots of somatic coaching and to nourish my quest for a thriving life. On a personal level, this has been an invaluable experience because this piece around embodiment was missing from all the other therapy modalities I had tried. Connecting with the body and getting back in touch and in tune with it has been invaluable, and I have had some of my biggest breakthroughs thus far. I am aware that this has spilled into how I practise as a coach: first, as a result of my body becoming a more finely tuned instrument, I see a parallel in my own practice to that of the themes that emerged for my co-enquirers, such as embodied presence, holding space and co-regulation (see Workshop 1 p.00 and Workshop 2 p.00). Furthermore, as I have integrated my own trauma further, I am able to hold more space and meet the other, such as my clients when they disclose without being triggered, which I would have been the case previously if their story was close to my own.

In addition, through this research and from wanting to understand stress and how trauma may sit closely with it, I attended a trauma-informed coaching course certified through the ICF, where I learned about psycho-education and gained tools such as nervous system regulation tools, for example, utilising exteroceptive sensations to ground "five senses" (Treleaven, 2018) or understand the "Window of Tolerance" (Siegel, 1999), and how this relates to the client being able to become engaged in coaching.

I also studied for a Trauma-Informed Coaching Certificate (TICC) in the course of this research, which is relevant to navigating the grey space; once more drawing a parallel to Grant's (2007) quadrant from the Engagement/Well-being Matrix, 'Distressed but Functional'. Through this training, I am more relationally attuned, with a greater capacity to 'hold' space. My training was delivered by a Canadian company, Moving the Human Spirit. "Trauma-Informed Coaching is the practice of understanding the presence of trauma in a coach-client relationship and how to use it as a guide for resilience and solution-forward resolution". The depth of information and skill necessary to hold space for profound coaching work is what gives trauma-informed coaching its nuance and strength. Trauma-informed coaches have training in client regulation, brain-body connection, behavioural reaction, different types of traumas, leading causes and subsequent symptoms. They have learnt the proper channels for referral and about the growing relationship between clinical professionals, therapists and coaches. To become a trauma-informed coach, one must have authenticity, strong values and beliefs that are not limiting and do not suppress working in this area. Trauma-informed coaches will have "learned methods to help 'regulate' the nervous system, discard shame and guilt through powerful questions, and recognize and promote wellness as it starts to develop" (Moving the Human Spirit).

As a result, this has enabled me to have a framework for working if trauma is present. The training has also helped me to respond to a disclosure, by thanking the person for sharing and asking what they would like to do with this information; 'handing back' to the client how they would like to proceed. Some clients may then feel that they want additional support beyond the remit of coaching, and for others it is an exercise in informing.

I incorporated aspects into my practice from the 'cross-boundary' themes (see p.159) such as further defining my coaching offering and niche, so that I can clearly communicate this to potential clients (see my broader definition below). I also formed a peer-to-peer supervision group, in addition to my one-to-one supervision with a chartered coaching psychologist; thereby maintaining my CPD and training.

Most significantly, I experienced a parallel process similar to my co-enquirers, relating to the 'arc of transformation'. Fook (2010) proposes that the first stage of developing critical awareness of practice is to expose "(unsettling or 'shaking up') of fundamental (dominant) assumptions and their sources; the second stage develops this awareness into possible practice strategies" (p.41). In this sub-theme, the arc of transformation presents how coaches experiencing this exposure phased it, describing being unsettled and shaken up, with a sense of deconstruction taking place, as a result of critically reflecting on themselves as practitioners in the grey space. Coaches depict a groundlessness taking place; much like being in a "liminal space" (Turner, 1974), as one transitions between what was and what will be. This was something I experienced myself: a sense of the deconstruction and reconstruction of how and which terrain I can work with my clients; ground shifting beneath me. My sense of self as a practitioner became shapeless as I investigated and reflected on how I am in my practice. I experienced moments of seeing everything as grey space, questioning whether coaching in and of itself is different to therapy, and whether any of it was ethical. Should I be working as I do?

The original questions that brought me to this research (see p.54–55) became exaggerated. I have come through this liminal space of reflection, my sense as a practitioner and of how I work has settled and a new 'shape' has emerged. The change is subtle. I now embrace the questions that brought me to this research. I see them as an ally, ensuring that I am being aware and reflexive, rather than anxiety-inducing. As a result, I feel more confident in my practice, allowing me to step into a greater presence with my clients.

Diary extract: 11 September 2020

This process of workshops, reflections and reflective practices has impacted the construction of 'self' as a coach! I have experienced a de-construction of 'self' as a coach, through reflecting on my practice regarding the grey space. To the point that I question whether I should use the word 'psychologist' in my title as a coach? Does this attract clients that hear psychologist and think it is therapy? I have felt at moments that everything feels like the grey space, wondering if I should/we should be here at all. I have now settled and come back to my original starting point, not as the same person, but feeling more sure, more robust, with the feeling of greater capacity to hold space and to be more comfortable in the grey space. I really felt a loss of sense of self for a while, in a liminal space as a result of this deep reflection. I feel more confident in myself as a practitioner, firmer in living my values of empowerment and authenticity. This has been supported through engaging in all the CPD over the last year or so, impacting me both personally and professionally. Through the somatic psychotherapy, I have developed greater boundary awareness and boundaries. I have a greater sense of myself and my ability, when I am capable of holding space for my clients and knowing my limits and how to be comfortable with that.

The greatest change is how I view coaching and how it can work alongside other helping professions. As part of the trauma-informed coaching training, they shared with us their model of practice: how they work alongside a psychiatrist, a clinical psychologist and a therapist as a wellness team with veterans who suffer from PTSD. The veteran moves through the team, first working with the psychiatrist, the clinical psychologist and the therapist, then moving on to a six-month coaching programme. Trauma-informed coaching works with the veteran to implement life and professional goals, with the added difference of being aware of how trauma may show up in the sessions. Furthermore, the coaches work to fortify the awareness the client has gained about their trauma responses and triggers through therapy; reinforcing this through psycho-education and practical goals related to resilience. What was beautiful for me was that there was room to move back and forth between the wellness team, should it become apparent that the client was moving into a state of distress beyond the scope of coaching; demonstrating how coaching and other helping professions can work in alliance.

As I come to the end of this research process, where I began and where I am now within myself as a practitioner feel very different. Where I will go within my practice as this change continues to 'ripple out', I am not sure. However, I have begun to investigate the concept of personal consulting, transpersonal psychology and am considering becoming a trauma-informed trauma therapist. In what modality I am not sure yet; some time and exploration is needed. "Personal Consulting is a general framework for different types of 'one to one' (or 'helping by talking') practices that enable integration" (Popovic & Jinks, 2014, p.47). "An integration of one-to-one practices – not only integration between counselling and coaching, but also integration between different counselling approaches" (Popovic & Jinks, 2014, p.49).

I have also begun to reflect on my ontological positioning once more. Having investigated Dr Jessica Taylor's work where she discusses that she would have described herself as having a social constructionism view, but, through her work regarding victim focus and trauma-informed work, she sits more comfortably with critical realism, so as to acknowledge the "real harm, real abuse, real danger and risk" (Taylor, 2022). This has left me contemplating my own ontological stance. On reflecting on this with a critical friend, I received the following feedback.

> I see (and experience you) as a critical realist; but what does that mean for you in principle (with respect to coaching?). For me, you sit between subjectivity and objectivity, and navigate the tension between structuralism (stability) and change. You are a change agent (a disruptor), but at the same time you bring stability and order to others' chaotic worlds (physical worlds, and subjective life-worlds). My sense is that the polarities operate at different levels of analysis. In other words, when you are focused on the individual at an intra-personal level (psycho-biology), you are objective, possibly even a positivist? But not in the traditional sense, more in an action learning (action research) sense, i.e. you're not bound by evidence; instead you seek to create evidence. When operating (coaching) at the inter-personal and social level, you then appear more a social-constructionist. When we couple that with your political agenda, you are a 'radical'.

I am still working out what this shift is that has happened. I am aware that my stance is important to my coaching work. As Flaherty (2010) highlights, "coaching is a principle-shaped ontological stance and not a series of techniques" (p.6); and states that coaches must be clear on their ontological stance. Otherwise, how can they prepare themselves to coach the person in front of them?

Research confessions

In conclusion, I share that the process of writing Chapters 1 and 7 has been a profound experience for me and has been the toughest part of this research process. I have had moments of frustration, doubt and confronting my shame. I have muttered the following countless times: "Why did I do the doctorate in professional practice? An academic doctorate would have been so much easier!" It has thrown up much for me to grapple with, such as how much of my story I want to disclose. How much is appropriate? How much do I convey to honour the importance that coaching holds for me and why? I have grappled with the term 'survivor' and my resistance to the identity surrounding this term. Taylor (2022) has suggested that many individuals do not align with this term, arguing that women and girls do not identify with the terms 'victim' and 'survivor' so as not to be defined by the crimes committed against them.

Having spent many hours speaking to my academic supervisors, my practice supervisor, my therapist, my husband and my friends (including my critical friends), through the telling of my story, I have come to see how far I have come on my journey to wellness and flourishing. I have battled with shame and have learned and am still learning to put down the shame and responsibility that is not mine to carry. I have had conflicting moments of wanting to say little because it affords me a level of control as to who gets to know my story, as well as holding true to my value of courage, which requires vulnerability (Brown, 2012). But I also recognise the need to speak out to 'shatter the chains' of shame and, in so doing, encourage others to not feel that they have to hide their experiences. Shame is a sneaky thing. It drives us to hide our experiences/ourselves from the world, yet the way to overcome it is to share it, for it to be heard and seen with compassion and empathy. In Brene Brown's 2012 TED Talk, 'Listening to Shame', she shares that shame grows under the conditions of secrecy, silence and judgement because shame is a focus on the self: "I am bad" (Brown, 2012). The antidote is sharing one's story in a supportive environment, and being received with empathy, concluding that vulnerability is the path through shame.

As I conclude this chapter, I reflect on how pleased I am to have had the opportunity to undertake the DProf. At the start of this research process, I was unaware of the links between my research topic and my own story and how deeply entwined they are. This process has enabled me to step back and consider what our motivations are to conduct any piece of research. Why this topic? Why this enquiry? Reason and Marshall (1987) suggest that, as researchers, we select topics consciously or unconsciously resulting from the "baggage" we carry around, with an underlying drive: "a bid for personal development" (p.115). Therefore, this glimpse into me and my practice was offered; I hope to inform other coaches and the wider profession.

Discussion points

1. In which ways do you empower your client decisions regarding engaging in coaching?
2. How do you maintain psychological safety and connection with your clients, particularly if they have a trauma history?

3. What effect has the shift from the term 'referral' to 'signposting' had on your [practice?

Recommended reading

Bailey, C.A. & Taylor, J. (2022). 'I needed to know I wasn't crazy': Exploring the experiences of women who sought support for their mental health after rape or abuse, Victim Focus, UK. Available at: https://irp.cdn-website.com/f9ec73a4/files/uploaded/VictimFocus%20Rep ort%202022%20I%20needed%20to%20know%20that%20I%20wasnt%20crazy%20 MH%20SV%20Bailey%20Taylor%20%20FINAL.pdf (Accessed: November 2022).

O'Broin, A. & Palmer, S. (2010). 'Building on interpersonal perspective on the coaching relationship'. In S. Palmer & A. McDowall (eds.), *The coaching relationship: Putting people first.* Abingdon: Routledge.

Vaughan-Smith, J. (2019) *Coaching and trauma. From surviving to thriving.* London: Open University Press.

References

Bailey, C.A. & Taylor, J. (2022). 'I needed to know I wasn't crazy': exploring the experiences of women who sought support for their mental health after rape or abuse, Victim Focus, UK. Available at: https://irp.cdn-website.com/f9ec73a4/files/uploaded/VictimFocus%20Rep ort%202022%20I%20needed%20to%20know%20that%20I%20wasnt%20crazy%20 MH%20SV%20Bailey%20Taylor%20%20FINAL.pdf (Accessed: November 2022).

Bassot, B. (2016). *The reflective practice guide: An interdisciplinary approach to critical reflection.* London: Routledge.

Bettelheim, B., 1976. *The uses of enchantment: The meaning and importance of fairy tales.* London: Penguin.

Brown, B. (2012a). *Daring greatly.* London: Penguin Books.

Brown, B. (2012b). 'Listening to shame – TED talk'. Available at: https://www.youtube. com/watch?v=psN1DORYYV0 (Accessed: October 2022).

Burr, V. (2003). *Social construction,* 2nd edn. London: Routledge.

Dall'Alba, G. & Sandberg, J. (2006). 'Unveiling professional development: a critical review of stage models'. *Review of Education Research,* 76(3), 383–412.

Flaherty, J. (2010). *Coaching.* London: Routledge.

Fook, J. (2010). 'Beyond reflective practice: reworking the "critical" in critical reflection'. In H. Bradbury, N. Frost, S. Kilminster & M. Zukas (eds.), *Beyond reflective practice: New approaches to professional lifelong learning.* London: Routledge.

Gergen, K.J. (1989). 'Warranting voice and the elaboration of the self'. In J. Shotter & K.J. Gergen (eds.), *Text of identity.* London: Sage.

Grant, A.M. (2003). 'The impact of life coaching on goal attainment, metacognition and mental health'. *Social Behavior and Personality,* 31(3), 253–264.

Hayes, S.C, Follette, V.M. & Linehan, M.M. (eds.). (2004). *Mindfulness and acceptance: Expanding the cognitive behavioral tradition.* New York: Guilford Press.

Hayes, C. & Fulton, J.A. (2015). 'Autoethnography as a method of facilitating critical reflectivity for professional doctorate students'. *Journal of Learning Development in Higher Education,* 8(8), 1–15.

International Coaching Federation (ICF). (n.d.). 'ICF definition of coaching'. Available at: https://coachfederation.org/about (Accessed: August 2020).

King, L. A. (2001). The health benefits of writing about life goals. *Personality and Social Psychology Bulletin*, 27(7), 798–807.

Mental Health Foundation (2018). *'Stress: are we coping?' Mental Health Foundation*. Available at: https://www.mentalhealth.org.uk/explore-mental-health/publications/stress-are-we-coping-report? (Accessed: October 2018).

Moving the Human Spirit https://www.movingthehumanspirit.com

O'Broin, A. & Palmer, S. (2010). 'Building on interpersonal perspective on the coaching relationship'. In S. Palmer & A. McDowall (eds.), *The coaching relationship: Putting people first*. Abingdon: Routledge.

Palmer, S. & Cooper, C. (2010). *How to deal with stress*. London: Kogan Page.

Palmer, S. & McDowall, A. (eds.). (2010). The *coaching relationship*: *Putting people first*. Abingdon: Routledge.

Paterson, M., Higgs, J., Wilcox. S. & Villeneuve, M. (2002). 'Clinical reasoning and self-directed learning: key dimensions in professional education and professional socialisation'. *Focus on Health Professional Education*, 4(2), 6.

Popovic, N. & Jinks, D. (2014). *Personal consulting*, 1st edn. London: Routledge.

Reason, P. & Marshal, J. (1987). 'Research as personal process'. In D. Boud & V. Griffin (eds.), *Appreciating adult learning: From the learner's perspective*. London: Kogan Page.

Rogers, J. (2008). *Coaching skills – a handbook*. Maidenhead: Open University Press/ McGraw Hill Education.

Sanderson, C. (2015). *Counselling skills for working with shame*. London: Jessica Kingsley Publishers.

Shotter, J. (1993). *Cultural politics of everyday life: Social constructionism, rhetoric, and knowing of the third kind*. Milton Keynes: Open University Press.

Shoukry, H. (2016). Coaching for emancipation: A framework for coaching in oppressive environments. *International Journal of Evidence Based Coaching and Mentoring*, 14(2), 15–30.

Siegel, D. J. (1999). *The developing mind: How relationships and the brain interact to shape who we are*. New York, NY: Guilford Press.

Taylor, J. (2022). 'Views and perspectives: on being trauma informed'. Available at: https://victimfocus.org.uk/publications/views-and-perspectives-on-being-trauma-informed (Accessed: January 2022).

Trede, F., Macklin, R. & Bridges, D. (2012). 'Professional identity development: A review of the higher education literature'. *Studies in Higher Education*, 37(3), 365–384.

Treleaven, D. A. (2018). *Trauma-sensitive mindfulness: Practices for safe and transformative healing*. New York, NY: W. W. Norton & Company.

Turner, V. (1974). *'Liminal to liminoid, in play, flow and ritual: an essay in comparative symbology'*. Rice University Studies. Available at: https://scholarship.rice.edu/handle/1911/62895 (Accessed: January 2022).

Vaughan-Smith, J. (2019). *Coaching and trauma. From surviving to thriving*. London: Open University Press.

Wilson, C. (2007). *Best practice in performance coaching: A handbook for leaders, coaches, HR professionals, and organizations*. London: Kogan Page.

Chapter 8

Regular navigational updates and conclusion

Given that the client brings the whole of themselves to the coaching room, it may be implausible to know when and what may be disclosed, and whether, at the outset, we are always able to gauge if the client is 'coachable'. We may hear themes of abuse, racism, bullying and relationship breakdowns shared in our sessions. Therefore, it is essential across the helping professions that our skills in navigating these complexities are developed.

The world we live in has changed dramatically since starting this research. The impact of COVID-19 has been far-reaching – and we are yet to see the long-term effects socially, economically and personally. A pre-COVID-19 warning went out in the UK, with a call to tackle stress in an effort to mitigate mental health problems resulting from long-term stress such as anxiety and depression (Mental Health Foundation, 2018) and the negative implications of the mental health factors mentioned above through to physical health problems and disturbance (Crouter et al., 2001; Palmer & Cooper, 2010).

Emerging research is highlighting the impact that COVID-19 has had and is having in terms of mental health. Mind (2021) reports that 65 per cent of adults over 25 and 75 per cent of young people (aged 13–24) with a pre-existing mental health problem have reported worsening mental health, with reports of greater risks of suicidal ideation during the pandemic due to lack of social connection and loneliness (Lewis et al., 2023). Furthermore, those who experienced higher COVID-related stress are predicted to have an increased risk of developing Generalized Anxiety Disorder and Major Depressive Disorder (Monistrol-Mula et al., 2022)

One in five adults who had no experience of poor mental health prior to the pandemic is now describing their mental health as poor or very poor. As lockdown lifted, Bupa (2020) found that 65 per cent of British workers were anxious about returning to work, the cost of living and future impacts yet unknown. Additionally, a greater burden on mental ill health was reported as a result of the economic implications and worries related to the pandemic (Orestis et al., 2021, p.3832; Lanz et al., 2023).

Globally, the United Nations released a policy, 'COVID-19 and the Need for Action on Mental Health' (2020), reporting higher levels of symptoms of anxiety

DOI: 10.4324/9781003509776-9

and depression than usual, documented in various countries – suggesting that the full extent of the psychological impact is yet to be seen.

Moreover, seismic social events have taken place such as the impact of movements like Black Lives Matter, Me Too and Reclaim the Night. They have demonstrated how, as a society in the Western context, we talk about mental health and abuse, such as racism and violence against women. We, as coaching professionals, need to keep updated and equip ourselves to work with these movements.

Based on this evidence, the idea that mental health *should* not show up in the coaching space and that coaches *should* only be working with clients who have no mental health problems is obsolete and unrealistic. The map of the terrain that coaches are presented with due to the contextual issues is outdated. We must remember that "the map is not the territory" (Bateson, 1972). Bateson and Bateson further suggest that there is a tendency to mistake the map for the territory: "The name is not the thing named" (Bateson & Bateson, 1988, p.21), and that we must at times reconsider the map-like boundaries, as the landscapes and terrain shift. Consequently, our maps need to be updated.

I propose that we will have more and more coaches bumping up against the grey space, consciously or unconsciously. Therefore, being aware and prepared is the best way to ensure the safety of our clients and coaches. Sweeping this under the rug and suggesting that coaches do not navigate this terrain is a fool's errand and only serves to put both client and coach in harm's way. Better that we accept, acknowledge and learn to take the appropriate steps to navigate this space safely than argue about whether coaches should or should not be there in the first place.

Coaching and the coaching approach are permeating all walks of life. Examples include: managers being trained using a coaching style and approach; the Crisis homeless charity utilising structured coaching (Crisis, 2021). Corrie and Parsons' (2021) proposal for mental health coaches. The coaching field is growing and perhaps growing up into its own profession; "individuating" (Jung, 1976), one might say.

This research 'facilitated voice' to the concerns and standpoints of coaches and the clients they represent. Belenky et al. (1997) suggest that oral and written forms of narratives must pass back and forth between speaker and listener in order to reflect and "expand on each other's experience. Such interchanges lead to ways of knowing that enable individuals to enter into the social and intellectual life of their community" (p.26).

Many themes were presented in this research. They highlighted the complexities of the terrain, the concerns coaches have about managing boundaries between the therapeutic and coaching space, mental health, and that their clients are not left without support, and that they should act as a bridge – stepping into the role of 'helper' to facilitate finding support – through to their disillusion with systemic issues and inherited terms such as 'referral'; further suggesting that the term 'referral' is outdated within the future profession of coaching. As we grow up as a profession, we have the opportunity to choose which narratives, discourses and rhetoric we keep – and those we discard – and call for training such as foundational mental health, basic psychology and trauma-informed training. This goes to highlight the need for robust supervision, such as dual-trained supervisors who can illuminate the path that coaches traverse.

The real-life implications for different parts of the coaching sector are as follows:

1. Professional bodies need to recognise this complexity of the grey space consider how they could support coaches; ethics and codes of conduct will need to reflect this. As discussed in Chapter 2, most professional associations' ethical frameworks are created in a normative, punitive and prescriptive manner (Garvey & Stokes, 2023). Drawing on ethical thinking rather than defined codes may be a preferred choice. From this standpoint, the coach has the capacity to weigh up benefit versus harm on a case-by-case basis (Garvey & Stokes, 2023, p.282). Furthermore, bodies and associations would need to ensure that coaches have an appropriate levels of knowledge and training in emotional literacy, are trauma-informed and have a good knowledge base of various types of therapies (what they do and how they support individuals) to ensure signposting is done appropriately.

2. Supervisors should be open, aware and able to navigate the complexities of the grey space themselves; they should also have developed ethical thinking (Garvey & Stokes, 2023) to help guide their supervisees through the complexity of this terrain. Being dual-trained as a therapist and coach may offer a wider lens through which to support supervision work, in addition to being trained to be trauma-informed/sensitive.

3. Coaches of all kinds working in the grey space should be actively engaging in reflective and reflexive practice, bringing to light "everyday taken-for granted" (Schön, 1983), as demonstrated through this research. In addition, in the discoveries section of the research (see Chapters 4 and 5), a map is offered as a result of the lived experience of all the co-enquirers, to assist coaches in navigating this space. Lessons can be learnt by utilising the ways in which co-enquirers navigated this terrain and sought to improve their own practices.

4. It is vital that practitioners gain clarity on what both their professional and personal values are, where they align and where they might misalign, as practices are viewed as being informed by our values, and our values act as a benchmark within our practice (McNiff & Whitehead, 2010). In addition, appropriate supervisors should be sought and supervision increased when working with a client in the grey space. Coaches would also do well to acquire knowledge regarding emotional literacy, become trauma-informed/sensitive and have a wide knowledge of various types of therapies, should they need to signpost.

5. Policymakers, academics, researchers, writers and the coaching field would be well advised to remove the term 'referral' from their practice and replace it with 'signposting'. Not only would this be more in alignment with what coaching is, it may also support ethical thinking (Garvey & Stokes, 2023) when coaches inevitably face ethical dilemmas in practice.

6. As the world we live in becomes more complex, we as coaches need to ensure that we have the necessary tools to map our terrain so that we can navigate it ethically. This responds to the request for coaches to avoid the "tyranny of the positive" (Einzig, 2011) or that of denial or avoidance.

Rather than being afraid of encountering difficult emotions as they navigate the terrain of the grey space, coaches can "assist clients to entertain a different perspective; one that assists in finding meaning. Rather than fearing and avoiding emotional content with our clients" (Einzig, 2011, p.41). Furthermore, coaches in this space can act as allies to the therapeutic profession, rather than thwarting their efforts!

I suggest that coaches can and do play a dual role when it comes to mental health issues, particularly in relation to stress. Either they can take preventive measures, drawing on Grant's models or they can help the client gain greater psychological strength so that they feel more resourced to carry out deeper work in a therapeutic setting, and/or to destigmatise and normalise the situation, thus helping the profession and coaching the client 'towards therapy'.

This research was born out of knowing that I was doing positive ethical work with my clients, but in an undefined space. One that left me questioning my practice – when turning to textbooks, and seeking advice, responses were contradictory and not always in the best interest of the client. Therefore, it has highlighted a variety of new ways in which co-enquirers and I are able to navigate this grey space to be of service to our clients, while remaining within the ethical bounds of coaching. Moreover, through this research process, we, as co-enquirers, have developed greater ethical thinking (Garvey & Stokes, 2023). Therefore, addressing my motivation and purpose of this research, which consisted of questions arising from working with several clients who I would have been advised to 'refer' to therapy, while seeing the positive impacts of coaching. Furthermore, through this research I have been able to experience coaching acting as a stabiliser, through empowerment and the development of resource and resilience, so that it becomes a preventative element regarding stress-related ill health. What this research has highlighted is that we as coaches can and do work in productive ways with our clients within this complex area where the boundaries between therapy and coaching intersect: the grey space.

Ultimately, this research aimed to address how we do no harm and work ethically. In doing so it strives to ensure that we do not unintentionally reinforce shame or unhelpful beliefs the client may have; thereby, holding space for what our clients may share, seeing beyond the trauma our clients may disclose. This frees us to reflect to our clients the strengths and capabilities they have. Through this we offer that restorative experience of meeting our clients with compassion, love and kindness, which is intrinsically a therapeutic experience, even if our principal objective is to work on their coaching goals.

In conclusion, this research investigates how coaches experience the intersection between coaching and therapy – the grey space – and how I and other coaches can improve the practice of dealing with ethics and managing boundaries in the grey space when working with clients experiencing stress. This may go some way to further understand and attempt to address how we can work as coaches in service to our clients while safely navigating the terrain of the grey space. This calls for the coaching profession to update its position so that we can be better equipped to work with our clients and the inevitable complexities of life.

As McNiff (2002), so eloquently posits:

> My own view is that we live in a deeply unified universe, where all things are connected. Often in very distant ways, but their effects are evident in the lives of everyone – the 'butterfly effect' – where the beat of a butterfly's wing locally can have repercussions in far-flung global terms. For me, all open-ended systems have the potential to transform themselves. Humans and human interactions, by the fact that they are living, are open systems.
>
> (p.12)

Contribution to practice: framework

This research was undertaken to facilitate improvement for the following three stakeholders: 1) for me: research contributes to my personal development; 2) for coaches: research is a cooperative endeavour, which enables us to act effectively in the world; and 3) for the profession: research contributes to the fund of knowledge (Reason & Marshal, 1987, p.113).

This research/enquiry has assisted all three stakeholders: it has improved my own practice and the navigation of the grey space; through taking part in the research for the co-enquirers have gained reflective and reflexive practice to improve their navigation of the grey space; and the coaching profession have been given a body of knowledge to add insight into how coaches can improve their practice by ethically navigating the grey space.

Below I have presented my contribution to practice by pulling together the threads of data generated in this research to create a framework. In addition to the recommendations made by the cross-boundary experts, I propose the following:

Supervision

- Dual-trained supervisors who can support in charting and mapping the territory of the grey space, and who themselves have the competency and capacity to navigate this territory.
- Increased supervision when working with clients in the grey space.

Knowledge acquisition

- Further training is vital to navigate the grey space, to support the coach in mapping the terrain, including foundational psychology training, trauma-informed training, a basic understanding of mental first aid and training regarding emotional literacy.

- Training is needed to give a good level of knowledge on the variety of therapies so as to be able to support clients when signposting. Lou Lebentz (2021a, 2021b), a therapist, trauma specialist and speaker has compiled a document that supports practitioners and individuals when signposting and selecting support.

Peer and community support networks

- Working as a coach can be isolating because of the nature of the work. Peer-to-peer groups in the community, particularly where discussions can be held in a safe, non-judgemental space regarding some of the complexities encountered when working in the grey space, may decrease the sense of loneliness many of the coaches in this research expressed. Among other factors, one of the greatest benefits expressed by the co-enquirers was having a safe space within the workshops to discuss these complexities.

Reflective and reflexive practice

- Time needs to be given for reflection in action and on action (Schön, 1983) to become more consciously aware of practices and decisions when entering the grey space; bringing to light "everyday taken-for granted" (Schön, 1983).
- Additionally, it is important to have a clear view of one's personal and professional values regarding the grey space, reflecting on how they may align or conflict; as a result, the coach becomes reflexive about how to navigate these "living contradictions" (Whitehead, 1988) when encountering the grey space.

Discussion points

1. How would further training in the navigation of the grey space benefit your practice?
2. How will you reflect upon your professional and personal values regarding the grey space in the future?

Suggested reading

Belenky, M.F., Clinchy, B.M., Goldberger, N.R., & Tarule, J.M. (1997) *Women's ways of knowing: The development of self, voice and mind.* New York, NY: Basic Books.
Garvey, B. & Stokes, P. (2023). 'Ethics and professional coaching bodies'. In W. Smith, J. Passmore, E. Turner, Y. Lai & D. Clutterbuck (eds.), *The ethical coaches' handbook: A guide to developing ethical maturity in practice.* Abingdon: Routledge.

Schön, D.A. (1983). *The reflective practitioner: How professionals think in action.* New York, NY: Basic Books.

Whitehead, J. (1988). 'Creating a living educational theory from questions of the kind, "How do I improve my practice?"' *Cambridge Journal of Education*, 19(1), 41–52. Available at: https://www.actionresearch.net/writings/livtheory.html.

References

Bateson, G. (1972). *Steps to an ecology of mind.* London: The University of Chicago Press.

Bateson, G. & Bateson, M. (1988). *Angles fear: Towards an epistemology of the scared.* New York, NY: Bantam Dell Pub Group.

Belenky, M.F., Clinchy, B.M., Goldberger, N.R. & Tarule, J.M. (1997). *Women's ways of knowing: The development of self, voice and mind.* New York, NY: Basic Books

Bupa. (2020). 'Returning to the office: How to handle anxiety' Available at: https://www.bupa.co.uk/newsroom/ourviews/return-to-work-anxiety (Accessed: August 2020).

Corrie, S. and Parsons, A.A. (2021). The contribution of coaching to mental health care: An emerging specialism for complex times. In M. Watts & I. Florance (eds.), *Emerging conversations in coaching and coaching psychology* . Abingdon: Routledge.

Crouter, A.C., Bumpus, M.F., Head, M.R.M. & McHale, S.M. (2001). 'Implications of overwork and overload for the quality of men's family relationships'. *Journal of Marriage and the Family*, 63(2), 404–416.

Crisis. (2021, October 6). 'Structured coaching at Crisis. Crisis: Together we will end homelessness'. Available at: https://www.crisis.org.uk/get-involved/philanthropy/journeys-home-fund/structured-coaching-at-crisis (Accessed June 2022).

Einzig, H. (2011). 'The beast within'. *Coaching at Work*, 6(3). Available at: https://hett yeinzig.co.uk/wp-content/uploads/2019/10/Hetty-Einzig-The-Beast-Within-2011.pdf (Accessed: October 2017).

Garvey, B. & Stokes, P. (2023). 'Ethics and professional coaching bodies'. In W. Smith, J. Passmore, E Turner, Y. Lai & D. Clutterbuck (eds.), *The ethical coaches' handbook: A guide to developing ethical maturity in practice.* Abingdon: Routledge.

Jung, G. (1976). *Collected works of C.G. Jung, Volume 6: Psychological types.* Princeton, NJ: Princeton University Press.

Lanz, M., Caliciuri, R., Iafeate, R., Regalia, C., Rosnati, R., & Sogente, A. (2023). 'Covid-related stress in the financial, relational and health domains. Which longitudinal effects on present and future perception?', *Psychological Reports*, 128(2), 1–25.

Lebentz, L. (2021a, February). 'Solutions to trauma: Part I: Psychosomatic and holistic methods [pdf]. *Therapy & counselling*. Available at: https://therapyandcounselling.co.uk/wp-content/uploads/2021/02/SOLUTIONS-TO-TRAUMA-PART-I.pdf

Lebentz, L. (2021b, February). 'Solutions to trauma: Part II: Complementary therapies and new technological methods [pdf]'. *Therapy & counselling*. Available at: https://therapyandcounselling.co.uk/wp-content/uploads/2021/02/SOLUTIONS-TO-TRA UMA-PART-II.pdf

Lebentz, L. (n.d.). 'Home'. Available at: https://loulebentz.com (Accessed: 17 June 2022).

Lebentz, L. (n.d.). 'Resources'. Available at: https://loulebentz.com/resources (Accessed: 17 June 2022).

Lewis, K.C., Roche, M.J., Brown, F., & Tillman, J.G. (2023). 'Attachment, loneliness, and social connection as prospective predictors of suicidal ideation during the COVID-19 pandemic: A relational diathesis-stress experience sampling study'. *Suicide & Life-Threatening Behavior*, 53(1), 64–74.

McNiff, J. (2002). *Action research for professional development: Concise advice for new action researchers*, 3rd edn. Available at: https://www.jeanmcniff.com/userfiles/file/Publi cations/AR%20Booklet.doc (Accessed: August 2020).

McNiff, J. & Whitehead, J. (2010). *You and your action research project*, 3rd edn. London: Routledge.

Mental Health Foundation (2018). 'Stress: are we coping?' Available at: https://www.menta lhealth.org.uk/publications/stress-are-we-coping (Accessed: October 2018).

Mind. (2021). 'Coronavirus: the consequences for mental health. The ongoing impact of coronavirus pandemic on people with mental health problems across England and Wales'. Available at: https://www.mind.org.uk/media/8962/the-consequences-of-coronavirus-for-mental-health-final-report.pdf (Accessed: August 2020).

Monistrol-Mula, A., Felez-Nobrega, M., Domenech-Abella, J., Mortier, P., Cristobal-Narvaez, P., Vilagut, G., Olaya, B., Ferre, M., Gabarrell-Pascuet, A., Alonso, J., & Haro, J.M., (2022). 'The impact of COVID-related perceived stress and social support on generalized anxiety and major depressive disorders: moderating effects of pre-pandemic mental disorders'. *Annals of General Psychiatry*, 21(1), 1–7.

Orestis, Z., Butter, S., Bennett, K., Hartman. T.K., Hyland, P., Mason, L., McBride, O., Murphy, J., Gibson-Miller, J., Levita, L., Martinez, A.P., Shevlin, M., Stocks, T.V.A, Vallieres, F., & Bental, R.P. (2021) 'How does the COVID-19 pandemic impact on population mental health? A network analysis of COVID influences on depression, anxiety and traumatic stress in the UK population'. *Psychological Medicine*, 52(16), 3825–3833.

Palmer, S. & Cooper, C. (2010). *How to deal with stress*. London: Kogan Page.

Reason, P. & Marshal, J. (1987). 'Research as personal process'. In D. Boud & V. Griffin (eds.), *Appreciating adult learning: From the learner's perspective*. London: Kogan Page.

Schön, D.A. (1983). *The reflective practitioner: How professionals think in action*. New York, NY: Basic Books.

United Nations. (2020). 'COVID-19 and the need for action on mental health'. Available at: https://unsdg.un.org/sites/default/files/2020-05/UN-Policy-Brief-COVID-19-and-men tal-health.pdf (Accessed: May 2023).

Whitehead, J. (1988). 'Creating a living educational theory from questions of the kind, "How do I improve my practice?"' *Cambridge Journal of Education*, 19(1), 41–52. Available at: Living Educational Theory 1989, Living Contradictions (actionresearch. net) (Accessed: August 2019).

Index

For Product Safety Concerns and Information please contact our EU
representative GPSR@taylorandfrancis.com
Taylor & Francis Verlag GmbH, Kaufingerstraße 24, 80331 München, Germany

9 781032 835341